More Praise for Nation on the Take

"*Nation on the Take* is a timely and inspired book about a uniquely American problem. But Penniman and Potter don't merely draw our attention to the ways money dominates politics—they expertly show how the crisis connects with our daily lives and offer a path forward that includes people from all walks of life and all political persuasions."
—**Arianna Huffington**

"This book will make you mad, but you're probably already mad, so it will make you mad and informed." —*St. Louis Post-Dispatch*

"A well-written must-read for those ready to give up hope about politics and government in the United States." —*Kirkus Reviews*

"A rallying cry to bring government back under the control of the people ... Their argument is impassioned and accessible." —*Library Journal*

"Whether Republican, Democrat, or independent, we are, first of all, Americans. This book makes a powerful case that dark money darkens our democracy, and we must rise and join as patriots to reclaim our cherished right to self-government." —**Senator Alan Simpson (R-WY, 1979–97)**

"*Nation on the Take* is a tour de force, a work of immense importance in the seminal debate at the core of all debates: Will our nation be sold to the highest bidder or will the American people reestablish the republic our founders intended? A gripping and frightening exposé of the crisis, along with profound yet practical suggestions to repair the dysfunction, *Nation on the Take* should be required reading for all who care about America."
—Jack Abramoff, author of *Capitol Punishment: The Hard Truth about Washington Corruption from America's Most Notorious Lobbyist*

"The biggest challenge surrounding the issue of politics and money is that so many recognize it is a problem but so few can articulate why and what we can do about it. Penniman and Potter have cut through the clutter and distilled the essence of the challenge in a way that should have people marching in the streets. They make a compelling case that Americans across the political spectrum, from MoveOn Democrats to

Tea Party Republicans, should care about this issue because it is an existential threat to our very democracy." —**Mark McKinnon, former communications adviser for George W. Bush**

"If you're among of the 90 percent of Americans who think our political system is broken, *Nation on the Take* is made for you. Wendell Potter and Nick Penniman have compiled a fact-packed handbook for political reform: the nitty-gritty on how billionaires' campaign contributions and corporate cash have captured both political parties and bought policies for the 1 percent; how each of us pays a price in our daily lives for the runaway political money game; and, most important, specific suggestions on how we can reform our broken system and get our democracy back on track." —**Hedrick Smith, former Washington bureau chief for the *New York Times* and author of *Who Stole the American Dream?***

BOOKS BY WENDELL POTTER

Deadly Spin: An Insurance Company Insider Speaks Out on How Corporate PR Is Killing Health Care and Deceiving Americans

Obamacare: What's in It for Me?

Nation on the Take

How Big Money Corrupts Our Democracy and What We Can Do About It

WENDELL POTTER AND
NICK PENNIMAN

BLOOMSBURY PRESS
NEW YORK · LONDON · OXFORD · NEW DELHI · SYDNEY

Bloomsbury Press
An imprint of Bloomsbury Publishing Plc

1385 Broadway	50 Bedford Square
New York	London
NY 10018	WC1B 3DP
USA	UK

www.bloomsbury.com

BLOOMSBURY and the Diana logo are trademarks of Bloomsbury Publishing Plc

First published 2016
This paperback edition 2017

ISBN: HB: 978-1-63286-109-2
       PB: 978-1-63286-111-5
     epub: 978-1-63286-110-8

Library of Congress Cataloging-in-Publication Data is available.

2 4 6 8 10 9 7 5 3 1

Typeset by RefineCatch Limited, Bungay, Suffolk
Printed and bound in the U.S.A. by Berryville Graphics Inc., Berryville, Virginia

To find out more about our authors and books visit www.bloomsbury.com. Here you will
find extracts, author interviews, details of forthcoming events and the option to sign up for
our newsletters.

Bloomsbury books may be purchased for business or promotional use. For information on
bulk purchases please contact Macmillan Corporate and Premium Sales Department at
specialmarkets@macmillan.com.

To our dear families, and the country we all love.
And in loving memory of Emily Jacqueline Potter.

Contents

Preface to the 2017 Paperback Edition

When we set out to write this book, we had no idea what an unprecedented mess the 2016 election would be, but suspected that money would play a huge role. And it did, both in terms of the amount raised and spent, and the ways in which public concern about the "rigged" political system fueled the rise of unconventional candidates.

The total amount spent—roughly $7 billion—broke all records. Seemingly bolstered by the Supreme Court's 2010 *Citizens United* decision, centimillionaires and billionaires poured money into super PACs and "dark money" groups as never before. Of the more than $1.5 billion raised by super PACs, at least $260 million came from just ten individuals. The amounts would have been even higher had Donald Trump, who many deep-pocketed conservative donors found repellant, not been the nominee.

One of the flawed notions put forth in *Citizens United* was that large donations flowing to groups like super PACs can't have a corrupting effect on the political process because such donations are going to "independent" groups—they aren't flowing directly into candidates' campaign coffers. Yet, 2016 saw the proliferation of candidate-specific super PACs. Most of the major-party presidential contenders had a "personalized" super PAC, run by close associates or former aides, and while campaign law nominally prohibits coordination between a candidate's campaign and independent groups, campaign lawyers found creative ways to get around that rule in ways that leave the modifier "independent" virtually meaningless.

Some of the amounts spent last year seem almost bizarrely out of proportion to where they were spent, like the more than $100 million pumped into the tiny state of New Hampshire to influence the Senate contest between Republican incumbent senator Kelly Ayotte and her Democratic challenger, Maggie Hassan. Tellingly, more than 75 percent of the funding in last year's Senate elections came from out of state. If you were a voter in New Hampshire, or any battleground district, you either felt flattered by all of the attempts to get your attention, or disgusted by the deluge of negative ads. More likely, you were disgusted. And that disgust was compounded by the lack of any good legislation—or any legislation!—coming out of Washington. It's easier to tolerate the mudslinging of politics if it seems like progress is otherwise occurring. But mudslinging in the midst of a years-long government snarl is a recipe for upheaval.

Which is the other way Big Money—and its effects on our democracy—molded 2016. Just imagine: Members of Congress, on average, spend half their time raising money. You'll read more about the phenomenon later in this book. So if you multiply four hours of fundraising a day, by 260 working days a year, by 535 members of the House and Senate, you get 556,400 hours that members of Congress collectively spend each year fundraising; or more than one million hours within every two-year cycle of Congress.

That's one million hours they're spending with donors and lobbyists, not studying policy, attending committee hearings, checking in with constituents back home, or reaching across the aisle to forge the bipartisan relationships necessary to govern. It's a soul-crushing experience for most of them, driving the best of them from office, and inhibiting potentially great public servants from running in the first place. And, although the public might not know every disturbing detail (unless they read this book!), they get it. Thus, the rise of candidates who want to "drain the swamp."

In early 2015, who would have expected a scrappy, little-known senator from Vermont to come within striking distance of stymying Hillary Clinton's second run at the Oval Office? Who would have expected Donald Trump to even make it through the early rounds of a primary in which he shared the stage with twelve former senators and governors? Two quotes connect their successes. Bernie, being interviewed in March of 2016: "Today we have a corrupt campaign finance system with Wall Street and billionaires spending unlimited sums, which is undermining democracy." Trump, tweeting two months later: "Crooked Hillary Clinton is bought and paid for by Wall Street, lobbyists, and special interests. She will sell our country down the tubes!"

Yet while Bernie came forward with bold policy ideas that would help reduce the influence of Big Money—ideas that forced Clinton to take a stronger stance on campaign finance reform—Trump only offered limited tweaks to lobbying laws. Now, cynical political operatives would say that the general public doesn't care whether or not the policy fixes are sweeping or small. Joe Sixpack doesn't know the difference. But few can deny that anti-Big-Money populism is on the rise, and has been fomenting for many years. In the same way that it unites Trump and Sanders, it links the Tea Party and Occupy Wall Street.

And that's why we wrote this book. We believe our country is on the precipice of a revolt against the system, and we want to help lay the system bare.

While there have been other books about money and politics in the last decade, although fewer than one would hope, none do what we have set out to do—craft an accessible guide that shows in detail how the system really works, and chronicles the real-world outcomes. Part 1 presents the big picture and traces the history of the problem. Part 2 connects the dots to show the downstream effects on us all. Then part 3 discusses solutions and how a new kind of bipartisan movement is emerging to get those solutions passed into laws. Throughout, we provide graphs and charts, and believe we've written in a way that avoids esoteric and academic references.

Both of us have reported on government and politics at different times in our careers. As a young reporter in Washington during the 1970s, Wendell covered national politics when Gerald Ford and Jimmy Carter were in the White House and congressional leaders included Senate Minority Leader Howard Baker from Wendell's home state of Tennessee. It was a time when there were far fewer lobbyists on Capitol Hill and when the vast majority of campaign contributions came from people who could actually vote for the candidates they supported.

Wendell's longer career, after he left Scripps-Howard's Washington bureau, was in corporate public affairs. Among his responsibilities at Cigna, where he served as head of corporate communications until he left in 2008, was administering the company's PAC and coordinating efforts with the industry's lobbyists.

When Wendell left his job at Cigna after a crisis of conscience, which was described in his first book, *Deadly Spin*, he played a key role in the debate to reform the U.S. health care system, testifying before several congressional committees. During one hearing he told lawmakers that if they caved to pressure from insurance industry lobbyists they might as well call their bill the "Health Insurance Industry Profit Protection and Enhancement Act."

It turned out to be a prescient warning.

The ability of small groups of people to bend the levers of power away from the common good and toward their own narrow goals is what drew Nick to this cause, too. For more than a decade, working as a journalist, investigative reporter, and magazine publisher in D.C., he saw how great ideas—from balancing the budget to improving public health—never got a hearing on the Hill, not because they lacked public support, but because they lacked the support of well-financed special interests. We, the people, he concluded, know how to fix many of the problems before us; we just don't have the power to enact and then implement those fixes. It's akin to the profound frustration that many recovering stroke victims must feel: the ideas and desires are in the head but it's nearly impossible to move the mouth or limbs.

It's time to end the paralysis.

PART 1

INTRODUCTION

America is a dream.
The poet says it was promises.
The people say it is promises—that will come true.
　　　　　　　　—LANGSTON HUGHES, "FREEDOM'S PLOW"

Our country is indeed a dream—a dream created during a period of time
known as the American Enlightenment, which came to a focal point during
the American Revolution and lasted until the early nineteenth century.

The leading political thinkers of the day were the ones we know so
well: Thomas Jefferson, John Adams, James Madison, Thomas Paine,
George Mason, Alexander Hamilton, Benjamin Franklin. Their dream
was to create a democratic republic, in which ultimate power rested with
the citizens. Just after the Declaration of Independence asserts the
unalienable rights to "life, liberty and the pursuit of happiness," it states:

> That to secure these rights, governments are instituted among
> Men, deriving their just powers from the consent of the governed,
> That whenever any Form of Government becomes destructive of
> these ends, it is the Right of the People to alter or to abolish it,
> and to institute new Government, laying its foundation on such

principles and organizing its powers in such form, as to them
shall seem most likely to effect their Safety and Happiness.

They knew that self-government would be messy and inefficient at times,
but they had faith that common ground would be regularly found and
that people would slowly but surely build a better nation together. As
Jefferson said: "Sometimes it is said that man cannot be trusted with the
government of himself. Can he, then, be trusted with the government of
others? Or have we found angels in the form of kings to govern him? Let
history answer this question."

In addition to the Declaration of Independence, the Constitution of
the Commonwealth of Massachusetts is a shining example of the idealism
that defined the era. Ratified in 1780, it is thought to be the world's oldest
still-functioning written constitution. Drafted in part by John Adams, it
inspired and informed the U.S. Constitution, forged seven years later.
Part I, Article VII, of the Massachusetts charter reads: "Government is
instituted for the common good; for the protection, safety, prosperity,
and happiness of the people; and not for the profit, honor, or private
interest of any one man, family, or class of men; therefore, the people
alone have an incontestable, unalienable, and indefeasible right to institute government; and to reform, alter, or totally change the same, when
their protection, safety, prosperity, and happiness require it."

Government for the common good, not for the "profit, honor, or
private interest of any one man, family, or class of men."

Those words don't seem to ring true today. Not just for those who
follow politics, but for all of us. A profound shift has occurred—one that,
perhaps because it has occurred slowly, has yet to fully register as the
serious crisis it is. But it has by no means gone unnoticed.

A few years ago, CBS News conducted a poll about Americans' percep-
tion of government. The headline of the resulting story they published:
ALIENATED NATION: AMERICANS COMPLAIN OF GOVERNMENT DISCON-
NECT. The first sentence reads: "Americans see their leaders in Washington
as overpaid agents of wealthy individuals and corporations who are
largely disconnected from the concerns of average Americans."

We, the people, are losing our faith in the dream of democracy. As our
collective power is increasingly eclipsed by a rigged system of politics and
governance dominated by a handful of billionaires and a phalanx of well-
financed special interests, we are growing skeptical that the promises will
come true.

Right now there is no credible outside threat to our American way of life. No other nation is sounding the death knell of ours. But the rapid proliferation of a system akin to oligarchy—within our own country— threatens to cripple our march forward.

It's a threat the Founding Fathers knew we would always have to guard against. In the summer of 1787, when delegates to the Constitutional Convention were in the heat of their debates, they were obsessed with bribery, influence, and corruption. James Madison, who kept meticulous notes, recorded the word "corruption" fifty-four times. To them, the notion of corruption was both the corruption of the individual and the corruption of the system of governance. They were less obsessed with corrupt individuals—with bad apples—than with the system itself, with the orchard. The rotting of the fruit of liberty was seen as the dominance of private interests over the public interest. It was the bending of governing priorities away from the common good—a process that would, over time, fatally damage the whole project of a democratic republic—of "We, the people," of the "consent of the governed."

Seen in this light, government is us. Or it should be. We give our government our money, in the form of taxes. Then we hire its executives, through elections. Then we imbue it with directions and instructions, in the form of legislation. If all goes well, our politicians utilize our tax dollars to manifest our brightest ideas. The most exquisite dynamic is achieved when the common good is served while individual liberty is protected. No kings, no dictators. Us, in charge of ourselves, leveraging our resources behind our highest hopes, while protecting each other's freedoms, shaping our country, forever working to form "a more perfect union."

Yes, of course: there were—and always will be—bad people and bad pieces of legislation. The factions and special interests will fight for their legislative handouts and carve-outs, and politicians will lose their virtue. Corrupt moments in our future are inevitable.

And, of course, for centuries, women, people of color, and nonland-owners were legally excluded from voting and running for office. But powerful, popular grassroots movements like suffrage, abolition, and civil rights—fueled by the early American Enlightenment's dreams of liberation and equality—forced profound course corrections that are among this country's greatest accomplishments, not just for United States citizens but for humankind.

Today we all seem to feel as if we need another such profound course correction, one that is focused on reclaiming our right to self-government and renewing our hope in the American dream. Correctly, we suspect that the system is rigged, our government has become coin-operated, and that we've been sidelined.

Obviously, money's dominance of politics and governing isn't the only factor behind the dysfunction of our democracy. Gerrymandered congressional districts, presidential elections entirely focused on a handful of states, low voter-turnout rates, petty and polarized political parties, superficial and partisan media, and an increasingly rude public arena all contribute to the breakdown of our ability to govern together. But Big Money makes a lot of these factors worse, and it's time for the political class—which has grown way too cozy with the status quo—to step out of its elite bubble and recognize that the crisis we are in is eating away at the country.

In 1998, the total amount of money spent on federal elections was $1.6 billion. By 2012, it had nearly quadrupled to $6.2 billion.

The Supreme Court's 2010 *Citizens United* ruling was akin to crop-spraying gasoline onto a wildfire. In a narrow 5–4 decision, the majority of justices asserted that corporate spending in politics is an act of free

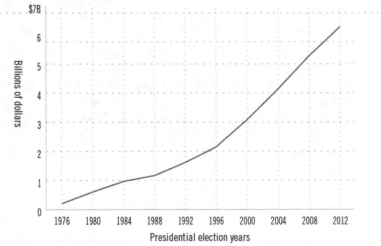

Increasing Cost of Elections
Sources: Federal Election Commission, Center for Responsive Politics, Campaign Finance Institute
Methodology: *Nominal dollars. Includes spending by presidential, Senate and House candidates, political party spending, outside groups' independent expenditures.

speech and should therefore be unlimited. Subsequent lower court rulings have expanded that rationale to reduce some limits on political campaign contributions, which has put the chase for political money on steroids.

At times, the news seems almost surreal. Take for instance, how a single family—the Kochs—which owns Koch Industries, has forged a small but very wealthy network of donors who have pledged to spend nearly $900 million influencing the outcome of the 2016 elections. That's $500 million more than the Republican National Committee spent in 2012.

WHERE THE MONEY IS SPENT

Total Spending in 2012 Election **$6,285,557,223**

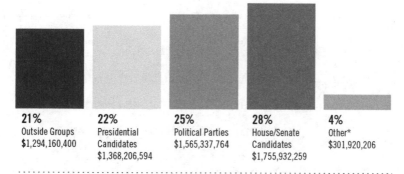

21%	22%	25%	28%	4%
Outside Groups	Presidential	Political Parties	House/Senate	Other*
$1,294,160,400	Candidates	$1,565,337,764	Candidates	$301,920,206
	$1,368,206,594		$1,755,932,259	

Source: Center for Responsive Politics (opensecrets.org)
Methodology: *FEC convention outlays, delegate candidate spending, etc.

Where the Money is Spent
Source: Center for Responsive Politics (opensecrets.org)
Methodology: *Nominal dollars. Category spending in graphic doesn't equal total election spending because political conventions, PAC overhead money left out.

On the other side of the Big Money equation—the fundraising side— the nonstop scramble for campaign cash is distracting and exhausting our elected officials as never before, and perpetually repelling good people from office. Members of Congress simply don't spend as much time thinking about us as they once did. They spend most of their time thinking about how to get enough money from wealthy individuals, lobbyists, and political action committees to get reelected—it's what political operatives refer to as a "permanent campaign" mentality.

In January 2013, newly elected Democrats in the House of Representatives were being given an orientation session by the Democratic Congressional Campaign Committee about how they should spend their time serving in the House—what was once referred to as the "People's House." Among the materials they were presented with was a "model daily schedule." That schedule provided for four hours of "call time," one to two hours of "constituent visits," two hours of committee hearings or floor votes, one hour of "strategic outreach," and one hour of "recharge time." You have no doubt already guessed what "call time" and "strategic outreach" are: fundraising. Which means that new representatives are expected to spend half of their time either dialing for dollars or attending fundraising events.

Who are they calling? Probably not you. Certainly not us. Mostly, very wealthy donors in the richest cities in America. And who's throwing the

MODEL DAILY SCHEDULE - DC

- ☑ **4 hours** Call Time
- ☑ **1-2 hours** Constituent Visits
- ☑ **2 hours*** Committee/Floor
- ☑ **1 hour** Strategic Outreach
  Breakfasts, Meet & Greets, Press
- ☑ **1 hour** Recharge Time

How Members Spend their Time: How House Democrats were told they should spend their time in Washington
Source: PowerPoint delivered by the House Democrats' campaign committee, 2013, obtained by the *Huffington Post*.

daily fundraisers for them? Often, the very industries they are supposed to be regulating, based on their congressional committee assignments. The Finance Committee members rake in contributions from the bankers and their lobbyists, the Natural Resources Committee members from the oil and coal executives and their lobbyists. That's why these types of committees on Capitol Hill are referred to as "cash committees." In 2014, for instance, the top industries contributing to members of the House Financial Services Committee, formerly known as the Banking Committee, were finance, insurance, and real estate. Individuals and PACs from those sectors collectively chipped $30 million dollars into the committee members' coffers.

As Ray Plank, the former founder and chairman of the Apache Corporation, told the conservative journalist Peter Schweizer, whose book *Extortion* was later turned into a *60 Minutes* episode, campaign cash and corporate contracts with well-connected lobbying firms are "protection money. It's what you expect from the mafia."

Yet, in Washington and the state capitals, such activity is not seen as mafia-like. It's run-of-the-mill. It's the way things get done. Anyone who questions it, or wants to change it, is deemed naïve or—even worse!—idealistic.

And it's done in broad daylight. Although an estimated 5 to 10 percent of money in the political system is what's called "dark money," which is much harder to trace, all of the direct contributions to politicians' campaigns, all of the PAC and superPAC money, and the large checks to the political parties are disclosed. They're not disclosed in real time, which is one of the commonsense reforms that need to be passed. But otherwise you can track 95 percent of the money in the system and pretty easily deduce who's likely feeling beholden to whom.

One of the many pernicious effects of this endless extraction of campaign cash from lobbyists and wealthy individuals is that politicians have little time to form strong relationships with one another, particularly across the aisle. For all of the newspaper editorials and Press Club forums about gridlock, partisanship, and polarization in Washington, and all the appeals to politicians to get along, too little attention is paid to whether they have time to get along. When announcing in early 2013 that he wouldn't be seeking reelection in 2014, Senator Tom Harkin (D-IA) remarked, "The time is so consumed with raising money now, these campaigns, that you don't have the time for the kind of personal relationships [between lawmakers] that so many of us built up over time."

Our legislators—our employees, remember—also have less time to draft, study, or pass legislation. The more than nine thousand registered lobbyists in D.C. are keenly aware of this vulnerability, and they are poised to take advantage of it. Collectively, they annually disclose more than $3 billion in expenses—including the many events they hold for members of Congress. The nonprofit transparency group the Sunlight Foundation tracks categories of influence peddling. One category is called "Hill coverage," which is defined as the "average percentage of incumbent members of Congress receiving contributions from the organization over the course of the 2008, 2010 and 2012 election cycles." AT&T, for instance, has 88 percent Hill coverage—meaning that 88 percent of members of Congress have received contributions from AT&T sources. Honeywell International also has 88 percent coverage. United Parcel Service has 87 percent. Lockheed Martin has 80 percent. Comcast, General Electric, Boeing, and Verizon all have around 70 percent.

How much coverage do you have? How much coverage do we, the people, have? How much do Main Street businesspeople have? How much attention do people who have little or no money get in such a system? We know that the banks wield enormous power over politics and policy decisions in D.C. But who's representing the families facing foreclosure? As Bob Dole once famously quipped: "There is no poor people's political action committee."

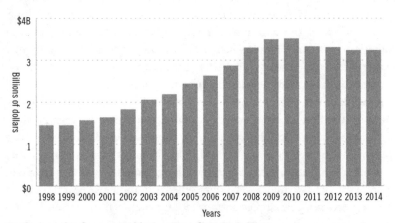

Explosion of Influence: Lobbying Spending Over Time
Source: Center for Responsive Politics (opensecrets.org)
Methodology: *Nominal dollars. Includes federal spending data only.

There are also few members of Congress who, upon leaving the Hill, have any interest in starting a poor people's political action committee. In 1974, around 3 percent of former members became lobbyists. Now, half of them pass through Washington's "revolving door" and stroll from the Hill down to K Street, many of them to lobby for the industries they once oversaw, based on their congressional committee assignments. Served on the Finance Committee? Become a bank lobbyist. As the *New York Times*'s Mark Leibovich observed: "In some sense, [they are] living proof of the thing that most voters loathe about Washington: the notion that membership in its political class guarantees a win-for-life lottery ticket."

Throughout this book, we will talk about both lobbying and campaign contributions and expenditures. Big Money is both. And well-financed special and corporate interests deploy both as a means of bending the apparatus in Washington and the state capitals to their will. It's worth pointing out early in the book that large corporations—along with wealthy corporate executives and the lobbyists the corporations hire—really dominate the game. Yes, unions play the game, and any meaningful reforms of the system should include them. Just look at the inability to accomplish meaningful education reforms. But in 2014, as an example, business interests outspent union interests 15 to 1.[1]

It's also important to point out early on that lobbying in its purest form is not bad. Making arguments to members of Congress is part of the democratic process. Sharing information and expertise is a good thing. It's a form of free speech, and a healthy democracy should have plenty of lobbying going on, as long as it is occurring on behalf of *all* sides of an issue. Our concerns about lobbying involve the relationship between lobbying and political cash, the lobbyists who have little or no fealty to the broader public interest, and those politicians or Hill staffers who see public office as a pathway to a lucrative influence-peddling career. We are also disgusted by lobbying groups that knowingly leverage millions of dollars into false and misleading communications campaigns, which destroy the possibility of having a thoughtful, genuine debate about weighty policy ideas.

Stanley Collender, who has had extensive experience on Capitol Hill and in the private sector, is widely considered to be one of the leading experts on U.S. budget policy. He remembers when the lightbulb went on for corporate lobbyists. In a piece titled "How Big Money Corrupts the Budget," published by the *Democracy Journal*, he chronicles one of the most crucial moments in the saga of American politics and money.

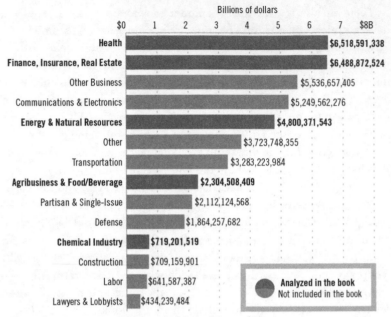

Billions of dollars

| | $0 | 1 | 2 | 3 | 4 | 5 | 6 | 7 | $8B |

Health — $6,518,591,338
Finance, Insurance, Real Estate — $6,488,872,524
Other Business — $5,536,657,405
Communications & Electronics — $5,249,562,276
Energy & Natural Resources — $4,800,371,543
Other — $3,723,748,355
Transportation — $3,283,223,984
Agribusiness & Food/Beverage — $2,304,508,409
Partisan & Single-Issue — $2,112,124,568
Defense — $1,864,257,682
Chemical Industry — $719,201,519
Construction — $709,159,901
Labor — $641,587,387
Lawyers & Lobbyists — $434,239,484

● Analyzed in the book
Not included in the book

Where the Money Comes From: Lobbying Expenditures
Source: Center for Responsive Politics (opensecrets. org), authors' analysis (1998 to first quarter 2015).

In 1975, the Democratic Senate Budget Committee chairman, Ed Muskie, from Maine, successfully led a charge against a defense authorization bill. At the time, Collender was an intern for the committee. It was customary for defense authorization bills coming out of the powerful Armed Services Committee to become law without being challenged. But Muskie saw an opportunity to bring more scrutiny to the budget process. According to Collender,

> That was the moment when lobbyists discovered the congressional budget process. It was also the moment when budget committee decisions free of lobbyist influence ended and action on the deficit, debt and federal priorities started to be determined more by those who could devote resources to getting what they wanted than by national need and appropriate fiscal policy.

Let's pause for a moment on that last part of that sentence: *more by those who could devote resources to getting what they wanted than by national need and appropriate fiscal policy*. If it is functioning well, our country's project in self-government would be mainly driven by, among other virtuous objectives, *national need* and *appropriate fiscal policy*. We would not only know the right policies to enact—we would also enact them. But when government is coin operated—when America becomes a nation on the take—the nation's needs get shoved aside like neglected children.

Which brings up another crucial link that isn't discussed often enough: Although the system creates special economic benefits for those who can pay to play, the overall well-being of the economy does not necessarily improve. For too long, campaign finance reform has been viewed as an "anti-corporate" cause. Instead, it should be seen, in part, as pro competition and anti-cronyism.

Luigi Zingales, a conservative economist at the University of Chicago Business School and author of *A Capitalism for the People*, compellingly documents how the system of lobbying and legislative favors is dangerously reducing economic competitiveness and opportunity. He writes:

> American capitalism . . . grew in a unique incubator that provided it with a distinct flavor of competitiveness, a meritocratic nature that fostered trust in markets and a faith in mobility. Lately, however, that trust has been eroded by a betrayal of our probusiness elites, whose lobbying has come to dictate the market rather than be subject to it, and this betrayal has taken place with the complicity of our intellectual class.

Who suffers from this betrayal? Consumers (you and us), small- and medium-sized business owners, big corporations whose lobbyists get beat by their competitors' lobbyists, and entrepreneurs—that is, nearly everyone. As John Arensmeyer, the founder of the group Small Business Majority, said: "With the *Citizens United* decision, the political system has become even more stacked against the interests of small firms. Small businesses end up paying the price for big money politics that allow large firms to secure special perks and advantages over their smaller, less politically connected competitors."

You see, wherever you are, and whatever you do, whether you love politics or hate politics, whether you devour news or never look at the news, whether you see yourself as an environmentalist or a business leader (or both), as a conservative or a liberal, every moment of your life is being affected by the system of Big Money.

Imagine a baby named Eve, born this morning in a hospital whose regulations—medical equipment, pharmaceuticals, staff training, and certification—were partly created by the system.

Little Eve will ride home tonight in a car that was engineered by the system as much as it was by engineers. The mileage it gets, how safe it is, the materials it's made of, what goes into the gas tank, how it's taxed, what comes out of the tailpipe.

Eve will arrive at a home built to standards established, in part, by the system. Lobbyists, trade groups, phony "citizens" groups and corporate executives have waged massive campaigns for decades that have determined the quality of every breath of air Eve draws into her new lungs.

Her mother's breast milk has already been infused with pesticides, herbicides, and hormone disruptors that chemical companies and their representatives have fought to keep on the market.

Once Eve starts eating solid food, what other chemicals will she be consuming? Spoiler alert: less than a third of the eighty thousand chemicals on the U.S. market today are regulated at all, so it's ultimately an unanswerable question. Was the food inspected, and if so, to what degree and by whom?

The banking lobby has its fingerprints all over the regulations that shape her parents' mortgage, their taxes, their medical bills, their job opportunities.

Eve can't escape the reach of the system. You can't. We can't. Government is us, and it's either working for us, or it's working for those who are trying to rig it to get what they want, sucking our employees (our legislators) into their agendas and often diverting our resources (tax dollars) into their pockets.

The middle of this book is dedicated to exploring the connections between political and policy manipulations in Washington and the price we all pay for those manipulations. We present case studies to demonstrate how the bending of—or outright obstruction of—the legislative process creates kitchen-table problems. We hope you'll see that we have to first fix our democracy and put ourselves back in the driver's seat of governing, if we want to fix the other problems we all face.

So is it fixable? Yes, if we are clear about what success means. The reformers' slogan, "Get Money Out of Politics," is misleading. We can't get money completely out of politics, but we can create a much, much higher-functioning and responsive system. It requires money to run campaigns, to hire door knockers, to print lawn signs, and to run TV, radio, and online ads (the bulk of the spending). Groups like the NRA, the Sierra Club, and the National Association of Manufacturers will always want to weigh in on key public policy debates. And they should.

What we can do is restore our power—the people's power—within the system by limiting the most egregious sources of the money, by creating new ways of financing politics that reorient politicians to their voters back home, by demanding total transparency in the giving and spending of political cash, by enacting new ethics and lobbying laws that reduce conflicts of interest and shut down the most transactional forms of political giving, and by making sure that campaign and lobbying laws are evenly and effectively enforced.

These things shouldn't seem so hard to achieve. We've won similar fights before. We're Americans, after all. We're the ones who make dramatic course corrections when things are going wrong or when new and revolutionary ideas emerge. We're not a defeatist or cynical people (although our level of cynicism is rising fast). We know that we can accomplish extraordinary things.

The reforming spirit that has fueled successful fights against Big Money was perhaps best embodied a century ago by Teddy Roosevelt. His time, just like ours, was one of unprecedented technological change when wealth and power were aggregating at the top of society. Massive corporate conglomerations—the bank, oil, railroad, and mining trusts, especially—threatened free and competitive markets. The rich were getting richer by the year. And the public felt outraged, yet exhausted, by the increasing pace of industrialized life and by the sense that their voices no longer mattered.

Roosevelt was a master at drawing battle lines:

> At many stages in the advance of humanity, this conflict between the men who possess more than they have earned and the men who have earned more than they possess is the central condition of progress. In our day it appears as the struggle of freemen to gain and hold the right of self-government as against the special interests, who twist the methods of free government into machinery for defeating the popular will.

He saw political reform as the precursor to winning other reforms—antitrust, public health, consumer safety.

As most who have read about TR know, he was not just talk. In fact, quite the opposite. In 1907, he helped ram through the first major campaign finance reform bill of the modern era, called the Tillman Act, which banned corporations from contributing directly to political campaigns.

These days, there are signs that Roosevelt's spirit might be coming back to life. As of the writing of this book, all of the Democratic presidential candidates have embraced money-in-politics reform as a central pillar of their campaigns. Many Republican candidates have acknowledged the increasing severity of the problem, although have been less clear about solutions. Love him or hate him, Donald Trump has been refreshingly blunt about what political money buys.

There are signs, too, that the Washington establishment is starting to come around. In the spring of 2015, the dean of Washington journalism, Bob Woodward, who as a young *Washington Post* reporter broke the Watergate scandal, said at a commencement address at Loyola University:

> There is a new governing crisis here and it is getting worse. It is about money in politics. It involves both political parties. I won't name names. If you follow the news at all, you know . . . It is important that the next president be able, unfettered and unbought, to find and move the country to the next stage of good.

A *governing crisis*. This is a dramatic statement for a careful wordsmith like Woodward.

Inhabiting a totally different part of the political ecosystem from Woodward's is a guy like John Feehery. Feehery was Dennis Hastert's chief of staff when Hastert was the Republican Speaker of the House in the early 2000s. He's now an executive at a big D.C. lobbying and public relations firm. Yet the same week that Woodward gave his Loyola commencement speech, Feehery wrote in the *Wall Street Journal*:

> I don't have anything against billionaires. It would be nice to have access to that kind of money. But our political system shouldn't be run by the super-rich for the super-rich's pet causes.

Run by the super-rich for the super-rich's pet causes is another way of saying *oligarchy*. America, an oligarchy. It's almost sickening to see those words next to one another. Imagine the heartbreak that John Adams and his compatriots would feel if they were alive today.

Then there are public servants of both the executive and legislative branches of government, such as John Kerry. Before he left the Hill to head the U.S. Department of State, Kerry delivered a moving speech to his colleagues from the floor of the Senate, in which he asserted:

> We should not resign ourselves ... to a distorted system that corrodes our democracy. This is what contributes to the justified anger of the American people. They know it. We know it. And yet nothing happens. The truth requires that we call the corrosion of money in politics what it is: it is a form of corruption and it muzzles more Americans than it empowers, and it is an imbalance that the world has taught us can only sow the seeds of unrest.

They know it. Indeed we do. A growing number of people, of all political stripes, are increasingly fed up. Last year, CBS News partnered with the *New York Times* on a poll, the conclusion of which was: "In a rare show of unity, Americans, regardless of their political affiliation, agree that money has too much influence on elections, the wealthy have more influence on elections, and candidates who win office promote policies that help their donors."

But it's no longer true that nothing is happening. More than at any time since Watergate, regular people are realizing that this situation has to change.

Since 2010, more than six hundred anti–*Citizens United* resolutions have been passed by cities and states. New campaign finance systems are already functioning in places including Connecticut, Arizona, and New York City. In 2014, led by the reform group Represent.Us, 67 percent of voters in Tallahassee, Florida, supported a major reform package, including lower campaign contribution limits, creation of a new, independent ethics commission, and a program to empower nonwealthy people to participate in funding politics. The coalition that was assembled to win consisted of progressives, independents, and Tea Party members.

Similar coalitions are forming around ballot measures in cities and states throughout the country. And there's the possibility for immediate progress at the federal level. Even if Congress isn't ready to legislate, the White House can act, and it should use its authority to do so. Hundreds of thousands of people have urged President Obama to sign an executive order that would require federal contractors—given that they are receiving taxpayer dollars—to disclose their political activities. If such an order were signed, 70 of the Fortune 100 companies would have to do so.

The Securities and Exchange Commission could also help. More than a million comments have been submitted to pressure the SEC to issue a rule requiring publicly traded companies to disclose the political dollars they spend on behalf of investors. Former Republican SEC Commissioner William Donaldson and former Democratic SEC Commissioner Bevis Longstreth are among the chorus calling for change.

But for these types of executive actions and state-based efforts to take root, we must immediately build a much stronger—and politically broader—citizen army. There is already a battalion of reformers working hard every day. But they are waiting for major reinforcements to arrive. That means you. And your friends. It will take you, and us, and millions of other kindred spirits to create a patriotic force powerful enough to reorient the power in this country back to "We, the people."

What are we up against? First or foremost, our own cynicism and resignation. Too many people—rich and poor, political and apolitical— have decided that we simply can't overcome the power of monied interests and have given up trying.

In fact, fixing this is *technically* remarkably simple compared to other things we need to fix—we could do it in a day with a single piece of legislation. No pipes or wires or army bases have to be moved. No new power plants need to be built or retrofitted. No cyber attacks need to be defended against. No international humanitarian missions need to be launched. No families or individuals have to change the way they eat or drive or raise their children. No new federal agency needs to be funded. No school needs to alter the way it educates our children. No hospital or health center needs to amend the way it cares for patients or bills insurance companies. No trade agreements need to be nullified. No workers need to be retrained. Those things—transportation, education, public health, national security, good jobs—are complicated. And, by the way, most of them are harder to fix because of the influence of money in politics. This, though—how money flows in and around our political system and our government—should be something we routinely clean up, like making sure the gutters on our homes are clear of leaves.

After all, what are we up against? There are maybe a hundred thousand political power brokers in this country who are truly invested in the perpetuation of a coin-operated government. They see no problem with it. They are unabashed about their participation in it. They figure that's how the world works. Money buys access. More money—and fundraising events and favors and nice trips—engender a sense of obligation between politicians, political donors, and lobbyists. So be it. Such people will say that spending money is an act of free speech. And some who say that genuinely believe it.

A few specific foes of reform: Senator Mitch McConnell (R-KY), although he used to be less antagonistic. The U.S. Chamber of Commerce has attacked most attempts to improve the system. More inside-the-Beltway Republicans are opposed to major reforms than Democrats, although that dynamic is changing. Outside the Beltway, more than a decade of public opinion polling shows that regular Republicans feel just as disturbed about the problem as do Democrats and independents. Many people who work on K Street—Ground Zero of the lobbying community in D.C.—like the system the way it is, although they will never say so publicly. Others on K Street would be happy if they didn't have to make campaign contributions and constantly attend political fundraisers.

It's possible that a hundred thousand might be too high a number. But, for the sake of argument, let's stick with it. That's 0.03 percent of the United States' population. We, the other 99.97 percent, have to push aside our cynicism and exhaustion and join with others from all walks of life to create a new, surprising, mighty reform moment in history.

Just as we won our right to self-government by fighting the British monarchy more than 240 years ago, we will lose it if we fail to fight to reclaim it now.

Imagine what would happen if we don't. Can any one of us truly claim that we will be able to revitalize our country as long as this problem worsens? Does anyone believe fixing our democracy is optional? Who among us would surrender ourselves, our children, our communities, to an oligarchy?

America is indeed a dream.

The poets are right: it is promises.

Once again it's time to prove that the people are also right: it is promises—that will come true.

CHAPTER 1

How We Got Here

I hope we shall take warning from the example and crush in its birth the aristocracy of our monied corporations which dare already to challenge our government to a trial of strength, and bid defiance to the laws of their country.

—THOMAS JEFFERSON, LETTER TO GEORGE LOGAN, 1816[1]

Money has a long history in American politics. Not even George Washington was immune. Before he earned a spot in every history book, on every map, and in every wallet across America, Washington was a victim of unchecked campaign spending. He lost his first race—for the House of Burgesses in 1755—by an enormous margin after his opponent supplied would-be voters with an admirably large and diverse selection of liquor. Not to be bested twice, Washington fought back with a vengeance three years later, coasting to a commanding victory after supplying voters with his own stash of booze.[2]

Washington's behavior was not out of the ordinary. Landed, wealthy men had the vote, and they were the ones who typically ran for office, largely funding their own campaigns. Back then, phrases like "campaign finance reform" or "money in politics" didn't exist—the Founders could not have imagined the scope and scale of today's political races, nor the massive buildup of the lobbying industry. Back then, campaigns were local and fundraising was minimal.

But larger questions about the role of wealth in the republic were in the air. In 1816, for instance, Thomas Jefferson had been out of office for seven years, having served two successful terms as president. Like many of the luminaries of his generation, he wrote extensively about politics. In a letter to his friend and colleague, the former senator George Logan of Pennsylvania, he expressed concern about the threat posed to the national interest by the growing influence of corporate wealth. He—and his contemporaries—were beginning to see trends emerge that could threaten the system of government they had bled for in the Revolution, helped construct at the Constitutional Convention, and worked to implement as elected officials.

Some of what they predicted—those "monied corporations which dare already to challenge our government to a trial of strength"—emerged full force in the middle of the nineteenth century, as the nation's economy modernized and industrialized at a breathtaking pace. With the manufacturing boom—and the shift away from what we today call "family farming"—came the rise of the transnational corporation. The men behind these powerful businesses have been woven into the fabric of the American story—Rockefeller, Carnegie, Morgan.

Americans were unsettled by the breakneck changes they were experiencing. They saw how a handful of aggressive businessmen could control swaths of the economic landscape. As the big corporations grew richer, they began to exert greater control over the political realm, too. History has shown that when wealth aggregates, it has a tendency to assert its power in order to protect itself.

Expanding voting, first to men without property, and then, over time, to nonwhite men after the Fifteenth Amendment in 1870, broadened the electorate. This process diluted to some extent the political power of the wealthy, who had once exclusively controlled the right to vote. But a populist groundswell was also brewing, built in opposition to the corporate titans of the era. As industrialization and corporate consolidation filled their coffers, elites sought to counter the forces opposing their continued political dominance through political contributions. If they couldn't be in power themselves, they could fund those who would be.

Senator William Chandler of New Hampshire, who had been one of the founders of the Republican Party as a young man in the mid-1850s, understood the public's concerns. In a 1904 letter to Wisconsin governor

Robert La Follette, Chandler gave voice to the zeitgeist at the turn of the century: "When corporations can furnish money to carry elections from corporate treasuries, individualism in government is gone. . . . When the custom grows broad enough the whole character of government is changed, and corporations rule, not men."[3]

Chandler echoes Jefferson. The Founders thought intensely about the character of the government they were creating, grappling with notions of individual and systemic corruption. As we discuss throughout this book, the distinction between the two is crucial for analyzing the state of the American political system. As the Founders saw it, the Fordham University law professor Zephyr Teachout writes, "corruption—writ large—is the rotting of positive ideals of civic virtue and public integrity."[4] This isn't the much-maligned, Jack Abramoff–style quid pro quo corruption—this kind of systemic rot goes much deeper than bribery. When citizens lose faith in their government, the government has been corrupted, and this can bring down even the mightiest democracy. In the late 1800s, the rise of the corporate economy brought with it the rise of the corporate campaign—and some Americans worried that the character of their government *had* been changed. As the historian Doris Kearns Goodwin quotes in *The Bully Pulpit*, Republican president Teddy Roosevelt saw the same problem during the Gilded Age, later noting, "the power of the mighty industrial overlords of the country had increased with giant strides, while the methods of controlling them, or checking abuses by them on the part of the people, through the Government, remained archaic and therefore practically impotent."[5]

The First Corporate-Funded Campaign

The election of 1896 might be considered the first modern presidential contest, thanks largely to the efforts of Marcus Alonzo Hanna. Hanna was a successful businessman, running a prosperous coal and iron business in his home state of Ohio. He also had an interest in politics—which, combined with his deep pockets, landed him a position as a fundraiser for the Republican National Committee. Hanna used his checkbook to wield massive influence in the party primary, bankrolling his friend William McKinley's campaign almost entirely with his own money.

Hanna's big innovation was to travel to New York to solicit contributions from the big banks and trusts that operated there—essentially seeking money in exchange for assurance that government policies would favor their interests. The business community would fare better, he argued, if McKinley were elected president.[6] This strategy was unprecedented: in previous cycles, candidates had dedicated a percentage of their salaries to fund their campaigns. But such novel ideas often end up working. Big business responded to Hanna by opening its collective wallet, hoping to shield its growing fortunes. McKinley raked in $96 million in today's dollars using the new approach, including the equivalent of $6.9 million from Standard Oil. The contest kicked off a pattern of rising campaign costs that would come to define American elections.

The election of 1896 was truly a watershed moment. As a percentage of GDP, no election before or since has seen spending levels as high.[7] The rise of outside contributions triggered fundamental questions about politics and elections in the minds of many Americans.

As the historian Robert Mutch, author of *Buying the Vote*, argues, questions of campaign finance are fundamentally inseparable from broader questions of democracy, and the era's economic inequality and powerful corporations brought this discussion into focus. He writes:

> [It] opened a new phase of the old debate about how our democracy should work, turning it into a question about money as well as votes. Like earlier differences about how far to extend the suffrage, the debate over where campaign funds should come from is part of the constitutional issue of deciding who should govern.[8]

Much as they do today, people had begun to worry that a handful of wealthy men had co-opted the political system. Indeed, as Hanna famously said, "There are two things that are important in politics. The first is money and I can't remember what the second one is."[9] By the turn of the century, big business had established itself as a force to be reckoned with in the political system.

Teddy and Pitchfork Ben

When the irascible Teddy Roosevelt took over after McKinley was assassinated by the anarchist Leon Czolgosz in 1901, he would prove to be an entirely different type of leader. As president, he would pursue campaign finance reform—the first president to take up the cause—as one of many means of fighting the monopolistic corporations.

In 1903, two years after taking office, Roosevelt was in full trust-busting mode. The previous year, he had invoked the all-but-ignored Sherman Antitrust Act of 1890 to take on J. P. Morgan's behemoth railroad holding company.[10] The case, *Northern Securities Co. v. United States*, would eventually result in a landmark Supreme Court decision restricting corporate consolidation.[11] Roosevelt commended the decision, but he realized the need for additional change. In a lengthy speech delivered at the State Fair in Syracuse, New York, in 1903, he railed against monopolistic power:

> The death-knell of the republic had rung as soon as the active power became lodged in the hands of those who sought, not to do justice to all citizens, rich and poor alike, but to stand for one special class and for its interests as opposed to the interests of others.[12]

Roosevelt's opposition to corporate consolidation and his reputation for independence, along with a strong stance on foreign policy, helped him breeze through the 1904 election to win a second term.[13] But that year's campaign also hit a strong note of irony. Soon after the election, the press reported that his campaign had received possibly nefarious corporate contributions, including an alleged $100,000 donation from John D. Rockefeller's Standard Oil Company.[14] The *New York Times* attacked with a scathing editorial, mercilessly headlined THE ROOT OF ALL EVIL, that is worth quoting extensively from here:

> Certainly the virus has penetrated deeply and has wrought subtly when a man of Mr. Roosevelt's native scorn for corruption can be the willing, the eager beneficiary of funds paid into the campaign chest through his former secretary and former Cabinet officer with the undisguised hope that it will be repaid in favors to the subscribers . . . When we make Governmental action a source of private profit we invite, we compel, large numbers of men to seek to influence that action for their own advancement or defense. And since such action depends on the party in control of the government, the first effort of those who would influence it is toward the success of the party that will favor them. Thus we have not merely the class of eager, aggressive, sometimes unscrupulous business men who depend on the policy of the government and on the party control of the Government, but we have also the

vast number of politicians and place holders all animated by the same interest, all pursuing practically the same end, combining, plotting, working together to bend the minds of those responsible for public action away from the general and common good and toward their own private advantage. No more potent force, or complex of forces, tending toward substantial corruption has ever been known in political history.[15]

Roosevelt was quick to call for the complete prohibition of corporate donations to campaigns. In his 1905 message to Congress, he proclaimed, "All contributions by corporations to any political committee or for any political purpose should be forbidden by law."[16] Taking the lead in fulfilling this mandate was Senator Benjamin Tillman of South Carolina.

Tillman, a Democrat, may not have been the likeliest choice to help push Roosevelt's agenda, given the checkered history between them. The two had begun clashing when the notoriously fiery "Pitchfork Ben," as he was known, got into a fistfight with another senator on the Senate floor. Roosevelt, who thought such behavior unbecoming of a senator, had rescinded Tillman's invitation to an upcoming state dinner. Tillman was terribly offended and had resolved to be a thorn in Roosevelt's side.

Thanks to some political gamesmanship, however, Roosevelt's proposed ban on corporate campaign contributions bore Tillman's name. Though the Tillman Act passed the Senate with ease, the House proved a tougher crowd—but Roosevelt, beloved for his tenacity, did not falter. The first item on the agenda in his 1906 message to Congress: admonishing the House for their failure to pass the bill. Roosevelt left no room for misunderstanding of his position. "Let individuals contribute as they desire," he proclaimed, "but let us prohibit in effective fashion all corporations from making contributions for any political purpose, directly or indirectly."[17] The House passed the bill shortly thereafter, and Roosevelt signed it into law in early 1907. With the Tillman Act, America had passed its first major campaign finance law.

As the 1908 election loomed, big donations still weighed heavily on the public's collective conscience. Both major candidates—William Jennings Bryan and William Howard Taft—committed to disclosing their donors, in part because of the embarrassing revelations Roosevelt had suffered in the wake of his 1904 election. Taft, the Republican, looked beyond big business in New York to a larger web of smaller donors, and he translated that broader support into a winning campaign.

In 1910, congressional Republicans passed additional campaign finance laws, which restricted House campaign spending and required political parties to report their expenditures and donations, but only after the election had occurred. A coalition of Republicans and Northern Democrats amended the law in 1911 to mandate pre-election disclosure by candidates as well as parties for primary and general election campaigns, and they extended the spending limits to Senate candidates.[18]

In 1925, Congress amended the 1910 law again—this time to remove the disclosure mandate for primary elections and require political committees to report contributions that were made between election cycles.[19]

Going After the Unions

All was relatively quiet on the reform front until the late 1930s, when the Hatch Act—which officially bore the rather grandiose title of "An Act to Prevent Pernicious Political Activities"[20]—gained momentum. Introduced by New Mexico senator Carl Hatch, the legislation was a response to reports of New Deal relief workers doubling as campaign operatives. The Hatch Act, still in effect today, explicitly banned the intimidation or bribery of voters and restricted political campaign activities by federal employees.

By the early 1940s, both parties had cemented their main donor bases, with Republicans relying on big business and Democrats relying on organized labor. Just as corporate contributions at the turn of the century spurred Democrats to call for reform, conservatives moved to check the rising union power that had lifted FDR into the White House.

In 1943, when the United Mine Workers union broke its promise not to go on strike during the war, congressional Republicans mobilized to pass the Smith-Connally Act, which allowed the federal government to seize striking industries involved in the war effort and banned union contributions to federal campaigns. The Congress of Industrial Organizations (CIO) responded with a campaign finance innovation that survives to this day—the political action committee, or PAC. Rather than drawing from its treasury to contribute directly to campaigns, the union set up a PAC that was able to raise donations from members. It was a work-around of sorts—the unions were no longer making contributions to political campaigns, the PACs were. It's worth noting that unions could still make direct political *expenditures*—just not campaign contributions.[21]

Corporations had been engaging in similar practices—*strongly recommending* that employees vote for certain candidates and donate to specific campaigns—to work around their own ban on direct campaign contributions. Congress reacted to the CIO PAC by moving to end such a stratagem, including a provision in the anti-union Taft-Hartley bill that would ban both corporations and unions from *directly* spending money on politics.[22] The *indirect* spending, though, through PACs, was just beginning.

The bill enjoyed conservative support in the newly elected 80th Congress, which inaugurated in January of 1947, where Republicans controlled both the House and the Senate for the first time in fifteen years. Northern Democrats were less enthused; the vote on the bill split cleanly along partisan lines. President Harry Truman, a Democrat, sided with his party. He vetoed the bill on June 20, pulling no punches in his accompanying message to Congress:

> I would have signed a bill with some doubtful features if, taken as a whole, it had been a good bill . . . But the Taft-Hartley bill is a shocking piece of legislation. . . . Under no circumstances could I have signed this bill . . . The restrictions that this bill places on our workers go far beyond what our people have been led to believe. This is no innocent bill.[23]

Unions didn't take the new restriction lying down; the CIO immediately challenged the constitutionality of the expenditure ban. *United States v. Congress of Industrial Organizations* has provided precedent for campaign finance law ever since. As the government wrote in its brief, corporate and union contributions and expenditures could be classified and banned together, since Congress had passed the laws to "control the power represented by the aggregate wealth of entities, organized primarily for nonpolitical purposes . . . in a position to exercise a disproportionate influence on federal elections."[24] The "aggregate wealth" argument was powerful. The law stood, and the classification of corporations and unions as similar aggregators of wealth for federal campaign finance restrictions has largely remained intact to this day.

For practical purposes, though, the laws on the books remained largely ineffective. Beginning with the Tillman Act, the enforcement of which Robert Mutch has called "a legal and practical impossibility,"[25] campaign finance laws in the first half of the twentieth century were rife with loopholes and widely ignored by political players.

Taft-Hartley ushered in a decades-long lull in reform efforts. There was little policy action to speak of until 1971, when President Richard Nixon signed the Federal Election Campaign Act into law. FECA was designed to join the separate, weaker campaign finance laws of previous decades into a strong, centralized piece of legislation. Taking full effect in April 1972, FECA required the complete reporting of campaign contributions and expenditures.[26] Along with the 1971 Revenue Act, it also instituted the first federal financing system for presidential campaigns. Ronald Reagan took advantage of the program for his winning bid in 1980, and all major party presidential candidates since then utilized matching funds in the general election, if not in the primary, until Barack Obama in 2008.[27]

The Revenue Act may have been intended to make sweeping changes to the system of campaign finance—but, like so many laws before it, it did not include sufficient means for administration or enforcement. After the 1972 election, more than seven thousand cases were referred to the Justice Department, which was able to prosecute just a few of them.[28] Campaign finance reform groups used FECA reporting requirements to bring more disclosure into the public view.

Money Becomes Speech

It took the Watergate scandal and the end of a presidency to make real progress with regard to enforcement. The revelation of the Nixon administration's wide-ranging abuse of power, including campaign violations and slush funds of illegal contributions, shook Americans' faith in their government. Once again, crisis would sow the seeds of change.

Out of the ashes of the scandal rose a means of enforcing the laws on the books. In 1975, Congress created the Federal Election Commission to oversee all aspects of the campaign administration and finance process. The FEC consolidated the administrative responsibilities and enforcement authority that, up to that point, had been split between agencies.[29] Everything about the group's operation is bipartisan by design. Of its six commissioners, three must be Democrats and three Republicans; in

FEC (established 1975) with a mission to administer and enforce:

- Public disclosure of funds raised and spent to influence federal elections

- Restrictions on contributions and expenditures made to influence federal elections

- The public financing of presidential campaigns

Basic Federal Campaign Finance Laws:

- Contributions to candidates limited to $2,700 from individuals and $5,000 from PACs.

- Contributions to candidates banned from corporations, labor unions, government contractors and foreign nationals

- Super PACs can raise and spend unlimited amounts of money. Such spending is not supposed to be coordinated with candidates or their committees.

Federal Election Commission (FEC)
Source: Federal Election Commission (fec.gov)

order for it to take action, at least four of the members must agree.[30] In theory, this system prevents partisan abuses. In practice, it has resulted in profound inefficiency and crippling deadlock, making meaningful enforcement difficult.

Perhaps the late 1970s' most significant legacy came not from government agencies or legislation, but from the courts. As the reform movement pushed for more and better controls on campaign contributions, those in favor of maintaining the status quo crafted a powerful, lasting rebuttal. As the historian Robert Mutch puts it, campaign-finance-reform foes "developed a First Amendment doctrine that so closely linked campaign speech with campaign money that it would have made any regulation of that money unconstitutional."[31] This is the intellectual wellspring of *Citizens United*: since campaign spending is a form of political expression, limits on it are impermissible. Armed with this line of thinking, anti-reformers challenged FECA.

In 1976, the Supreme Court handed down its landmark decision in *Buckley v. Valeo*. James L. Buckley, a first-term senator from New York and then a member of the newly minted Conservative Party, boasted an impressive conservative pedigree. His younger brother, William F. Buckley, was the founder of the *National Review*. Before James's election to the Senate, both brothers ran long-shot campaigns for Congress just to ensure that their ideas made it into the conversation.

Despite Buckley's often partisan ways, the lawsuit that bore his name was remarkably bipartisan. His rather unlikely bedfellow was former senator Eugene McCarthy of Minnesota—the liberal who had sought and lost the Democratic nomination for president just a few years earlier. The lawsuit aimed to overturn the post-Watergate reforms that limited the amount of money federal candidates could receive from an individual donor, as well as how much of their own money they could spend.

Many years later, Buckley would describe the case's outcome to the *Wall Street Journal* as "50/50." The Court ruled that a cap on individual campaign spending violated the First Amendment right to free speech. They also decided, however, that campaign contributions should be limited so as to avoid corruption, or the appearance thereof.[32] And they affirmed the need for disclosure and upheld the presidential public financing system—important tools for the reform efforts of today and tomorrow.

The idea that money is speech is by no means a universally held belief by the courts, though. In a 2000 case, the Supreme Court held that *Buckley*'s contribution limit principles apply to contribution limits in state elections. As Justice John Paul Stevens wrote in his concurring opinion, political money is protected, but not at the same level as speech:

> In response to [Justice Anthony Kennedy's] call for a new begin-
> ning, therefore, I make one simple point. Money is property;
> it is not speech ... The right to use one's own money to hire
> gladiators, or to fund "speech by proxy," certainly merits signifi-
> cant constitutional protection. These property rights, however,
> are not entitled to the same protection as the right to say what
> one pleases.[33]

Stevens's line of thinking—that money is property—is an important alternative constitutional reading. But *Buckley v. Valeo*'s precedent, that political spending is an act of speech, has informed many of the major Supreme Court campaign finance decisions of the last four decades.

The Advent and Explosion of Soft Money

Corporations, unions, and political parties took advantage of the Court's decision. The money began to pile up, fast.

"Soft" money, which was unrestricted and raised for nebulous "party building" activities, came into vogue in the 1990s. In contrast to the tightly regulated, disclosed "hard" money contributed directly to candidates' campaigns, soft money was tough to track and control. Parties built up massive war chests, exploiting the spotty federal regulatory apparatus and more generous state laws, and rewarded their big-money donors. In one egregious example, major Democratic donors were offered sleepovers in the Lincoln bedroom of the Clinton White House.[34]

The 2000 election was another leap forward for Big Money. George W. Bush declined to avail himself of the presidential public financing option in the primary election—primarily out of fear that the billionaire Steve Forbes would self-finance his way to a victory—and, to everyone's surprise, raised $100 million just for the primary. He then used the public financing system in the general election. According to Doug Weber of the Center for Responsive Politics, no one in Washington thought a candidate could rake in that much cash—conventional wisdom had dictated that presidential campaigns would raise some campaign money and then use public federal funds to boost their totals.[35]

Bush's bypassing of the presidential public financing system in the primary, plus the amount of "soft money" the political parties were pumping into the elections, led to another major wake-up call. It was the "extraordinary amount of soft money in the 2000 election that marked what many political scientists saw as the final collapse of FECA," Mutch writes.[36] Americans were unsettled by the soft-money explosion, and good-government groups agitated for change. Reform came two years later, with the Bipartisan Campaign Reform Act (BCRA) of 2002. This act is often called "McCain-Feingold" after its bipartisan duo of sponsors: Senators John McCain (R-AZ) and Russ Feingold (D-WI). McCain-Feingold extended pre-existing statutes prohibiting corporations from using company funds to broadcast advertisements advocating for or against a candidate for federal office within a certain period before elections. It also prohibited soft money (unlimited) contributions to national political parties.[37]

Analyses of McCain-Feingold are remarkably similar to those of the Tillman Act. Proponents of McCain-Feingold argued that with soft money contributions no longer allowed, smaller donations would replace the large sums that corporations had been able to donate.[38] Compare that with a June 1906 New York Times article about the Tillman Act, which at the time had not yet passed the House. A Republican

Hill staffer quoted in the item, after expressing sympathy for the corporations that had suffered "extortion" at the hands of the political parties,
added:

> Parties will be put to it to fill their coffers by really voluntary
> contributions. These will be smaller than the old ones, but they
> will answer all legitimate needs for the simple reason that needs
> which they do not satisfy will cease to seem legitimate.[39]

Both efforts aimed to revitalize the grassroots of the political parties by
forcing them to rely on a high volume of small donations instead of a low
volume of large ones.

Critics, meanwhile, warned that McCain-Feingold's soft-money ban
and transparency measures would simply reroute gargantuan donations
to outside groups, many of which operate in a largely unregulated, uncon-
trolled Wild West–style system. Those fears would come to fruition to a
greater extent than anyone imagined.

In 2004, "527" organizations, so named for the section of the tax code
they are registered under, boomed in popularity. The groups are not
bound by contribution limits, but they must disclose their donors. Most
of the 527s in 2004 leaned left, with Republican groups making up only
fifteen of the top fifty organizations. Americans Coming Together, a 527
created to boost John Kerry's unsuccessful campaign, pooled multi-
million-dollar donations from wealthy Democrats including George
Soros, Peter Lewis, and Stephen Bing.[40]

When Barack Obama ran for president in 2008, he became the first
major-party candidate to bypass the presidential public financing system
in both the primary and general elections. Jimmy Carter, Ronald Reagan,
George H. W. Bush, Bill Clinton, and George W. Bush were all elected
with public funds. (Their challengers also received public funds.) The
money for the program is furnished by taxpayers who check the
voluntary-contribution box on their tax forms. Had Obama opted into
the program, as John McCain did, he would have received about $85 million
for the general election but would have had to forgo the small-donor and
major-donor fundraising that his campaign was quickly mastering. In the
end, Obama raised $750 million in 2008, which is more than all of the
presidential candidates collectively spent in 2004. His lack of participation in the program—combined with the suddenly enormous sums of
money people now believe are necessary to run for president—has left

the system in limbo. Neither Mitt Romney nor Barack Obama utilized it in 2012, and there is no indication that anyone will in 2016. Reviving the program, in a way that offers presidential candidates enough money to run robust campaigns, would be a valuable goal for near-term policy reforms.

Hillary: The Movie That Created Super PACs

In 2010, the Supreme Court ruled in *Citizens United v. Federal Election Commission* that corporations' and unions' efforts to publicly communicate their support for—or opposition to—political candidates by means of the spending of money should be protected as speech under the First Amendment. Ever since then, *Citizens United* has become a shorthand way of referring to Big Money in politics.

Two years before the ruling, in 2008, the plaintiff in the case, a conservative nonprofit organization called Citizens United was blocked from advertising and broadcasting (as a cable TV video-on-demand selection) a film called *Hillary: The Movie* just as the Democratic primaries were about to start. A federal court in Washington ruled that airing the film, which was strongly biased against Hillary Clinton, would violate a provision of the 2002 McCain-Feingold campaign finance law that prohibited certain kinds of groups from spending money on "electioneering communications" thirty days prior to a primary election and sixty days prior to a general election. The rationale behind that piece of the law was to create an opportunity in the final days of an election for voters to hear more from the candidates' campaigns and less from outside groups.

Citizens United hired James Bopp, a lawyer from Terre Haute, Indiana, to bring suit against the FEC. Bopp had built a reputation for successfully peeling back other campaign finance restrictions, arguing they violated constitutional protections of free speech.[41] He compared his client's film to CBS's *60 Minutes* broadcasts and said that banning it violated the group's First Amendment rights.

In a 5–4 decision, the Court ruled that spending money on communications is an act of speech and therefore should not be restricted, as long as the money spent was independent from (not coordinated with) the candidates' campaigns. Justice Anthony Kennedy laid out the rationale: "Because speech is an essential mechanism of democracy—it is the means to hold officials accountable to the people—political speech must prevail against laws that would suppress it by design or inadvertence."[42] He later expanded on the reasoning, to touch on an argument that is really more about freedom of the press than freedom of speech: "Premised on mistrust of governmental power, the First Amendment stands against attempts to disfavor certain subjects or viewpoints or to distinguish among different speakers, which may be a means to control content."[43]

That's the most laudable aspect of the decision. There are all kinds of corporations—from global media conglomerates to one-person start-ups—that pump out content and ideas about politics and politicians in the context of elections. Trying to distinguish among the sources is fraught. In the wrong hands, it could potentially lead to outright partisan censorship on behalf of the government—something that should scare any American.

Fifty years ago—even fifteen years ago—it was easier to tell the difference between "the press" and others. The press was, for the most part, people who had the money to buy presses, radio towers, and TV stations. But in the age of the Internet, where publishing is essentially free, where can the lines be drawn? It's all a mixed-up mess of content and opinion. What's the difference between a Fox News special report that's critical of Hillary and a Citizens United movie that's critical of her? Should one be allowed, under the rules of McCain-Feingold, and one banned? What about a negative video about Donald Trump, sponsored by a progressive organization (a nonprofit corporation), and a negative piece about him on MSNBC (a subsidiary of a for-profit corporation)?

Michael McConnell is a senior fellow at Stanford University's Hoover Institution and the director of Stanford's Constitutional Law Center. Formerly, he served as a federal judge, nominated by George W. Bush. It was rumored that he was eyed by Bush as a potential Supreme Court nominee. He's no liberal. Writing in the *Yale Law Journal*, McConnell praises, for lack of a better term, the "free press" piece of the *Citizens United* decision:

> It is not constitutional for the government to punish the dissemination of such a documentary by a media corporation, and it therefore follows that it cannot be constitutional to punish its dissemination by a non-media corporation like Citizens United unless the freedom of the press is confined to the institutional

media. Precedent, history, and pragmatics all refute the idea that freedom of the press is so confined.[44]

But then he takes to task the rest of what Justice Kennedy wrote:

> The opinion is overly long and unfocused. It seems to stretch for unnecessarily broad interpretations of free speech law, beyond what the parties argued or what the facts demanded ... The opinion itself was written with a broad brush, turning its back on several plausible narrower grounds for decision. But the most important flaw—a flaw to which the parties and the lower courts contributed—was to analyze the case under the wrong clause of the First Amendment. If the Court had analyzed the case under the Press Clause, it could have avoided muddying the waters of campaign finance law governing contributions, which presents different constitutional considerations, and it would have side-stepped the controversy over whether for-profit corporations, in general, have constitutional rights.[45]

Justice John Paul Stevens, who penned the dissent for the four liberal justices, was so angered by the ruling that he made the rare move of reading his dissent aloud from the bench. His criticism, like McConnell's, includes a broadside against the reckless overreach of the majority:

> Today's decision is backwards in many senses. It elevates the majority's agenda over the litigants' submissions, facial attacks over as-applied claims, broad constitutional theories over narrow statutory grounds, individual dissenting opinions over precedential holdings, assertion over tradition, absolutism over empiricism, rhetoric over reality.[46]

Stevens goes a step further, asserting that the decision could at some point unleash gushers of corporate cash into the political debate that could drown out the marketplace of ideas and create a monopoly of opinion. He additionally argues, as some of the Founders might have, that such extensive—and expensive—political activity could have such a dominating effect on elected officials that it could corrupt the government: "At bottom, the Court's opinion is thus a rejection of the common sense of the American people."[47]

Stevens was correct about the common sense of the American people. A 2014 poll showed that 80 percent of Americans opposed the *Citizens United* decision. Only 18 percent supported it. The breakdown of opposition is hardly partisan: Republicans, 72 percent; Democrats, 82 percent; independents, 84 percent.[48]

On the potentially corrupting influence of the decision, we turn to Norm Ornstein, a resident scholar at the American Enterprise Institute, who is one of the most respected observers of the ways of Washington:

> Ask almost any lobbyist. I hear the same story there over and over—the lobbyist met with a lawmaker to discuss a matter for a client, and before he gets back to the office, the cell phone rings and the lawmaker is asking for money. The connections between policy actions or inactions and fundraising are no longer indirect or subtle. Now comes [another] component. As one Senator said to me, "We have all had experiences like the following: A lobbyist or interest representative will be in my office. He or she will say, 'You know, Americans for a Better America really, really want this amendment passed. And they have more money than God. I don't know what they will do with their money if they don't get what they want. But they are capable of spending a fortune to make anybody who disappoints them regret it.'" No money has to be spent to get the desired outcome . . . This is what Citizens United hath wrought. It is thoroughly corrupting.[49]

This kind of deep understanding of how money and politics interact is something that Ornstein has developed after decades of examining Washington up close. Notice, the senator who spoke to Ornstein didn't say: "Well, because Americans for A Better America is an independent-expenditure group, they have no effect on my thinking or behavior." And notice that there is no quid pro quo—no specific exchange of campaign contributions for legislative favors. As Ornstein notes, "no money has to be spent to get the desired outcome."

But the Supreme Court justices inhabit such a rarefied intellectual bubble that they don't understand how money works its way on the political system. Sandra Day O'Connor was the last justice to have held elected office. Their naïve assumption that "independent expenditures" have no potentially corrupting effect on the behavior of politicians is the most glaring example of such a blind spot.

FOR   **AGAINST**

Corporations and unions can now spend on ads advocating a candidate's election or defeat, without restriction.

Individuals can make unlimited contributions to super PACs.

Of the $1 billion spent in federal elections by super PACs in the five years following the ruling, almost 60 percent came from 195 individuals and their spouses, according to the Brennan Center for Justice.

What Citizens United Changed.

"The two most abrupt breaks with the historical meaning of corruption—*Buckley* and *Citizens United*—have occurred when no politicians were on the [Supreme] Court," writes Fordham University law professor Zephyr Teachout in her book *Corruption in America*. "While lower courts and state courts have consistently expanded the scope of corruption laws, an opposite movement has happened on high. The [Supreme] Court has become populated by academics and appellate court justices, and not by people with experience of power and politics, who understand the ways in which real problems of money and influence manifest themselves."[50] Teachout argues that the court has too narrowly defined corruption as quid-pro-quo corruption— the direct exchange of money for specific legislative favors or outcomes. This form of corruption is basically already forbidden by law. It's called bribery. And, as we stated earlier in the book, it's not the kind of corruption the Founding Fathers were most worried about. They were concerned with preventing systemic corruption, or the bending of the government away from the public good and toward private gain.

That's why Kennedy's massive overreach in the scope of the case was so dangerous—if you're going to go off trail and bushwhack in the dark, you'd better know the terrain—in this case, the terrain of money in politics. Justice Ruth Bader Ginsburg, who joined in Stevens's dissent, said in a 2014 interview: "I think the notion that we have all the democracy that money can buy strays so far from what our democracy is supposed to be . . . Members of the legislature, people who have to run for office, know the connection between money and influence on what laws get passed."[51]

The Supreme Court didn't stop with *Citizens United*, either. The money-as-speech argument spawned another case, in 2014: *McCutcheon v. FEC*. In a 5–4 decision, the Court struck down aggregate contribution limits—the caps on total donations to candidates and party committees in a given election cycle—on the grounds that if contributions are considered political speech, limiting the number of those contributions is unconstitutional. Now a wealthy donor can cut a $2,700 check, for both the primary and general elections, for every candidate in the country. *Citizens United* continues to metastasize.

Bipartisan Angst Over *Citizens United*

Members of Congress are speaking out about what the Court has wrought. Nearly every Democrat in both the House and Senate has condemned *Citizens United*. In a symbolic moment before the 2014 midterm elections, Senate Democrats staged a debate about amending the Constitution to reverse the ruling. And it's not just Democrats. The nonprofit group Free Speech for People has identified more than 150 Republican leaders—from former Bush and Reagan White House officials to governors and members of Congress—who have been critical of the decision.

In the summer of 2015, former Republican senator John Danforth of Missouri, a man widely respected by members of both parties, said: "The Supreme Court's decision in *Citizens United* undermines our republican form of government and should not stand . . . [It has] further separated candidates and voters by inserting interlopers between the two. These interlopers are well-heeled individuals and corporations that pour massive amounts of money into supposedly independent campaigns."[52] His statement was especially powerful given that he shepherded Justice Clarence Thomas's confirmation through the Senate. Thomas stood with the majority in *Citizens United*.

One technical point: The pouring of "massive amounts of money into supposedly independent campaigns" is actually not a direct result of *Citizens United*. It's the progeny of a case called *SpeechNow.org v. FEC*. In its March 2010 decision, the D.C. Circuit Court of Appeals ruled, based on the logic of *Citizens United*, that if *spending* by independent groups (organizations not directly affiliated with politicians' campaigns) should be unlimited, then *giving* to such independent groups should be unlimited, too. Super PACs were born of this *SpeechNow.org* decision. It sanctioned unlimited contributions to independent groups capable of spending unlimited amounts of money to elect or defeat candidates.

These types of rulings have sped up the decline of self-government, both because they have "further separated candidates and voters" and because they have created a political arena so dominated by colossal forces that nearly everyone, other than an elite group of politically motivated billionaires and special interest groups, is feeling irrelevant in our democracy.

A March 2015 Rasmussen poll found that 58 percent of Americans think most members of Congress will sell their vote for cash or campaign contributions, while 63 percent believe most incumbents are reelected because election rules unfairly benefit them.[53]

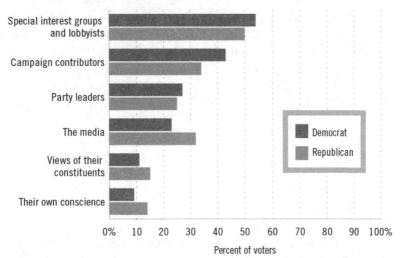

Who Does Congress Listen To? Constituents rank themselves near the bottom of the list
Source: Democracy Corps and Every Voice (everyvoice.org), 2014.

Another recent poll asked voters who has the most influence on how members of Congress vote. Fifty-four percent of Democrats and half of Republicans said "special interests and lobbyists." Coming in second were "campaign contributors." At the bottom of the list were "constituents," who 11 percent of Democrats and 15 percent of Republicans said were most influential.[54]

Ellen Miller has started three enduring good-government groups in the last thirty years—the Center for Responsive Politics, Public Campaign (now called Every Voice), and the Sunlight Foundation. She was the first to make campaign finance data more accessible to the public, back in the 1980s. When we asked her about the current movement, and about what she has witnessed with the rise of Big Money over politics in the last three decades, she was blunt: "I couldn't have imagined that it would get this bad. To suggest the situation is dire would be a vast understatement. Our electoral democracy has been steadily and effectively taken away from American people. Money has practically become the sole determinant of who runs for office, who wins, and what they say and do. It's a true American tragedy."

Looking back at the full span of our history, it becomes clear that we once again stand at a crossroads. We have to grapple with the role of money and power in our democratic republic. Campaigns, and campaign finance, have come a long way since landed aristocrats enticed voters with booze. But Jefferson's worries—about monied interests challenging "our government to a trial of strength"—are as valid today as ever.

CHAPTER 2

Rigged

"I won't dispute for one second the problems of a system that demands [an] immense amount of fund-raisers by its legislators," said Representative Jim Himes, a third-term Democrat of Connecticut, who supported the recent industry-backed bills and leads the party's fund-raising effort in the House. A member of the Financial Services Committee and a former banker at Goldman Sachs, he is one of the top recipients of Wall Street donations. "It's appalling, it's disgusting, it's wasteful and it opens the possibility of conflicts of interest and corruption. It's unfortunately the world we live in."

—"BANKS' LOBBYISTS HELP IN DRAFTING FINANCIAL BILLS,"

NEW YORK TIMES, MAY 23, 2013

It's unfortunately the world we live in.

Let's spend more time exploring the world our elected representatives live in. Although, as countless polls have shown, nearly all Americans believe money dominates politics, not many actually know the details, even fewer know how bad it's gotten, and too many think it's mostly attributable to *Citizens United*.

Make no mistake about it: as we stated a few pages ago, *Citizens United* was a bad decision that has created a great deal of reckless political behavior since it was handed down six years ago, especially among some billionaire political donors. But the role of money in politics, and its contribution to the decline of self-government in America, has been in the making for decades.

In 1998, the total amount of money spent on federal elections was $1.6 billion. By 2012, it had nearly quadrupled to $6.2 billion. In 1998, the average winning House candidate spent $650,000 and the average winning Senate candidate spent $5.2 million. In 2014 those numbers were $1.45 million and $10.6 million, respectively.

Spending by the influence industry in Washington to shape the decisions of policy makers has also increased exponentially in recent decades. In 1960, when John F. Kennedy was elected president, 289 lobbying groups spent a grand total of $30.4 million (in today's dollars) on lobbying activities.[1] The highest-spending group that year was the AFL-CIO, which shelled out the equivalent of just over $1 million. A report on the year's lobbying noted that a new power player, the American Petroleum Institute, had emerged. Adjusting for inflation, the API had spent $722,000.[2] In 1975, total revenue for Washington lobbyists was about $100 million. In 2014, lobbying spending reached $3.23 *billion*, more than a hundred times the 1960 total.[3] The biggest spender, the U.S. Chamber of Commerce, paid a staggering $124 million to a bevy of firms

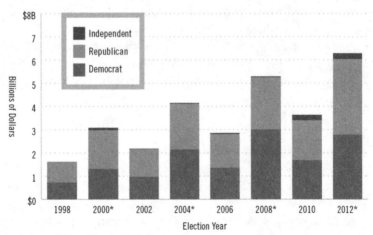

Total Cost of U.S. Elections by Party
Source: Center for Responsive Politics (opensecrets.org)
Methodology: *Presidential election cycle.

and a small army of lobbyists.[4] The top five sectors spending lobbying money in 2014 were health insurance ($533 million); finance, insurance, and real estate ($497 million); health industries ($488 million); communications and electronics ($379 million); and energy and natural resources ($346 million).

"Influence" is now the third-largest industry in D.C., behind government itself and tourism. According to Lee Drutman, a political scientist and author of the book *The Business of America Is Lobbying*, businesses spend more money lobbying Congress than we taxpayers spend funding the salaries, benefits, and expenses of all members of Congress and their staffers. Yes, that's right: more is spent each year in Washington lobbying the people who work for Congress than is spent paying and supporting the work of all those members of Congress and congressional staffers.

Drutman's book traces the rise of the influence industry:

> Starting in the early 1970s, corporate America began to devote attention and meaningful resources to politics. The current spending levels merely mark the latest moving capstone in a 40-year period of nearly continuous expansion of corporate political activity . . . Corporate lobbying expenditures now dwarf the comparable investments of unions and "diffuse interest" groups (my preferred term for what others more commonly call "public interest groups" or "citizen groups").

The gap in resources between corporate lobbyists and union and public interest group lobbyists is enormous. For every dollar spent by the unions and public interest groups, corporations and corporate trade groups spent $34 in 2012.

Once a sleepy and rather dowdy city, the nation's capital has been transformed into an expensive, nonstop influence-peddling battleground, full of restaurants that are happy to charge $40 for steaks and spas that will ease the difficulties of digesting those steaks with $150 massages. So much money has been pumped into the Beltway in recent years that, according to the Bureau of Labor Statistics, it is now the most expensive American city to live in. Yes: more expensive than even New York City.

Stroll around Capitol Hill in Washington and you can see the physical manifestations of the confluence of campaign donations and lobbying.

Just a few blocks east of the Capitol dome are street after street of stately townhouses that real families used to call home. Today, many of them house not families but comfortable spaces where members of Congress spend much of their time. Several of the townhouses are occupied by lobbyists, others by trade associations and big corporations. According to a 2010 analysis by the nonprofit Sunlight Foundation, 126 townhouses and offices around the Capitol are used for fundraisers. Seventy percent of those venues are run or owned by lobbyists or groups that hire lobby-ists. FedEx and UPS have "homes" on the Hill now, as does the U.S.

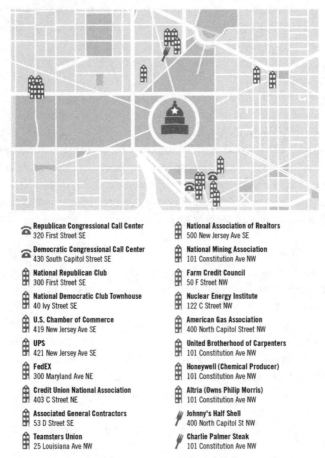

Republican Congressional Call Center
320 First Street SE

Democratic Congressional Call Center
430 South Capitol Street SE

National Republican Club
300 First Street SE

National Democratic Club Townhouse
40 Ivy Street SE

U.S. Chamber of Commerce
419 New Jersey Ave SE

UPS
421 New Jersey Ave SE

FedEX
300 Maryland Ave NE

Credit Union National Association
403 C Street NE

Associated General Contractors
53 D Street SE

Teamsters Union
25 Louisiana Ave NW

National Association of Realtors
500 New Jersey Ave SE

National Mining Association
101 Constitution Ave NW

Farm Credit Council
50 F Street NW

Nuclear Energy Institute
122 C Street NW

American Gas Association
400 North Capitol Street NW

United Brotherhood of Carpenters
101 Constitution Ave NW

Honeywell (Chemical Producer)
101 Constitution Ave NW

Altria (Owns Philip Morris)
101 Constitution Ave NW

Johnny's Half Shell
400 North Capitol St NW

Charlie Palmer Steak
101 Constitution Ave NW

Around the Capitol: A few of the places where money is raised and politicians are influenced.

Chamber of Commerce. Then there are groups with typical D.C. names such as Associated General Contractors, the National Association of Realtors, the National Automobile Dealers Association, and the National Pork Producers Council. About five hundred yards north of the Capitol is the headquarters of the Teamsters Union.

These townhouses have become especially valuable properties because they are a short walk from politicians' offices. Members of Congress are routinely whisked by their staffers to those houses for receptions at which—or after which—checks will be written. Many of the roughly nine thousand registered lobbyists in Washington provide much of the cash at such events.

An increasing number of those lobbyists are former members of Congress themselves. A study by the watchdog group Public Citizen found that around half of House and Senate members—and their staffs— went directly from being public servants to working as lobbyists.

It used to be that politicians would leave Congress and run quasi-public institutions such as colleges and universities and think tanks. Or they would return home and take up their former professions—lawyers, businesspeople. But lobbying is so lucrative. Take, for instance, former congressman Steve Bartlett (R-TX), who was making roughly $150,000 a year when he left the House of Representatives in 1999. While in Congress, he served on the House Banking Committee. The year he left, he was named the head of the Financial Services Roundtable, one of Wall Street's largest lobbying and advocacy groups. When he left the Roundtable, in 2011, he was making $2 million a year.

The members need such lobbyists for campaign cash, and they all but command their presence at fundraisers. Peter Schweizer, president of the Government Accountability Institute and a Republican political adviser, writes in his book *Extortion* that those lobbyists and political donors who want to play the game have to pay the toll. "If you are invited, you are expected to be there. There is an implicit aspect of the request that makes that clear. And when you get there, you better show up with a check," former Shell Oil president John Hofmeister told Schweizer.[5] "I feel extorted," he said.

D.C.'s Sweatshops

Not too far from the Capitol Hill townhouses are the call centers that both Democrats and Republicans use to dial for dollars. Endlessly.

This is how Senator Dick Durbin, Democrat of Illinois, described it: "We sit at these desks with stacks of names in front of us and short bios and histories of giving . . . and we make calls to our faithful friends and ask them to give money or host a fundraiser."[6]

National Public Radio tried to get access to the call centers for a story on fundraising in 2012 but got no further than a description of them from members of Congress.

Former representative Dennis Cardoza, a California Democrat, compared his party's call center to a sweatshop with thirty-inch-wide cubicles set up for the sole purpose of begging for money. He said the need for constant fundraising helped push him into retirement.

Peter DeFazio, a Democrat from Oregon, told NPR, "If you walked in there, you would say, 'Boy, this is about the worst looking, most abusive looking call center situation I've seen in my life.' These people don't have any workspace, the other person is virtually touching them."

Members of both parties say the time they have to spend in the cramped call centers is humiliating. Representative John Larson, Democrat of Connecticut, likened it to "putting bamboo shoots under my finger-nails." One female member of the House told us that, probably because she's a woman, when she makes her fundraising phone calls the donors are much more casual with her than she would expect—or hope. She recounted a call she made to a Hollywood mogul's home. The wife answered the phone. After the congresswoman introduced herself, "The wife launched into a tirade about some new curtains that had just arrived at her house, which were the wrong color of yellow. I had to sit and politely, sympathetically, listen to her so that I could get to the point of asking her for a twenty-five-hundred-dollar contribution to my campaign."

How much time do our elected representatives spend trying to collect money from wealthy people? Roughly 50 percent. One former congressman, Tom Perriello (D-VA), told reporter Ryan Grim at the *Huffington Post* that even that may be "low-balling the figure so as not to scare the new members too much."[7]

This feverish fundraising begins even before a freshman gets sworn in. After former representative Walt Minnick, a conservative Democrat from Iowa, won his first election to Congress in 2008, he took just five days off before heading back to the phones. He needed to raise $10,000 to $15,000 a day because his district is considered competitive and he knew he would face a tough reelection. Many freshman members get right to the townhouse circuit before they even move into a Washington apartment.

The constant need for campaign cash not only greases the wheels in Congress for the well-financed special interests but also reduces the amount of time our legislators spend considering or crafting legislation.

Dan Glickman (D-KS) has seen it all, from all angles. He served in the House for eighteen years, representing the people of Wichita, Kansas, then headed the Department of Agriculture for six years, during Bill Clinton's presidency, then became head of the Motion Picture Association of America, Hollywood's lobbying and advocacy arm in D.C. According to Glickman,

> The sad truth is that given the frenetic search for money in federal congressional elections, there simply isn't enough time in the day to stay competitive in campaign finance and do the actual job of policy making... I remember when I was first elected to Congress, I and many other House members would often go down to the floor of the House of Representatives and just listen to the debate. I may not have had an amendment to the bill or a particular interest in the issue but I always felt that watching policy discussions and witnessing the crafting of laws was an important part of my day. It gave me the chance to educate myself and interact with members of Congress on both sides of the aisle. Today most lawmakers would tell you that any free moment not used raising dollars is time wasted.[8]

This theme of members of Congress not being able to commit time to doing the increasingly complicated job of examining and deeply understanding legislation comes up over and over again. It's not just driving them nuts, it's also driving many of them out of office, and it's deterring good people from even thinking about running.

Senator George Voinovich, an Ohio Republican, left the U.S. Senate in 2010. At the press conference announcing his retirement, he said that it would be impossible to be an effective legislator while also meeting the fundraising demands of running for another term. "You can't do both of them," he said. "You're either going to do the job or you're going to be out there raising money."[9]

Of course, not all the fundraising occurs in dreary call center cubicles and trade-association-owned townhouses in D.C. As the *New York Times* investigative reporter Eric Lipton chronicled in 2014, "destination events" have become all the rage. Republicans join lobbyists and business executives for spa weekends in Las Vegas and ski trips at the Four Seasons resort in Vail. Democrats join lobbyists and business executives on the Ritz-Carlton's private beach in Puerto Rico and on quail hunts in Georgia.

Such trips are often sponsored by political campaigns or political action committees, which are funded, in part, by . . . you guessed it: the lobbyists and corporate executives who are attending the festivities, and who have business interests they think the members of Congress might be able to help them with.

As Lipton reported, among those attending a Vail event in January of 2014 were:

> Representative Edward Whitfield, Republican of Kentucky, and Katie Ott, a lobbyist for PPL Corporation, the single biggest contributor to Mr. Whitfield.
>
> Mr. Whitfield is chairman of the Energy and Commerce subcommittee that regulates energy utilities, making him one of the most important players in Congress for the industry. Only days after the Vail trip, he introduced legislation that would allow utilities like PPL to build new coal-burning power plants, over-riding environmental restrictions recently imposed by the Obama administration.

Super PAC Attack

Much of this type of activity—the endless fundraising phone calls, the in-person fundraising, the resort retreats—has been intensifying for years. Newer to the scene, though, are super PACs, which, as we discussed in the last chapter, are the progeny of *Citizens United*. One of the many things the five Supreme Court justices failed to envision was how closely super PACs would align with candidates' campaigns—how these alleg-edly "independent expenditure" entities are not really independent from the candidates at all. Through skilled lawyers, operating in the dim light of an under-resourced and dysfunctional FEC, the candidates have, for all practical purposes, been able to treat these "independent" groups as extensions of their own campaigns.

Presciently, Harvard Law School professor Lawrence Lessig, in a September 2010 commentary for the *Boston Review*, wrote, "No doubt, as corporations exercise this new right, candidates will become skilled in the dance necessary to get enormous corporate wealth spent for their political benefit."[10]

It was widely reported in the spring and summer of 2015 that former Florida governor Jeb Bush was working closely with Right to Rise, a super PAC backing his bid for the 2016 Republican nomination. The group, with Bush's direct help, raised $114 million in the first six months of its existence. Bush was able to coordinate with the group because he had not yet *officially* declared his candidacy. The rationale is laughably adolescent: if Jeb hasn't officially filed paperwork for his campaign, then he's not a candidate for office, so there's no question that Right to Rise is "independent" of his campaign, because there's no campaign to speak of. Kind of like a junior in high school saying to his parents, "I wasn't in Jimmy's basement when the cops broke up the party down there—I was in the kitchen."

Watchdog groups led by the Campaign Legal Center and Democracy 21 filed complaints with the FEC, calling out not only Bush but also fellow Republicans Scott Walker and Rick Santorum and Democrat Martin O'Malley for flouting the law.[11] "These 2016 presidential contenders must take the American people for fools—flying repeatedly to Iowa and New Hampshire to meet with party leaders and voters, hiring campaign staff, and raising millions of dollars from deep-pocketed mega donors, all the while denying that they are even 'testing the waters' of a presidential campaign," said Paul S. Ryan, senior counsel for the Campaign Legal Center, adding that all four "appear to be violating federal law."

In the spring of 2015, Bush's team was reportedly hatching a plan to use his super PAC in an unprecedented way. It would take on tasks that a more accountable, traditional campaign would normally handle: setting up and running phone banks, arranging television advertising, and managing get-out-the-vote operations.[12]

Richard L. Hasen, professor of law and political science at the University of California, Irvine, School of Law and author of *Plutocrats United: Campaign Money, the Supreme Court, and the Distortion of American Elections*, wrote for *Slate*, "By signaling that Right to Rise is his campaign arm, Jeb Bush has broken down the wall between his super PAC and his campaign committee in the eyes of donors."[13]

Outside spending on congressional races doubled from 2010 to 2014, when it reached a staggering $486 million, much of which went undisclosed. In 2004, the Center for Responsive Politics estimated about $5.8 million in dark money (undisclosed) spending. That's a hundredfold increase over the course of ten years.

Money Goes Dark

Super PAC money is disclosed. So when journalists and political pundits talk about "dark money," don't think of super PACs. Think of 501(c)(4) organizations, many of which appear to be set up principally to engage in politics.

Dubbed "social welfare organizations" by the IRS, 501(c)(4)s are tax-exempt groups that aren't required to disclose where their money comes from—a significant fact when you consider that some of the more powerful groups spend tens of millions of dollars each election cycle to advance a single issue or candidate.

In 1956, Alabama Attorney General John Patterson tried to compel the NAACP to disclose the names and addresses of its members in a blatant intimidation effort that would essentially shut down the organization's income. When the NAACP refused, the issue went all the way to the Supreme Court, which unanimously ruled that the organization did not have to disclose the names of its donors, arguing that "compelled disclosure of affiliation with groups engaged in advocacy" could lead to an effective "restraint on freedom" in the form of persecution or retaliation.

In recent years, political operatives have taken advantage of this exemption from disclosure—combined with inaction on regulating 501(c)(4)s by the FEC and IRS—to turn the groups into stealth political bombers. As Matea Gold reported in the *Washington Post* in the summer of 2015, "These tax-exempt groups—which can keep their donors secret even as they sponsor hard-hitting ads—are being increasingly embraced by campaign operatives looking for new ways to influence the political environment."

Groups like Priorities USA, founded by former Barack Obama staffers, and Americans for Prosperity, begun by the Koch brothers, have firmly taken root. The Republican political operative Karl Rove has run tens of millions of dollars through his (c)(4), called Crossroads GPS. New ones, with unmemorable names, are positioning themselves to play significant roles in 2016.

According to the Center for Responsive Politics, "spending by organizations that do not disclose their donors has increased from less than

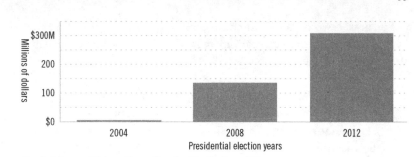

Dark Money Rising: Spending by Undisclosed Donors
Source: Center for Responsive Politics (opensecrets.org)
Methodology: Spending by 501(c)(4) organizations. Numbers are estimated because 501(c)(4) organizations are not required to disclose their donors.

$5.2 million in 2006 to well over $300 million in the 2012 presidential cycle and more than $174 million in the 2014 midterms." The *New York Times* editorial page noted, mournfully, that the 2014 midterm elections were affected by "the greatest wave of secret, special-interest money ever raised in a congressional election."

Although such dark money is a growing problem—an extra shot of poison in an already poisonous mixture—it constituted just 4.6 percent of all campaign spending in 2014.

No Help on the Hill

The Supreme Court is, of course, not solely to blame for problems associated with Big Money. Congress has passed up opportunities to enact commonsense laws for decades. Lawmakers have even failed to pass a bill that would require the funders of groups placing political ads on television to be identified in the ads so that we citizens can know who is trying to influence our votes. Congressional Democrats have introduced such a bill several times since the *Citizens United* decision, but Republicans have consistently blocked it, primarily because of Senator Mitch McConnell (R-KY), who claimed in 2010 that Democrats were behind the bill solely to *look* like reformers.[14] It's hard to tell if that's a fair criticism, but it seems the Democrats aren't taking passage of the bill terribly seriously. The House version of the legislation is called the KOCH Act—Keep Our Campaigns Honest—a personal jab at the wealthy Koch brothers, which shows the lack of seriousness of the effort.

For nearly two decades, Mitch McConnell has been a staunch opponent of campaign finance rules. In 1999, the *New York Times* opened a story about McConnell with this:

> A bill to overhaul the nation's campaign finance laws is being debated on the floor of the Senate. Its advocates and their many allies on the editorial pages are in full cry, demanding change for the sake of a cleaner, better, more democratic politics. And the senior Senator from Kentucky, Mitch McConnell, is doing his best to block the bill.
>
> So it went last week: Cheerfully, with conviction, with no apologies, Mr. McConnell stood in the well of the Senate, hour after hour, swatting back arguments that the system is corrupt, that it breeds cynicism, that it shuts out the little guy for the moneyed special interests.
>
> "I have sort of been the designated spear catcher on this issue," Mr. McConnell said, somewhat proudly.

McConnell has been more than a spear catcher on the issue; he's been jamming spears through the skulls of bills that could fix the problem, including the DISCLOSE Act, despite the fact that, as evidenced by the 2015 *New York Times*/CBS News poll, 76 percent of Republicans support disclosure of all campaign contributors to outside political groups.

In addition to obstructing legislation, McConnell has engaged in other forms of spear catching. He brought a lawsuit challenging the McCain-Feingold law the day Congress passed it in 2002, arguing that it violated the First Amendment. The Supreme Court in 2006 ruled against him, but he mushed on nonetheless, praising *Citizens United* when it came down and filing amicus briefs on behalf of others seeking to weaken campaign finance laws.

Why he turned so spitefully against reform is unclear.

Interestingly, he was not originally opposed to campaign finance reform. He supported disclosure for decades.[15] As a Republican Party county chairman in Louisville in 1973, he even advocated campaign spending limits and praised public financing efforts.[16] In 1987, McConnell said he would support a constitutional amendment to allow Congress to regulate independent expenditures.[17] In 1989, he sponsored a bill, with Senator Harry Reid (D-NV), that would have required outside groups to disclose their donors.

President Obama hasn't exactly been a champion of reform, either. Despite some of his strong rhetoric—for instance, his statement at a White House press conference in 2013 that "There aren't a lot of functioning democracies around the world that work this way, where you can basically have millionaires and billionaires bankrolling whoever they want, however they want, in some cases undisclosed"—he has failed to champion the cause. For instance, despite repeated requests from Common Cause and more than fifty other organizations, President Obama (as of the writing of this book) has been unwilling to sign an executive order requiring that all companies receiving federal contracts disclose their political spending.[18]

Other government entities that could help with some of the problems we discuss in this book never seem to get their act together. The Federal Election Commission is the most wretched of examples. The six members of the commission—three Democrats and three Republicans—must be approved by the Senate. As the atmosphere in Washington has become increasingly partisan, the FEC has, for all practical purposes, become paralyzed. A 2013 analysis by the Sunlight Foundation showed a sharp decrease in the dollar amount of fines levied against violators of campaign finance laws as well as a sharp decline in the number of cases commissioners could even agree to make a decision on.[19] "It is dysfunctional," a remarkably blunt Ann Ravel, the 2015 FEC chairwoman, told the *New York Times*. "The likelihood of the laws being enforced is slim."[20]

One of the main duties of the FEC, which was created by Congress in 1975 in the wake of Watergate, is to collect and disclose campaign finance information. Yet in recent years, Republicans and Democrats on the commission haven't been able to agree on how to do that.

Ironically—or perhaps we should say pathetically—members of both parties did unite on at least one issue: letting wealthy people donate more to political parties. Late in 2014, the offices of Harry Reid (who was still Senate majority leader) and House Speaker John Boehner feverishly negotiated the specifics of a $1.1 trillion spending bill. At the very end of their chess game, they agreed to slip in language allowing people to give $1.5 million to the national parties per election. The move was seen as an attempt to strengthen the political parties, which have been overshadowed and outspent by outside funding. CNN called the measure "the latest in a string of setbacks for restrictions on money in politics." House Minority Leader Nancy Pelosi, a Democrat, said it "would work to drown out the voices of the American people." Boehner countered that it and other provisions were "worked out in a bipartisan, bicameral fashion or they wouldn't be in the bill."

Big Money Goes Local

We wish we could claim that coin-operated government exists only at the national level. Sadly, that's not the case. Just as the influence industry has mushroomed in Washington in the last two decades, influence peddlers and political operatives have sought new ways to accomplish their agendas at the state and local levels. You will read, in future chapters, about specific ways in which money and influence place pressure on state and local legislators and regulators, but we want to flag the trend here:

> Four years after the Supreme Court ruled that Congress cannot restrict spending by political groups not directly affiliated with candidates, the "Super PACs" and other spending committees that [have] sprung up in the wake of that decision are becoming a fixture in races farther down on ballot sheets, where their money can have a greater impact.
>
> In some cases, they are looking to bypass a gridlocked Washington . . . In other cases, local operators are adopting tactics first developed at the national level.

That's from a Reuters report, published in October 2014. Journalist Nicholas Confessore wrote the initial "trend piece" about this phenomenon in the *New York Times* earlier that year. In it he quoted the Republican strategist Ed Gillespie: "People who want to see policies enacted, and see things tried, are moving their activity to the states, and away from Washington. There is a sense that you can get things done."

Another Ed—Ed Bender, who directs a watchdog group called the National Institute on Money in State Politics—called the migration of Big Money to the state and local level logical, but unfortunate. "It is less expensive than playing politics at the federal level and the odds of success are often way better," Bender told us. Paul Ryan, a senior attorney at the nonpartisan watchdog group Campaign Legal Center, concurred: "It's often the way things work in money and politics: practices are developed at the national and federal level, and those that work are replicated at the state and municipal level."

An investigation by the Center for Public Integrity found that just fifty individuals and organizations—from former New York City mayor Michael Bloomberg to the Democratic Governors Association—steered $440 million to state candidates and parties in 2014. Eighty-five percent of candidates who got donations from one of those fifty donors won.[21]

Giving directly to state candidates, who raked in $1.2 billion in 2011–2012, is often easier than giving to federal candidates, who can face tougher donation limits.[22] Six states allow limitless giving directly to candidates, and another six have only slight restrictions. Data show that in states like California, Georgia, and South Carolina, all of which have high contribution limits, elections are less competitive. By contrast, elections in Maine, Arizona, and Minnesota, all of which have some form of public financing, are typically much more competitive.[23]

State and local ballot measures attract some of the most deep-pocketed out-of-state business interests and individuals. In 2012, the amount that groups backing or opposing ballot measures raised approached $1 billion, an all-time high.[24] In 2014, a mere fifty donors pumped $266 million into such efforts. More than three quarters of the donors were corporations.[25]

Groups that represent well-financed business have been tilling the fields at the state level for quite some time. The American Legislative Exchange Council (ALEC) has promoted the causes of business interests who pay to be a part of its network for more than forty years. ALEC, which has been described as a "corporate bill mill," connects business lobbyists and state legislators at posh retreats and conferences. It helps the lobbyists build connections with state legislators, then furnishes the legislators with model legislation, often drafted by the corporate lobbyists, to file in the form of actual bills. Regrettably, the legislators, many of whom can't afford to travel to such resorts, and most of whom only work for the public part time, are more than happy to embrace the largesse of ALEC, as a reporter at a Savannah, Georgia, television station discovered while sitting at the bar at an ALEC retreat:

> When I asked the state representative how he pays for a trip like this, he told me that ALEC picks up the hotel room and $350 in expenses directly. He has to come up with the rest, or tap into his ALEC state reimbursement fund. "This is where you would come in, ma'am," he said, turning toward the lobbyist. "I'm the state chair of ALEC, and I look for financial supporters, lobbyists and

the like such as yourself, to send us a couple thousand bucks every so often."

Super PACs are also getting involved in city council and even school board elections across the country. A super PAC called the Committee for Economic Growth and Social Justice filed papers in Washington and promptly sent more than $150,000, funded largely by the bail bond industry, to unseat several members of a school board in Elizabeth, New Jersey. The PAC reportedly was launched by a state senator who wanted to kick his longtime rivals off the board.[26]

An ally of the losing candidates was shocked. "We've never experienced or expected that outside interest groups would come in and invest this kind of money into a local school board race," school board president Tony Monteiro told *USA Today*. "It boggles the mind . . . The whole landscape has changed."[27]

As the CNN reporter Teddy Schleifer, who covers money in politics, put it, "A century ago, party bosses ruled cities. Today, super PACs are in charge. Elections in the nation's cities are increasingly the territory of deep-pocketed donors who are finding that a dollar spent in a low-cost municipal race can easily put an ally in power."[28]

Weighting the Scales of Justice

Of the major trends that Ed Bender is watching carefully, efforts by political groups to elect state supreme court justices is at the top of his list— among all varieties of state races, judicial elections have seen the biggest percentage increase in independent-money expenditures over the past decade.

We Americans elect judges in thirty-nine states, including state supreme court justices. Between 2000 and 2014, these judges—the people we trust to be the fairest in our society—raised $275 million, according to *Politico*.[29] That means many judges are making the kinds of solicitations and phone calls to well-financed individuals and interests that our lawmakers make in Capitol Hill call centers. In the 2012 election cycle, outside spending in judicial races almost doubled from the previous cycle.

The nonprofit group Justice at Stake, which focuses on reducing the role of moneyed interests in judicial elections, asserts that "Since 2000, elected Supreme Courts have been Ground Zero of an unprecedented money war, in which competing groups have spent tens of millions on negative ads, in an attempt to pack courts with judges friendly to their agendas."

George W. Bush's former U.S. solicitor general, Ted Olson, has stated, "The improper appearance created by money in judicial elections is one of the most important issues facing our judicial system today." Olson should know. He once represented a man named Hugh Caperton. In 1998, Caperton, who owned a small coal company in West Virginia, filed a lawsuit against the Massey Coal Company. The suit stated that Massey illegally violated a contract to force Caperton's company out of business. When the case went to court, a jury ordered Massey to pay $50 million in damages.[30]

Soon after, Massey's then CEO, Don Blankenship, gave $3 million to help a judicial candidate named Brett Benjamin gain a seat on the West Virginia supreme court. When Massey's appeal came before his court, Benjamin overturned the $50 million ruling against the company.

Caperton took the case all the way to the U.S. Supreme Court, arguing that he hadn't had a fair trial because Judge Benjamin, although entangled in potential conflicts of interest with Blankenship, refused to recuse himself from the appeal. In July 2009, the high court agreed with Caperton in a 5–4 ruling.

After the campaign finance connections to the judge were exposed, Massey was found culpable in a tragic 2010 mine accident at its Upper Big Branch Mine resulting in the death of twenty-nine miners. The mine explosion resulted from excessive buildup of flammable coal dust gas. In its report to the governor, the investigating commission stated: "What is factual and well-documented is that Massey Energy CEO Donald Blankenship had a long history of wielding or attempting to wield influence in the state's seats of government." After $10.8 million in fines, the company was sold to Alpha Natural resources for more than $7 billion, and in 2014 Blankenship was indicted by a federal grand jury on four counts, including one of conspiracy with intent to circumvent mine safety regulations.

Caperton v. Massey, with Ted Olson's help, brought national attention to the issue of money in judicial elections. The other true champion of this cause is former U.S. Supreme Court Justice Sandra Day O'Connor, who was nominated by Ronald Reagan. She advocates replacing judicial elections—which she says have become "political prizefights"—with bipartisan judicial selection commissions.[31] "When you enter one of these courtrooms, the last thing you want to worry about is whether the judge is more accountable to a campaign contributor or an ideological group than to the law," she says. The public agrees: Justice at Stake cites a poll in which 93 percent of respondents said judges should not hear cases involving major campaign supporters.

A variation on that insight rings true for the whole of our democratic republic: the last thing we, or the Founders, would want is for our public servants—judges, elected representatives, government officials—to feel more accountable to a campaign contributor than to all of us.

CHAPTER 3

Oligarchy, Gridlock, Cronyism

Money is poisoning our political system. The people who matter most to a representative democracy—the ordinary voters in whose interests elected politicians are supposed to act—feel as though they've become an afterthought in the political process. The tidal wave of money washing over our elections, with no end in sight, is causing Americans to lose faith in the system. In that way, the course we're on threatens the core values and principles that define us as a nation.

—LEE HAMILTON, FORMER CONGRESSMAN AND
VICE CHAIRMAN OF THE 9/11 COMMISSION[1]

When reporters write about money in politics they often do so with a focus on the most wealthy political players—which super PAC is gearing up to back which candidate—or they focus on who's out-fundraising whom. Those reporters who are given the time by their editors to do more enterprising work—increasingly few—will sometimes try to connect the dots between Big Money players, specific legislative battles in D.C., and distorted policy outcomes. The middle section of this book is dedicated to such dot connecting. And we take it a step farther, showing how specific people are affected by those policy outcomes.

But here we want to dwell for a moment on other big-picture effects of the problem—specifically, the dominance of the wealthiest over policy making, intensified political polarization, and the rise of cronyism within our economy. We do so because we believe it's important to understand that money's influence isn't limited to just the financing of political campaigns or the influence of a few powerful industries over pieces of legislation. It has additional spillover effects as well that pose existential threats to the maintenance of vibrant political parties, bipartisan legislating, and a meritocratic economy.

"An Oligarchy"

Trevor Potter, who has served as the Republican chairman of the Federal Elections Commission, chief counsel to Senator John McCain, and chief political sidekick to Stephen Colbert, was being interviewed by a German television reporter early last year. Toward the end of the interview, the journalist said to Potter, "Tell us more about the oligarchs." Potter politely responded that he wasn't a specialist on Russia or Eastern Europe. The journalist responded, "No, the American oligarchs." As Potter told us, "It was like an out-of-body moment of awareness in which I realized that that's how people in other countries are starting to view our system of government."

Of all of the money-in-politics trends in the wake of *Citizens United*, the most alarming is the rapid and often brazen rise of the billionaire donor class. Reporter Dave Gilson calculated last year in *Mother Jones* magazine that between 1980 and 2012, the share of campaign contributions coming from the top 0.01 percent of political donors nearly tripled.

The sheer number of million-dollar contributions is reflective of this surge in political spending by wealthy Americans. According to the Sunlight Foundation, in 2010, fourteen people contributed $500,000 or more, while eight gave $1 million or more. By 2014, the number of donors who gave $500,000 had mushroomed to 134, while the number of $1-million-plus donors jumped to 63. That same year, according to *Politico*'s Ken Vogel, the one hundred largest campaign contributors donated $323 million. Compare that with the $356 million given by the 4.75 million people who donated $200 or less.[2]

The casino magnate Sheldon Adelson is a prime example of the dominance that a ballroom full of centimillionaires and billionaires now have over the system and the resulting fawning attention they receive from our most powerful elected officials. Chairman and CEO of the Las Vegas

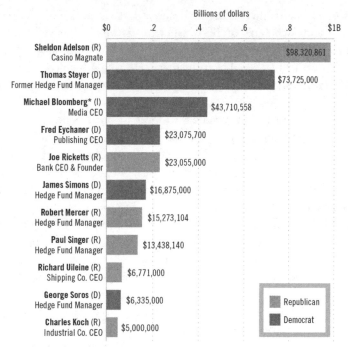

Notable Mega Donors
Source: Center for Responsive Politics (opensecrets.org)
Methodology: Totals include contributions by donors' wives.
* Bloomberg, an Independent who was previously a Democrat and then a Republican, has contributed primarily to super PACs supporting Democrats.

Sands Corporation and, according to *Forbes*, the eighteenth-richest man in the world, he hosts gatherings that attract not just wealthy political donors but also most of the leading contenders for the Republican presidential nomination.

Multiple GOP hopefuls flocked to an event held in 2014 at Adelson's Venetian Hotel and Casino in Las Vegas, including former Florida governor Jeb Bush and current governors Chris Christie of New Jersey and Scott Walker of Wisconsin. He invited all of them to meet with him privately so he could determine "what makes them tick," the *Washington Post* reported.[3,4]

Who would say no to the man with an estimated net worth of $27 billion and who spent a reported $100 million to influence the 2012 campaigns? The following year, additional presidential hopefuls, including Senator Ted Cruz of Texas and Governors Mike Pence of Indiana and Rick Perry of Texas, went to Las Vegas to have coffee and Diet Cokes with Adelson.[5] Whoever gets his financial support has a huge leg up in the Republican primary. He single-handedly made his favorite 2012 candidate, Newt Gingrich, a serious contender for several months.

Adelson is not merely a man who loves to meet politicians. He has several key economic interests to protect. Most important, he wants Congress to ban most forms of Internet gambling, for the sake of protecting his brick-and-mortar operations. He told *Forbes* he is "willing to spend whatever it takes" to do so.[6] Some of his money has been used to launch a group called the Coalition to Stop Internet Gambling.

Charles and David Koch, like Adelson, also host exclusive gatherings for wealthy conservative donors and candidates. *Forbes* estimates that the two brothers are *each* worth about $40 billion. Which means that, combined, they're worth more than Bill Gates, the richest man on earth. Koch Industries is a private conglomerate of paper mills and companies involved in fossil-fuel refining and chemical production. Together, their various enterprises spend millions of dollars on lobbying every year.[7] The Koch brothers vehemently deny that they or their representatives engage in any kind of rent-seeking behavior. They present themselves as free-market conservatives who lean more toward economic libertarianism. In a 2011 op-ed in the *Wall Street Journal*, Charles Koch ranted about businesses that "have successfully lobbied for special favors and treatment."

Among the estimated 450 who attended their "Freedom Partners" get-together in Palm Springs in January 2015 were Republican senators Marco Rubio of Florida, Rand Paul of Kentucky, Ted Cruz of Arizona and Governor Scott Walker of Wisconsin. The gatherings typically include a seminar at which the donors pledge large sums of money to finance one or more of the many groups in the Kochs' network.[8] At the Palm Springs get-together, the announced goal was to raise a total of $900 million to influence the 2016 elections.[9]

While there may not be comparably rich kingmakers vetting candidates on the Democratic side, there are several Democrats who spend big in elections. Tom Steyer is the largest. A hedge fund manager worth about $1.5 billion, he spent $74 million on the 2014 midterm elections, focused mainly on defeating foes of climate change legislation—Republican foes—and electing champions of the cause. Most of the races he engaged in lost. He says that his operation, NextGen Climate (which includes a super PAC), is in it for the long haul. "This is about consequences," he said in 2013. "If you have a pattern of voting for subsidies for oil and gas and voting against renewables and all this other stuff . . . there have to be consequences. That's the whole point of this exercise."[10]

Steyer is close to Hillary Clinton, opening up his home for a Clinton fundraiser early in her campaign. Soon after, one of his former aides had taken a job on her campaign team.[11] His super PAC dollars have often gone toward ads attacking the proposed Keystone XL oil pipeline from Canada's tar sands region in Alberta.

If you combine the amount of political money the Koch network, Steyer, and Adelson have spent in the last two election cycles, combined with what they are pledging to spend in 2016, it will likely outstrip the total cost of the entire 1998 election cycle. Let's repeat that: political spending from the networks of three American families is on track to eclipse the entire amount spent in 1998 to elect 435 members of the House and 34 members of the United States Senate (remember that only one third of the Senate is up for election every two years).

Even some long-term players within the political system are reacting with disgust to what they see happening at the top of the political giving pyramid.[12] John Feehery, who, as we mentioned earlier in the book, served as Republican Dennis Hastert's communications director when Hastert was speaker of the House of Representatives, is now head of public relations for the D.C. lobbying firm QGA Public Affairs. He wrote an op-ed in the *Wall Street Journal* in 2015 in which he asserted: "The campaign finance system is now completely in control of the super-wealthy on both the left and the right."

Mark McKinnon, who served for years as George W. Bush's communications director, has similarly written, "Let's call the system that *Citizens United* and other rulings and laws have created what it is: an oligarchy. The system is controlled by a handful of ultra-wealthy people, most of whom got rich from the system and who will get richer from the system."

Other political insiders—both Republican and Democrat—worry about the encroachment of oligarchy. Take, for instance, Rob Stein, who has a long résumé as a political insider. He served as a strategic adviser to the Democratic National Committee, chief of staff to the Clinton-Gore transition team, chief of staff at the Department of Commerce, and cofounder of the Democracy Alliance, a millionaire-billionaire liberal-donor network.

Late in 2014, Stein penned a piece in the *Huffington Post* titled "Voters, Billionaires and Elections for Whom?" In it, he lays out his concerns:

> The combination, on the one hand, of parties with diminished resources with which to support their candidates, and, on the other hand, of wealthy individuals able to create their own electoral machinery (1) is weakening the party as a mediating influence, (2) is contributing to the fracturing of each party into competing wings, (3) may eventually lead to three, four or more parties, and (4) is empowering super wealthy individuals to build their own electoral apparatus to promote their own personal messages and underwrite their preferred candidates.

Stein admitted that he can't predict what, specifically, the future will look like if these trends continue. But, in conversations with us, he was clear about the potential effects: "In this not so brave, unequal and dysfunctional new world of twenty-first-century politics, inequalities not just of income and wealth, but of democratic participation, political influence and economic and civic opportunity will be greatly exacerbated. The wealthy will not simply get wealthier, they will accumulate more and more political power and relegate America to a less inclusive, equitable and just country."

Stein's, McKinnon's, and Feehery's deep concerns about the wealthy accumulating more power are fortified by economic and political science studies that demonstrate that elected officials pay more attention to the concerns of the rich than to the concerns of the rest of us. Research by Martin Gilens and Benjamin I. Page, political scientists at Princeton and Northwestern Universities, explored whether it was empirically true that policy making bends toward the interests of the wealthy. In a much-lauded 2014 study titled "Testing Theories of American Politics: Elites, Interest Groups, and Average Citizens," the two professors examined decades of public opinion polls about policy preferences. They then compared public opinion with the policy preferences of elites, and then measured the two against which policy ideas actually became laws. What they discovered is that when the wealthy support a policy idea, it has a 45 percent chance of becoming law. When the wealthy oppose a given measure, even if it has majority support among the general public, its probability of becoming a law is 18 percent. Their conclusion:

Majorities of the American public actually have little influence over the policies our government adopts . . . Americans do enjoy many features central to democratic governance, such as regular elections, freedom of speech and association, and a widespread (if still contested) franchise. But we believe that if policymaking is dominated by powerful business organizations and a small number of affluent Americans, then America's claims to being a democratic society are seriously threatened.

A study by Jesse H. Rhodes and Brian F. Schaffner at the Massachusetts Institute of Technology expresses similar findings. Relying on data from a firm that specializes in microtargeting voters, they found that millionaires do indeed get more representation from their elected officials. In districts where millionaires comprise about 5 percent of the population and the poor about half the population, millionaires got "about twice as much representation."[13]

The hugely successful investor Warren Buffett didn't need to conduct an academic study to come to a similar conclusion. When asked in the spring of 2015 by CNN reporter Poppy Harlow if the wealth divide in America would continue to worsen, Buffett bluntly stated: "With *Citizens United* and other decisions that enable the rich to contribute really unlimited amounts, that actually tilts the balance even more toward the ultra-rich . . . The unlimited giving to parties, to candidates, really pushes us more toward a plutocracy. They say it's free speech, but somebody can speak twenty or thirty million times and my cleaning lady can't speak at all."

Polarization and Gridlock

The 112th Congress, which served from January 2011 to January 2013, was the least productive in modern history, passing just 283 laws in two years, a third of which were ceremonial acts such as naming buildings or issuing commemorative coins. The 113th Congress would have tied the 112th had it not managed to pass thirteen more laws.

To put this into historical perspective, the 112th Congress was less productive than the notorious "Do-Nothing Congress" of 1946 and 1947, which for decades had been the poster child for congressional inaction. President Truman used the lack of progress made during the 80th Congress as a main platform for his reelection campaign. And it worked.

Almost seventy years later, the need for action in our nation's capital has never been so great. The national debt has reached a staggering $18 trillion and the economy has not sustained consistent growth in the wake of the Great Recession. Income inequality is at the highest level since the Great Depression and racial tensions continue to rise in the wake of police brutality. The national student loan burden is $1.2 trillion and climbing, while the unemployment rate for recent college graduates in 2014 was more than 12 percent.[14] And those are just some of the domestic issues our elected officials have on their plate. If ever there was a time for our leaders to step up and lead, it's now.

Yet Congress is more divided today than at any time since Reconstruction; moderate politicians are an endangered species. So is the public. A 2014 Pew Research Center poll found that the number of people with "consistently conservative or consistently liberal opinions" has more than doubled over the past twenty years, jumping from 10 percent to 21 percent. Whereas in previous years there was some ideological overlap between people who were expressly Democrat or Republican, now 92 percent of Republicans find themselves to the right of moderate Democrats, and 94 percent of Democrats find themselves to the left of moderate Republicans.

Many members of Congress blame gerrymandering for the increasing levels of partisanship and polarization. Republican Aaron Schock, who represented Illinois's Eighteenth Congressional District until he resigned in 2015 after questions were raised about his use of federal funds for personal use, said this was his one major complaint about Congress.[15] "You know, if I had a magic wand, one thing I would love to change— which you can't do unless you're king—is the redistricting process by which our boundaries are drawn. Because what has happened over the decades is he who controls the mapmaking process, you know, creates hyper-partisan districts." Indeed, the 2014 Cook Political Report Partisan Voter Index found that after the 2012 elections, only one in four House districts was truly competitive—meaning that the makeup of the district was diverse enough that Republicans and Democrats each had a real shot at taking the seat.

Both parties are culpable, having been involved in redistricting to their own advantage for decades. Take Maryland's Third Congressional District, which one federal judge said was "reminiscent of a broken-winged pterodactyl, lying prostrate across the center of the state." For the past five years, Democratic officials in the state have taken every opportunity to redraw districts so they favor liberal candidates, slicing and dicing existing maps to reallocate Democrat voters where it would benefit the party most. In 1995, the state's congressional delegation was evenly split between Republicans and Democrats. Today, Democrats hold all but one of Maryland's eight congressional seats.

All of that said, Big Money—specifically super PACs and 501(c)(4) "dark money" groups—is also contributing to a more hostile political climate. Senator Sheldon Whitehouse of Rhode Island, a Democrat, had this to say about the phenomenon:

> If you're just a plain conservative Republican and not an extreme Tea Partyite, you are very anxious about the combination of the Koch brothers producing a candidate who has untold millions of dollars in outside money coming in for him, in your primary . . . And the next thing you know, you're all done. And it's not the merits of their ideas, it is not the appeal of their personalities—it is the raw political weight of *Citizens United* money.

President Obama has also expressed frustration with the polarizing effects of Big Money. During a particular high-water mark for extreme gridlock—the government shutdown of 2013—he said: "I've continued to believe that *Citizens United* contributed to some of the problems we're having in Washington right now. You have some ideological extremist who has a big bankroll, and they can entirely skew our politics." He added, "There are a whole bunch of members of Congress right now who privately will tell you, 'I know our positions are unreasonable, but we're scared that if we don't go along with the tea party agenda, or the—some particularly extremist agenda, that we'll be challenged from the right.' And the threats are very explicit. And so they toe the line."[16]

Many super PACs and "dark money" groups are here today, gone tomorrow. They have no brands to protect, no historical rootedness in Washington or the state capitals, no other institutional relationships to maintain. They come out of nowhere, with vague names like United for a Stronger America, put a few false or misleading attack ads on the air, and then vanish. It's easier to be extreme today in such an environment than it was when the groups doing the spending were more accountable—like the political parties—and the money was traceable.

Liberal *Washington Post* columnist E. J. Dionne picked up on this trend in the 2014 elections: "Structural changes in our politics are making campaigns more mean and personal than ever," he said. "Outside groups empowered by the Supreme Court's *Citizens United* decision are using mass media in ways that turn Americans off to democracy, aggravate divisions between the political parties, and heighten animosities among citizens of differing views."

We can always hope that, despite these extreme, unaccountable groups, politicians are able to forge meaningful relationships across the political aisle and get the work of the country done. But what if they have no time to forge such bonds? When Iowa senator Tom Harkin, an Ohio Democrat, announced he was retiring in 2013, he told the *Washington Post*:

> We used to have a Senate Dining Room that was only for senators. We'd go down there and sit around there, and Joe Biden and Fritz Hollings and Dale Bumpers and Ted Stevens and Strom Thurmond and a bunch of us—Democrats and Republicans. We'd have lunch and joke and tell stories, a great camaraderie. That dining room doesn't exist any longer because people quit going there. Why did they quit going? Well, we're not there on Monday, and we're not there on Friday. Tuesday we have our party caucuses. That leaves Wednesday and Thursday— and guess what people are doing then? They're out raising money.[17]

Creeping Cronyism

Throughout this book, we've described particularly egregious examples of how money in politics influences the bread-and-butter issues of the American people. It's tempting to chalk these case studies up to bad apples. The problem, though, is that the crisis facing the American public is not one of bad apples but of a diseased orchard.

All markets are formed in response to the demand and supply for goods and services. From the floors of the world's great stock exchanges to the hidden bazaars of ancient nations, markets have both informal and formal rules. In the words of the Nobel laureate Joseph Stiglitz, "Rules matter and power matters."[18] The problem, Stiglitz argues, is that in America today, the powerful are writing the rules—and for their own benefit. Their actions not only undermine the forces of competition that characterize real capitalism, they move us further and further away from the widespread prosperity of the post–World War II years.

By pressuring elected officials and regulatory agencies to bend the rules—or to rewrite them entirely—big businesses are opting out of the competitive marketplace. This practice not only limits competitiveness and innovation, it undermines our fundamental beliefs in an economy distinguished by a level playing field.

The net result: two entirely different sets of economic arrangements—one in which companies that have successfully manipulated Congress are insulated from competition, and another in which smaller firms with less capital are left to pick up the scraps left by their larger, more powerful counterparts.

David Stockman, who served as the director of the Office of Management and Budget in the Reagan administration and is a former Republican member of Congress from Michigan, expresses similar concerns. In his book *The Great Deformation: The Corruption of Capitalism in America*, he points out that the market system is anything but "free." Instead, he argues, "Crony capitalism is about the aggressive and proactive use of political resources ... to gain something from the governmental process that wouldn't otherwise be achievable in the market." He extrapolates from this hypothesis, reasoning that the sweetheart deals offered to big businesses fly in the face of democratic norms. In his words, "We pay for [crony capitalism] in the loss of political equality ... Money dominates politics and as a result we have neither capitalism nor democracy."[19]

When a progressive Nobel laureate like Stiglitz finds himself in the same camp as a Reagan Republican on this issue, it's obvious that opposition to crony capitalism has neither partisan affiliation nor ideological bent. Ours is a time when Tea Party Patriots and Occupy Wall Street share a belief that the game is rigged against the average American, that the individual's ability to chart their own course in the business world is constrained by forces beyond his or her control.

Luigi Zingales, a professor from the traditionally conservative Booth Business School at the University of Chicago, speaks passionately of the America that once was, and the America that now is, in his book *A Capitalism for the People*. Zingales was born in Italy, a land where networks of patronage and favors meant everything. He came to the United States for his graduate studies, lured by our country's meritocratic ideals and the promise of a graduate fellowship in Boston. Zingales describes the vision he had of "the land of opportunity":

In contrast to the rest of the world, where capitalism is too often the
creature of a rich elite who saw an opportunity to become richer,
America's brand of capitalism has survived and thrived because of
a unique set of circumstances: a government attentive to the interests of ordinary people, a set of values that have made accumula-
tion of wealth a moral responsibility rather than an end in itself,
and a belief that the system provides opportunities for all.[20]

Rather than pursuing government allies to buy up their products,
Americans invented new technologies that met the market's needs.
Instead of familial nepotism, Americans rose to higher positions largely
by their ability to put new ideas out into the world and work hard.

For many years, indeed for pivotal years, Zingales's ideal accurately
described the American economy. During the post–World War II era, the
United States presided over a period of unmatched economic growth and
stability. The economy throve, and more Americans were able to share in
that prosperity.

As we all know from so many newspaper headlines and books in recent
years, that economy has vanished. We now live in a time of wage stagna-
tion for the majority of working families, of pronounced inequities and
limited access to opportunity.

Over the past several decades, it's become the new normal for a handful
of companies to dominate each major industry. Desmond Lachman, a
senior fellow with the right-of-center American Enterprise Institute and
former International Monetary Fund director, reports, "The gross profits
of the 200 largest US corporations as a percentage of gross profits in the
economy has risen steadily from 15 percent in the early 1950s to 30 percent
by the early 2000s."[21] The goal of too many inventors and start-up
founders is no longer to make it big through competition in the marketplace but to be bought up—to be subsumed by global giants.

As Zingales points out, this tendency to aggressively acquire small
upstarts rather than develop new programs in-house is also characteristic
of some corporations' political strategies. He writes, "[These] incumbent
large firms [many of them tech companies] are politically powerful
but not necessarily the most efficient . . . they have a strong incentive
to manipulate the power of the state to preserve their market power
through political means."[22] He has additionally stated: "Traditionally,
corporations used to lobby to get the government off their backs. As
they grew more skillful, their efforts went from reactive to proactive,

and toward getting government in their pockets to obtain unique privileges."

While consolidating market power, many industries also work on rigging the tax code so that they can shield their income. In the introduction to this book, we mentioned the farewell address that John Kerry delivered to his Senate colleagues before he headed over to the Department of State. Lamenting the dominance of money over politics, he said, "The insidious intention of that money is to set the agenda, change the agenda, block the agenda, define the agenda of Washington. How else could we possibly have a U.S. tax code of some 76,000 pages? Ask yourself, how many Americans have their own page, their own tax break, their own special deal?"

There are a myriad of opinions about what taxes the government should levy, who should pay what, and how that money should be spent. But there is overwhelming agreement on one thing: our tax code—which was just twenty-seven pages long in 1913—is needlessly complex. There are tax breaks on everything from private jets to cat food and luxurious vacation homes. In 2012, the *New York Times* reported that loopholes in the tax code could have cost anywhere from $700 billion to $1 trillion the previous year.[23] Yet after years of debates to address what Senator Ron Wyden, chairman of the Senate Finance Committee, called the "dysfunctional, rotting mess of a carcass that we call the tax code," tax reform remains dead in the water because of the gridlock caused by wealthy special interests.

The poster child for tax preferences is something called "carried interest." This is the portion of income earned by a hedge fund manager's investments above a certain threshold. It is taxed at the current capital gains rate of 20 percent rather than at the upper bracket income rate of 39.6 percent.

The Real Estate Roundtable estimates that the revenue loss to the United States as a result of the carried-interest tax loophole is $13 billion annually. That's not just $13 billion that could go into deficit reduction or rebuilding the nation's crumbling infrastructure; that's 13 billion extra dollars—each year—that are going into the pockets of people who are already astonishingly rich.

Lynn Forester de Rothschild is the chief executive of EL Rothschild, a family-owned investment company. As you can imagine, she's a very wealthy woman who likely knows a lot of hedge fund managers. But in 2013 she wrote an op-ed in the *New York Times* stating:

> Of the many injustices that permeate America's byzantine tax code, few are as outrageous as the tax rate on 'carried interest' . . . This

state of affairs denies our Treasury much-needed revenue; fuels public cynicism in government; and is evidence of the 'crony capitalism' that favors some economic sectors over others. When plutocrats join with both parties to protect their own vested interests, the result is a corrosion of confidence in the free-market system.

As Warren Buffett once quipped, the loophole allows him to pay a lower tax rate than his secretary.

There have been multiple attempts to close the sweetheart tax deal down. In 2007, a bill to do so was introduced by Representative Sander Levin (D-MI). But the hedge fund industry blocked him. In 2010, there was another attempt in the Senate to remove the "carried interest" from the tax code. Lobbyists representing some of the most powerful hedge funds unleashed their dogs. Take just one of them—Blackstone. Working on its behalf were Drew Maloney, formerly a staffer for Representative Tom DeLay, and Moses Mercado, who used to work for Representative Dick Gephardt. They were joined by dozens of other Republican and Democratic lobbyists who were aligned in their desire to keep the loophole open. When the provision made its way to a vote, every single Republican voted against the change, joined by one Democrat, Senator Ben Nelson (D-NE). The bill failed to advance.

For our fellow Americans, the case of "carried interest" produces two entirely different sets of economic arrangements—one in which hedge fund managers who've successfully lobbied Congress are given an economic advantage with no economic justification, and another in which regular people are required to play by the normal rules.

Tim Carney is a reporter who writes for the Republican-leaning *Washington Examiner* and a fellow at the American Enterprise Institute. He is obsessed with these sweetheart deals and unfair advantages. He promotes the idea of "libertarian populism" and believes that "the game is rigged in America today, government is rigging it in in favor of the well connected, and that free and open markets are the way to unrig the game, and help the middle class."[24] In his book *The Big Ripoff*, he argues that big government and big business go hand in hand—the two operate in a mutually beneficial relationship that marginalizes small enterprises.[25]

In Carney's eyes, this is not an issue that is exclusively tied to Democrats or Republicans—both parties are at fault. In a 2013 article, he provides a laundry list of examples of corporate cronyism, spanning the latter Bush and early Obama years: ethanol, incandescent lightbulb bans, the automotive industry and Wall Street bailouts, the economic stimulus deals for green tech companies, and multiple provisions of the Affordable Care Act, or Obamacare.

You will read about more specific examples of cronyism later in this book. But the point we want to leave you with here is that a growing number of prominent thinkers—left, right, and center—are beginning to conclude that our increasingly rigged political system is leading to an increasingly rigged economy.

The combination of the two threatens the very promise of what America, and other Western democracies, offered to the world in the latter half of the twentieth century—a model in which "liberal" democracy and market-based, merit-based capitalism were seen as the only viable model for societies.

In 1989, the neoconservative writer and thinker Francis Fukuyama published his breakthrough essay "The End of History," in which he declared: "What we are witnessing is not just the end of the cold war, or a passing of a particular period of postwar history, but the end of history as such: that is, the end point of mankind's ideological evolution and the universalisation of western liberal democracy as the final form of human government."

In 2013, Fukuyama published an essay that can be seen as a course correction, or perhaps a lament, titled "The Decay of American Political Institutions." The first reason he cites for such decay is the lack of power within the executive branch to administer the government. The second:

> The accretion of interest group and lobbying influences has distorted democratic processes and eroded the ability of the government to operate effectively . . . Interest groups, having lost their pre-Pendleton Act ability to directly corrupt legislatures through bribery and the feeding of clientelistic machines, have found new, perfectly legal means of capturing and controlling legislators. These interest groups distort both taxes and spending, and raise overall deficit levels through their ability to manipulate the budget in their favor.

Crony capitalism can be fought only if we first regain our right to self-government. If we don't, it will be harder for us to recreate an economy that works for everyone, not just those who can afford to put coins in the machine.

PART 2

CHAPTER 4

Too Big to Beat

Let's take you back to early September 2008. The federal government had just done something previously unthinkable—committing nearly $200 billion of taxpayers' money in an emergency takeover of the troubled mortgage giants known as Fannie Mae and Freddie Mac.[1]

A week later, on Sunday, September 14, 2008, one of the country's most prestigious brokerage houses, Merrill Lynch, mired in billions of dollars of toxic assets nobody wanted and in danger of collapsing, agreed to sell itself to Bank of America.[2] On the same day, Lehman Brothers, another big Wall Street firm, collapsed. The following day, one of the world's largest insurance companies, AIG, accepted an $85 billion federal bailout, the largest of a private company in U.S. history.[3]

On Wednesday, September 24, with credit markets frozen and banks refusing to lend money, Republican presidential nominee John McCain suspended his campaign and called on Barack Obama to do the same. (Obama ignored the suggestion.) Then came the biggest bank failure in American history, when Washington Mutual was seized by federal regulators and sold, in part, to JP Morgan Chase. Other bankers were terrified, fearing that their institutions would go belly up, too. Many wanted capital from the government because, they said, that's what would let them start lending again.

Americans were anxious, and many already were suffering. Six in ten

people polled worried that a depression was likely.[4] Unemployment rose
to the highest levels since 1994. One in ten homeowners were either
behind on their mortgage payments or facing foreclosure.[5]

The federal government soon did come to the rescue, of course. The
recovery for the banks was so complete that within a few years after the
bailout they were posting near-record profits[6]—$40 billion in the second
quarter of 2014 alone. The stock market has surged. The Dow Jones
Industrial Average, in fact, has nearly tripled from its low point in 2009.
In 2015, it hit an all-time high, going above 18,000 for the first time.[7] In
2013, corporate profits reached their highest levels in eighty-five years.[8]

The recovery has been much less swift for regular folks, certainly for
the millions of people who lost their jobs and in many cases their homes.
Growth in real wages has been stagnant since 2009—near zero since the
depths of the recession.[9] In 2015, nearly three fourths of those polled by
the Pew Research Center said they believed government policies had done
little or nothing to help the middle class. Nearly one third said the recession had had a major effect on their finances and that they still had not
recovered.[10]

Washington's response to the financial crisis, which almost led to the
collapse of the U.S. and global economies, is our starting point for part 2
of this book. That crisis was perhaps our lawmakers' most important
moment to take big action, to correct the practices of an industry that
had brought us to the brink of financial collapse. But important reforms
to keep our economy safe did not make it out of Congress, and they
remain undone today.

The major congressional response to the crisis, the 2010 legislation
known as Dodd-Frank (its lead sponsors were Christopher Dodd of
Connecticut in the Senate and Barney Frank of Massachusetts in the
House), has brought some needed transparency to the banking industry
and contains important consumer protections, but almost no one believes
it will prevent another crisis in the years ahead. And that is precisely
because of the undue influence of the financial sector, which we will detail
in this chapter. It goes without saying that action that should have been
taken years earlier that could have prevented the crisis and resulting
recession didn't happen, either. That's because lawmakers and regulators
have long been more focused on helping the banks than on protecting
you and me from reckless lending practices.

In part 2, we will show how the unbridled power and influence of
numerous industries affects our government, our economy, and by

extension, all of us. And, as you read in part 1, that power and influence have only grown in recent years as the cost of elections has skyrocketed, drawing elected officials ever closer to the donors they need in order to get reelected. It is a self-perpetuating system that benefits a few at the expense of the many.

In this section, we offer glimpses into how Big Money manipulates much of our government and affects our daily lives: our financial security and the roofs over our heads; the medications many of us rely on to stay alive; the quality of the air we breathe, the water we drink, and the food we eat; and the sickening toxins we can't avoid because of their pervasiveness in thousands of products, from flooring to pesticides to hair spray.

When it became clear that the $200 billion takeover of Fannie Mae and Freddie Mac, which Treasury Department officials announced on Sunday, September 7, 2008, would not be sufficient to steer the nation's economy away from the cliff, the Bush administration began putting together what would be called the Troubled Asset Relief Program (TARP), a $700 billion government investment in banks, insurers, and automakers.

The proposed plan sparked a full-on blitz by lobbyists, who knew they had only a short time to shape the program to their liking. "This is not following any normal process," the then chief executive of the American Bankers Association (ABA), Ed Yingling, told the *New York Times*. "It's like a big Category 4 hurricane coming through."[11]

The interest groups had the resources to meet their goals. The ABA alone had a roster of nearly a hundred hired lobbyists.[12] Pressure also came from groups such as the U.S. Chamber of Commerce, the biggest lobbying kingpin in Washington, which spent $92 million in 2008 alone.[13] In all, financial, insurance, and real estate interests dropped more than $450 million lobbying Washington that year to make sure the bailout package met their needs.[14,15]

According to Yingling, the ABA had never wanted TARP, which was unveiled on September 19. But it was clear "we had to help it pass" because, as he wrote in an email, "its defeat would cause a huge market panic." He added, "We did have some success in keeping it clean as it went through Congress."

The legislation, which essentially would make the government the owner, at least temporarily, of billions of dollars in toxic assets, did not sail smoothly through Congress, however. On September 29, 2008, after a contentious debate, the House stunned Wall Street when it rejected the bailout. The Dow Jones dropped 778 points that day—the largest ever single-day fall.[16] That was not the only record set that day: $1.2 trillion in market value had vanished on Wall Street by the time the markets closed. Days later, a spooked Congress finally passed the bill.

What was not in the bailout plan: any tax on financial institutions to finance it. Nor did it include a provision, opposed by the banks, that would allow judges to renegotiate mortgage terms to help homeowners facing foreclosure. And as a result of lobbying by the U.S. Chamber of Commerce, it did not contain the limits on executive compensation that many lawmakers felt were warranted.

Banks Benefited When Democrats Turned Right

This crisis, of course, didn't happen in a vacuum. In the decades leading up to the Great Recession, Wall Street's power over Washington had grown steadily. A major reason for that was a change in attitude among Democratic lawmakers and candidates. Many Democrats, who had sometimes stood up to the big banks in Congress, had become as close to Wall Street as many Republicans. That's understandable when you consider that the financial sector has become the biggest source of reelection dollars. Since 1990, it has fed $3.89 billion in contributions to federal candidates and super PACs, far more than any other industry.[17] And of the one hundred firms that have contributed the most to federal campaigns since 1989, there are more financial companies than energy, healthcare, defense, and telecom companies combined.[18]

Democrats in Congress had once often served as a check against the bank lobbyists' efforts to loosen regulations, including their goal of weakening or even repealing the Glass-Steagall Act of 1933, which prohibited commercial banks from participating in the investment banking business. When commercial banks pushed for a repeal in the early 1980s, for example, congressional Democrats helped block it.[19] Later, when the Federal Reserve ruled that banks could, in effect, dedicate small percentages of their revenues to investment banking, a Democratic-led House and Senate passed a bill declaring a moratorium on the Fed's approvals of banks' applications to deal in securities.[20]

But a slow shift began during the Reagan administration. One of the factors leading to the shift was the emergence of the Democratic Leadership Council, formed in response to Ronald Reagan's 1984 land-slide victory over Walter Mondale. The DLC sought to move Democrats more to the right, especially in the South, as a way to win more seats. Another reason was the fact that the Democratic National Committee was deep in the red at the time.

The DLC was formed in 1985 by a political operative named Al From, who felt the party should be more business-friendly and centrist. Two of its early devotees were Bill Clinton of Arkansas and Al Gore of Tennessee. The group's goal was to turn the Democratic Party away from activists, labor unions, and hot-button social issues and toward fiscal restraint, smaller government, and a free-market outlook, as Robert Dreyfuss reported in the *American Prospect* in 2001.[21] If Democrats had to look beyond labor unions for funding, banking was a more palatable business than, say, coal. The "New Democrats," as the DLC members called them-selves, raised money by bringing wealthy donors into the same room as elected officials. By 2000, the group was raising about $5.5 million per year for like-minded candidates.[22]

With many New Democrats befriending Wall Street just as much as Republicans did, the financial industry poured more and more money into congressional coffers throughout the 1990s. Political contributions from the finance, real estate, and insurance sectors have skyrocketed since then, from $62 million in 1990 to $320 million in 2000 to nearly $675 million in 2012, according to the Center for Responsive Politics.[23]

Taking a Page from the GOP's Money-Raising Playbook

The Democrats' desire for new and bigger sources of reelection cash contributed to a turn toward a number of policies favorable to Wall Street. In terms of fundraising, the Democrats were getting slaughtered by the GOP, whose three big national committees had nearly five times as much revenue as the Democrats by 1986, as documented in the book *Winner-Take-All Politics* by the political scientists Jacob S. Hacker and Paul Pierson.[24]

That also began to change in the early 1980s, when Representative Tony Coelho of California was appointed chair of the Democratic Congressional Campaign Committee. Coelho was a much more aggressive fundraiser than his predecessors at the DCCC, developing a reputation as "the guy who sucked up all the PAC money in the world,"[25] as the *Los Angeles Times* reported.[26] Coelho tripled the DCCC's fundraising by 1986.[27]

As Marjorie Williams wrote in the *Washington Post* in a postmortem about Coelho's time at the DCCC:

> The positive way of summarizing what Coelho accomplished is to say that he placed a limit on the GOP realignment, preserving the House as a seat of Democratic resistance to Reagan's realignment all through the '80s. Less generous accounts conclude that Coelho sold the party's soul in the process, by vastly expanding the contributions of business political action committees—and the expectations those contributors felt in return . . .
>
> The crux of Coelho's appeal to businessmen was the unsubtle reminder that Democrats already controlled the House. He went to business and said, in effect, "You might not like us, but we've got our hands on the levers right now; you have to give to us." . . . He also started the "Speaker's Club," which offered business PACs, for a contribution of $15,000, the chance to "serve as trusted, informal advisers to the Democratic Members of Congress."

In a similar piece in the *New Republic* in 1995, Ruth Shalit wrote of Coelho that he

> aggressively marketed the once pro-labor Democratic Party as increasingly pro-business, often during candidate forums for corporate PAC managers. The contradictions of policy or philosophy never slowed him down. During these forums—nicknamed meat markets or cattle calls—Coelho forced candidates to stand behind tables, each with a name card and a place to display his or her literature.

Among the industries Coelho embraced most: finance. Specifically, the savings and loan industry, where Coelho cultivated deep relationships with unsavory—but very wealthy—characters, some of whom ended up going to jail in the wake of the savings and loan collapse in the late 1980s and early 1990s. Some of his fundraising adventures were well chronicled by the *Wall Street Journal* reporter Brooks Jackson in his book *Honest*

Graft. Here is Williams's summary of what Jackson and other journalists uncovered:

> Most damningly, Jackson and other reporters also exposed Coelho as he stepped blindly into bed with the savings and loan industry. He appointed as the DCCC finance cochairman one Dallas multimillionaire, Thomas Gaubert, who was eventually convicted of S&L fraud and barred from the Texas thrift business by federal regulators. Another major DCCC donor was Donald Dixon, later convicted of looting Texas's Vernon Savings & Loan, which ultimately cost U.S. taxpayers $1.3 billion. Coelho was given the use of Vernon corporate aircraft and a luxury yacht, the *High Spirits*, for travel and party fund-raising; when this was reported, he was forced to reimburse almost $50,000—more than half of it from his personal campaign committee—to Vernon, which was by then run by federally appointed conservators. Speaker of the House Jim Wright tried to intercede with federal regulators on behalf of both Gaubert and Dixon—in the latter case, at Coelho's direct urging. And in 1987, Coelho also helped S&L owners by scaling back a bill authorizing funds that bank regulators desperately needed to stay on top of the exploding crisis.

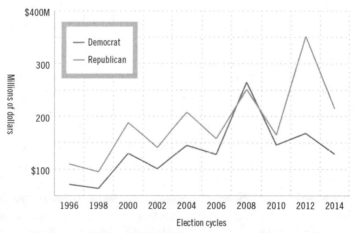

Financial Sector Donations to Each Party
Source: Center for Responsive Politics (opensecrets.org)
Methodology: Donations to federal candidates and parties from financial, insurance, and real estate interests.

In 1989, Coelho resigned from Congress after the exposure of a personal financial scandal in which he failed to disclose a financial transaction with an investment company that Coelho had helped while in office.[28] He was never charged with any specific crime. Soon after resigning, he became an investment banker for a New York firm.[29]

But the trend that Coelho started—aligning the Democratic Party with industries that, throughout most of the twentieth century, it had approached with greater caution—certainly continued. In 2008, for instance, during the height of the financial crisis and the Obama-McCain presidential race, the Democratic Senatorial Campaign Committee (led by New York senator Chuck Schumer) raised about three times more from Wall Street than the Republican Senatorial Campaign Committee did.[30]

The Cash Committee

The number of members serving on the House Financial Services Committee has increased significantly in recent years—from fifty members in 1995 to sixty in 2015—not so much because of its importance to the nation's financial well-being but because of its importance to the political parties' financial well-being. If party leaders think a rank-and-file member in a competitive district might need a big campaign war chest to get reelected, he or she stands a good chance of getting appointed to the committee, which the *Huffington Post*'s Ryan Grim and Arthur Delaney dubbed the "Cash Committee."[31]

The Cash Committee members are especially reliant on Wall Street money. Of all the contributions to House Financial Services Committee members, the money they received from finance, insurance, and real estate interests increased from 26 percent in 1999–2000 to 35 percent in 2013–2014, according to the Center for Responsive Politics. They're also very likely to be poached by lobbying firms offering them much higher salaries than the government can, which is another incentive for the members to be viewed as helpful to the financial sector.

"Traditionally, the money committees as a whole have always been the most valuable places to jump from the Hill to K Street," Ivan Adler of the headhunting firm the McCormick Group told the *Huffington Post*.[32] The *Huffington Post* looked at the staffers who have left the House Financial Services Committee between 2000 and 2009. Of the 126 people identified, 62 went on to register as lobbyists.[33] It works the other way, too.

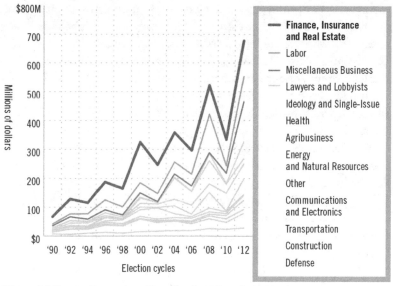

Financial Sector Campaign Contributions Dominate
Source: Center for Responsive Politics (opensecrets.org)

In 2009, 18 percent of the Financial Services Committee aides had worked on K Street before getting to a job on the Hill.[34] This all leads to tight collaboration between the overseers and the overseen.

Members of Congress, Tear Down This Wall!

By the late 1990s, with Democrats now fully on board with Wall Street, the stage was set for what would become a tragedy for millions of Americans a few years later. A deregulatory fever had taken hold in Washington.

The Financial Crisis Inquiry Commission, which was commissioned by Congress to look into the origins of the crisis, began its January 27, 2011, final report with these words: "We conclude that this financial crisis was avoidable."[35]

One of the key reasons, the FCIC concluded, was the failure of regulators to police the industry. "More than 30 years of deregulation and reliance on self-regulation by financial institutions, championed by former Federal Reserve chairman Alan Greenspan and others, supported by successive administrations and Congresses, and actively pushed by the powerful financial industry at every turn, had stripped away key safeguards, which could have helped avoid catastrophe."[36]

Glass-Steagall was the biggest of those safeguards. And it did not fall in one fell swoop. The banking lobby had been chipping away at it for years, resulting in Federal Reserve Board regulatory changes in the 1980s that allowed federally insured banks to earn a percentage of their profits from investment banking activities.

As noted earlier, Glass-Steagall was enacted in the midst of the Great Depression. It forced banks to choose between being either a commercial bank that could make loans to borrowers, or an underwriter of stocks and bonds. In essence, it erected a firewall between commercial and investment banking. That law also created the Federal Deposit Insurance Corporation, providing government insurance of bank deposits (a part of Glass-Steagall that, fortunately, remains intact).

On the floor of the U.S. Senate on November 5, 1999, just before the Senate was about to vote to repeal Glass-Steagall, Senator Byron Dorgan, a North Dakota Democrat and one of the few congressional opponents of its repeal, warned of the consequences: "I think we will look back in 10 years' time and say we should not have done this but we did because we forgot the lessons of the past, and that that which is true in the 1930s is true in 2010."[37]

Another opponent of the repeal measure was Democratic senator Paul Wellstone of Minnesota, who, as reported by the New York Times, said that Congress "seemed determined to unlearn the lessons from our past mistakes." He added: "Scores of banks failed in the Great Depression as a result of unsound banking practices, and their failure only deepened the crisis. Glass-Steagall was intended to protect our financial system by insulating commercial banking from other forms of risk. It was one of several stabilizers designed to keep a similar tragedy from recurring. Now Congress is about to repeal that economic stabilizer without putting any comparable safeguard in its place."[38]

Dorgan and Wellstone were among just eight senators to vote against repeal. Ninety of their colleagues voted for it.

After the House voted that same night, 362 to 57, to repeal Glass-Steagall, the bill was on its way to the White House, where President Clinton signed it a week later. Among the biggest cheerleaders of the repeal bill had been Clinton's Treasury secretary, Lawrence H. Summers.

Enter Sandy Weill

Glass-Steagall might still be in place had it not been for the influence of a Wall Street executive with close ties to the Clinton administration: Sandy Weill, a big fundraiser for the Democratic Party who was the CEO of Travelers Group. In 1998, Weill and John Reed, the CEO of Citicorp, announced that their two companies would merge to form the world's largest financial services company, which would be called Citigroup Inc. Although the merger would have been in violation of Glass-Steagall, Weill and Reed were able to complete the deal—the biggest corporate merger in history—by agreeing that the new company would divest itself of its insurance business in two years.

In the weeks leading up to the merger announcement, Weill made calls to the president, Treasury Secretary Robert Rubin, and Federal Reserve chairman and former JP Morgan director Alan Greenspan, who ultimately approved the merger under existing precedent giving corporations two to five years to divest before officially violating Glass-Steagall.[39]

After the merger was announced, Citigroup and other financial lobbyists pushed to remove the parts of Glass-Steagall that would force them to spin off the insurance industry. They had strong partners in the White House's two pro–Wall Street regulators—Rubin and Summers (who at the time reported to Rubin as deputy secretary of the Treasury)—and in GOP senator Phil Gramm of Texas, who guided the legislation through the Senate. From 1989 to 2002, Gramm received more campaign contributions from commercial banks than any other senator.[40] (After retiring in 2002, he was hired as a lobbyist for Swiss Bank UBS, earning an undisclosed sum, and was still a consultant there in 2015.)

Citigroup had upped its political game to help make sure the repeal vote would succeed. Just look at its flow of money over the course of less than a decade: In the 1992 election, Citicorp contributed about $1.5 million to federal candidates and political parties.[41] By the 1999–2000 election cycle, its contributions had increased to more than $4 million.[42] It spent another $16.5 million in lobbying expenses from 1998 to 2000, more than any other bank.[43]

In all, according to the *New York Times,* the financial sector devoted more than $300 million to lobbying and campaign contributions in 1997 and 1998 as part of its effort to get rid of Glass-Steagall.[44]

Good Fixes Proposed, but Never Passed

The too-big-to-fail banks that had to be bailed out because of their reckless practices were certainly not the only financial institutions that caused the near meltdown of the U.S. economy. In fact, the loosely regulated mortgage lending companies that began to proliferate in the 1990s and early 2000s may have contributed more to the dire straits many Americans found themselves in than the Wall Street companies.

Many of those companies granted subprime loans to people who would likely have difficulty making repayment; in exchange for the added risk, lenders charged higher interest rates. In 2006, at the height of the subprime bubble, the nonpartisan Center for Responsible Lending projected that 2.2 million of the 14 million subprime loans made between 1998 and 2006 would end in foreclosure, destroying as much as $164 billion of wealth.[45]

These lending companies included big names like Countrywide and Ameriquest. Ameriquest's political action committee and its employees and their relatives dispensed more than $20 million to state and federal political groups from 2002 to 2006, according to the *Wall Street Journal*, and they played a big role in weakening existing lending laws in the states, Georgia and New Jersey in particular.[46] As Countrywide dived deeper into subprime lending, it bought Washington protection, increasing its lobbying budget from $60,000 in 1998 to more than $1.5 million seven years later.[47]

In the early 2000s, several state legislatures passed laws to protect their citizens against predatory lenders. Georgia passed one of the toughest in 2002. But lobbyists for surging mortgage lending companies—led by Countrywide and Ameriquest—flocked to the states to persuade legislators to relax the new laws, and Georgia's law was soon clawed back.[48] Lobbyists for big banks, some of which also originated subprime loans in the mid-2000s, also argued against state laws curbing predatory lending.[49]

Members of Congress had many opportunities to rein in the subprime bonanza but always turned the other way. Former Maryland Democratic senator Paul Sarbanes, who chaired the Senate Banking, Housing and Urban Affairs Committee, introduced the Predatory Lending Consumer Protection Act in 2000 and again in 2002, but the bill was never enacted because of industry opposition. One of the most outspoken critics of Sarbanes's bill was the top Republican on the committee—once again, Senator Phil Gramm.

The money was always stacked against Sarbanes and other advocates of fair lending. Though Sarbanes's bill was endorsed by more than a dozen civil rights and consumer groups in 2002, most had little if any money to spend on lobbying, and only two—AARP and the Leadership Conference on Civil Rights—had a lobbying budget above $300,000.

The ultimate authority to curb subprime lenders lay with the Federal Reserve Bank, which is charged with the responsibility for the "safety and soundness" of our financial system and "protecting the credit rights of consumers." But under former chairman Alan Greenspan's leadership, the Fed didn't show much interest in what was happening in the mortgage business, despite calls from housing advocates to take action.[50] It wasn't until Greenspan left the chairmanship that the Fed, in 2007, finally proposed a rule prohibiting lenders from making mortgage loans without considering borrowers' ability to repay them.[51]

"We Are Not Represented in This Melee"

The 2010 Wall Street Reform and Consumer Protection Act, better known as Dodd-Frank, was our best chance to address the fundamental flaws in the U.S. financial services industry and prevent another crisis from developing. The legislation made serious strides despite Wall Street opposition—including the creation of the Consumer Financial Protection Bureau, greater oversight of payday lenders, more transparency into derivatives markets, and the reserve requirement, which has shored up the capital of lending institutions. But, regrettably, the law did not sufficiently address the underlying causes of the crisis.

As a consequence, it may be only a matter of time before we find ourselves at the brink of another financial meltdown. When asked by the journalist Bill Moyers in 2012 whether that is likely, *New York Times* business reporter Gretchen Morgenson replied: "It will happen again, and the unfortunate fact is we did not fix the problem."[52] When asked why, she responded:

> Well, a big part of it is the money problem, that money—the big powered, moneyed institutions are in control in Washington, there's no doubt about it. You and I don't have a lobbyist and so we are not represented in this melee, call it what you will, that happens, you know, when laws are created.[53]

Former senator Ted Kaufman, a Delaware Democrat, went so far as to call the final version of Dodd-Frank a victory for the bank lobby. "Look at what their financial reports and bonuses look like since Dodd-Frank," Kaufman said, adding that the banks' change in behavior lasted "about 48 hours."

Lobbyists were hugely influential in the drafting of the Dodd-Frank law, which passed in July 2010. They were able to kill proposals that they considered especially onerous, and they were able to write the law in a way that gave regulators too-wide discretion. They were betting that their close relationships with regulators would enable them to influence the rule-writing process—which is used to create greater specificity about the intention of the legislation—and even slow down the implementation of the law. It was a safe bet.

As Congress was finalizing and implementing provisions of Dodd-Frank, financial industry lobbyists vastly outnumbered consumer lobbyists.[54] The industry and its allies also spent an estimated $1 billion on lobbying in the months leading up to the passage of the bill, and it continues to spend millions more to undo and weaken reforms, provision by provision.[55] Among the industry's well-heeled allies: the U.S. Chamber of Commerce, which spent $132 million on lobbying in 2010 on Dodd-Frank and other matters.[56] The biggest spender among groups defending Dodd-Frank, by contrast, has been the nation's largest union of public sector workers, known as AFSCME, which spent less than $3 million on lobbying that year.[57]

What the Money Buys: Face Time with Regulatory Agencies

Number of lobbyist meetings since passage of the Dodd-Frank law. July 2010-April 2013

Top 5 consumer protection groups

Americans for Financial Reform: **47**
Consumer Federation of America: **41**
Center for Responsible Lending: **15**
AFSCME: **11**
U.S. Public Interest Research Group: **2**

116

Top 5 commercial banks

Goldman Sachs: **238**
JP Morgan Chase: **222**
Morgan Stanley: **189**
Bank of America: **153**
Wells Fargo: **99**

901

Money Buys Face Time with Regulators
Source: Infographic by Tracy Loeffelholz. Research by the Investigative Fund at the Nation Institute from sunlightfoundation.com.

As we have seen, banks also rely on former congressional staffers who can leverage their relationships and expertise gained while on taxpayer-paid salaries. The financial sector, which comprises finance, real estate, and insurance firms, has had more employees go through the revolving door than any other clearly defined sector, according to the Center for Responsive Politics. The six biggest banks and their trade associations employed more than 240 former government staffers and members of Congress as lobbyists during the two years after the first bank bailout in 2008.[58] By 2014, nearly nine out of ten Citigroup lobbyists were former government staffers.[59]

The banks' lobbyists take advantage of many lawmakers' inch-deep understanding of the financial sector. When members of Congress oppose reform, industry lobbyists convince many of them that finance is too complicated to treat with simple rules and principles. "They try to make this stuff out to be way more complex than it really is," said former senator Kaufman. "It isn't."

Cramdown Goes Down, Again and Again and Again

While the financial sector has thrived since the bailout, millions of American families are still struggling to recover. As we have noted, the crisis hit many homeowners particularly hard: there were 2.3 million foreclosures in 2008, far more than in previous years. The following year saw 2.8 million more foreclosures, and the year after that, 2.9 million more.[60]

Although there have been efforts to help those affected, many have found the efforts inadequate, especially if they have had to file for bankruptcy. Consumer and civil rights advocates and some congressional Democrats promoted a bill in 2008 and 2009 that would have allowed people facing foreclosure an option to stay in their homes. It would have closed a loophole that bars judges from decreasing homeowners' mortgage payments if they file for bankruptcy on their primary residence. It's a loophole because bankruptcy judges can write down the value of nearly all other forms of debt.[61] As a presidential candidate in 2008, Senator Barack Obama called the bankruptcy exemption for mortgages "the kind of out-of-touch Washington loophole that makes no sense."[62]

Many experts think that this reform, known in Washington as "cramdown," a term that means imposing terms on creditors they had not accepted, is needed. Georgetown University law professor and Consumer Financial Protection Bureau advisory board member Adam Levitin wrote that it is the "best and least invasive method of stabilizing the housing market" and would have "little or no impact on mortgage credit cost or availability."[63] But the cramdown legislation was not approved because of opposition by the banking industry. Despite a strong push in 2009 by Dick Durbin and other members of Congress and a thumbs-up from President Obama, it was defeated 51–45 in April 2009. Twelve Democrats joined the entire Republican caucus in voting against it. "Every now and again an issue comes along that we believe would so fundamentally undermine the nature of the financial system that we have to take major efforts to oppose [it], and this is one of them," the American Bankers Association lobbyist Floyd Stoner told ProPublica.[64]

One of the most determined opponents of the bill was the Mortgage Bankers Association, a trade group that had twenty-eight lobbyists in 2009, almost three fourths of whom were former government staffers. "We led the way on [the legislation] and we are clearly responsible for defeating this for the third time in the last year," David Kittle, former chair of the Mortgage Bankers Association, told the *American News Project* following the vote. It's little wonder that Kittle's group prevailed on all three occasions. It has spent $38 million lobbying government officials and, along with mortgage bankers and brokers, has contributed nearly $68 million to federal campaigns since 1990.

The defeat of the cramdown bill forced the Obama administration to take a different tack. Early in 2009, Obama had proposed the $75 billion Home Affordable Modification Program (HAMP), which gave banks financial incentives to write down mortgages. But HAMP is entirely voluntary and has been of little help to many homeowners. Near the end of its first year, even Treasury Department officials admitted HAMP was not working well.[65] Overall, it aimed to help three or four million homeowners, but by 2014 it had resulted in only about 1.3 million loan modifications.[66]

One of the homeowners affected by HAMP's shortcomings was Lisa Douglas, a forty-seven-year-old mother of six living in the Chicago area. Years before applying for a loan modification, in 2006, Douglas and her now ex-husband were given a subprime loan with an adjustable interest rate, a common tactic of the subprime industry.

By 2009, Lisa's life had taken an unfortunate turn. Her husband was injured at work and would soon move out. She soon realized that he hadn't been paying the mortgage. The mortgage payment, including fees and insurance, was close to $1,900, an amount she couldn't afford on her own. But she believed she could pay $1,400 a month under a loan modification.

Douglas applied for a HAMP mortgage modification in 2009, hoping to get quick approval, but six years later she remains in limbo. She described the experience of trying to get approval as "hell." She said she has repeatedly sent "stacks and stacks of paper" to the bank, only to be sent more letters seeking additional documentation. At one point, she did obtain what the bank referred to as a "trial modification." She said she made all of her payments of about $1,000 a month for three months but was then turned down for a permanent loan modification.

Douglas maintains, however, that she was never informed that she hadn't been approved. She says she never received a denial letter. The first she learned of it was when she received an advertisement that her home was being auctioned in a foreclosure sale in late 2012. She fought back with the help of the Legal Assistance Foundation (LAF) in Chicago. It was worth the effort: a judge later found that the foreclosure sale was invalid because her bank's failure to send her a denial letter violated the terms of its agreement with her.

That didn't end her nightmare, however. In 2015, the company that bought her mortgage from Chase Select Portfolio Services rejected her application for yet another HAMP modification. She has not been forced out of her house, at least not yet, thanks in part to the LAF's support.

The LAF says Douglas's story is very common among their clients. It is also very common across the country. An investigation by the *Huffington Post* found dozens of homeowners with similarly frustrating stories.[67] In fact, in 2009 and 2010, 2 million homeowners seeking HAMP modifications were rejected by lenders. Of that number, most were not even granted a trial modification, and about 700,000 had their trials canceled. The most common reason for a rejection, according to ProPublica, was that banks said documents were missing.[68]

What is frustrating to Levitin and others familiar with those homeowners' plight is that cramdown could have helped many families stay in their homes. It also could have had a positive effect on neighborhoods—and housing prices—according to Kathleen Engel, a research professor specializing in mortgage finance and regulation and consumer protection at Suffolk University Law School.

"They Frankly Own the Place"

The Mortgage Bankers Association held its annual "fly-in" conference—when mortgage bankers fly to Washington from across the country to discuss issues of importance to them with members of Congress—the day before the cramdown vote. During the conference, Kittle warned that

Millions of Dollars

Booker, Cory (D-NJ) Senate	$4,115,184
McConnell, Mitch (R-KY) Senate	$3,717,082
Boehner, John (R-OH) House	$3,289,421
Warner, Mark (D-VA) Senate	$2,707,781
Cotton, Tom (R-AR) House	$2,557,139
Markey, Ed (D-MA) Senate	$2,482,902
Cornyn, John (R-TX) Senate	$2,329,636
Gardner, Cory (R-CO) House	$1,972,504
Sullivan, Dan (R-AK)	$1,894,690
Brown, Scott (R-NH)	$1,801,568
Perdue, David (R-GA)	$1,783,665
Tillis, Thom (R-NC)	$1,717,373
McFadden, Mike (R-MN)	$1,714,563
Cassidy, Bill (R-LA) House	$1,694,968
Schumer, Charles E (D-NY) Senate	$1,689,091
Cantor, Eric (R-VA) House	$1,675,470
Ryan, Paul (R-WI) House	$1,629,456
Hensarling, Jeb (R-TX) House	$1,627,086
Graham, Lindsey (R-SC) Senate	$1,576,558
Udall, Mark (D-CO) Senate	$1,551,420

Republican
Democrat

Top 20 Recipients of Financial Sector Contributions
Source: Center for Responsive Politics (opensecrets.org)
Methodology: The numbers above are based on contributions from PACs and individuals giving $200 or more. All donations took place during the 2013–2014 election cycle and were released by the Federal Election Commission on March 09, 2015.

even if they succeeded in killing the bill the next day, it would resurface at some time in the future. To keep their string of victories going, he said, they would need to open their checkbooks to help the MBA wage the noble fight against cramdown whenever it reappeared. "We need to keep fighting it," he told them. "We need to keep giving to the PAC. On a regular basis." He was referring, of course, to his group's political action committee, which has doled out millions of dollars in recent years to influence the outcome of elections. The PAC spent almost $1.3 million during the 2014 election cycle alone. Of the money it gave to federal candidates, 55 percent went to Republicans and 45 percent to Democrats.

It was following that May vote on the cramdown bill that, in exasperation and disgust, Durbin uttered during a radio interview what might be his most memorable quote in recent years:

> The banks—hard to believe in a time when we're facing a banking crisis that many of the banks created—are still the most powerful lobby on Capitol Hill. And they frankly own the place.

CHAPTER 5

Drugged

Bill and Faith Wildrick have never heard of Billy Tauzin, but they're paying dearly for Tauzin's tireless work for the pharmaceutical industry. So are Faith's employer and all of her co-workers. We all are. And in the future, so will our children and grandchildren.

Thanks in large part to Tauzin and Washington's infamous revolving door, the Wildricks are paying so much to fill Bill's prescriptions every month—even with their insurance—that they're barely able to make ends meet. They and most of the rest of us, including the executives and employees of MCS Industries, the Easton, Pennsylvania, company where Faith works, also have to fork over more money to health insurance companies every payday because of the deals Tauzin cut for Big Pharma.

We can also thank Tauzin and many of his friends in Washington for increases in both our taxes and the national debt. In fact, by 2023, the U.$ government's debt will likely be more than a trillion dollars higher than otherwise would be because of the way Tauzin and other lobbyists—v the blessing of President George W. Bush and Republican leader Congress—wrote the Medicare drug bill in 2003.

And in large part because of Tauzin's deal making and the milli dollars at his disposal, the Affordable Care Act—with the bles President Barack Obama and Democratic leaders in Congr written in a way that boosts drug company profits while doir make prescription medications more affordable for the vast majority of Americans. In fact, drug prices are going up at a faster clip than ever before.

As drug industry profits soar, millions of people—including most of our elected officials—continue to accept as gospel Big Pharma's talking points that (1) any constraint on pharmaceutical companies' ability to gouge us would "stifle" or "have a chilling effect" on innovation and (2) they have to charge Americans more because other countries won't let them gouge their citizens. For the success of this propaganda we can thank the millions of dollars in dark money the industry spends every year on deceptive PR campaigns.

Americans pay far more for their prescription medications than citizens of any other country. In fact, we pay almost 40 percent more than Canada, the next highest spender on drugs, and twice as much as many European countries, including France and Germany. In 2013 we spent exactly 100 percent more per capita on pharmaceuticals than the average of the 34 countries that comprise the Organization for Economic Cooperation and Development (OECD), of which the United States is a member. And the portion of our tax dollars that go to Medicare likely will continue to increase because Congress, under the influence of the pharmaceutical industry's cash, made it impossible for Medicare to negotiate with drug companies in order to lower costs.

In 1980, spending on health care in the United States totaled $255.8 billion. Of that total, we spent 39.3 percent on hospital care, 25.3 percent on physician/professional services, and 4.7 percent on prescription drugs. In just a little more than three decades, our total spending on health care exploded to $2.9 trillion. Between 1980 and 2013, the percentage of the total that we spent on hospital care dropped to 32.1, while spending on physician/professional services increased slightly, to 26.6 percent. Spending on prescription drugs, by contrast, almost doubled, to 9.3 percent.[1]

Partly because of that steep increase, health care spending reached 17.4 percent of the U.S. Gross Domestic Product in 2013, nearly double the average of 9.3 percent[2] of the OECD countries. Spending on health care per person in the United States reached $9,255 in 2013, compared to the $3,484 average spent on health care per person in the OECD as a whole.[3]

If you're a young, healthy person you probably can't even remember the last time you had to get a prescription filled. You may be wondering why you should even care about the rising cost of drugs and the ability of big corporations and their lobbyists to keep the status quo firmly in place.

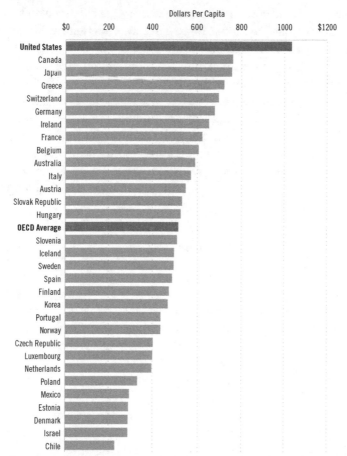

U.S. Pharmaceutical Spending, Per Capita, Compared to Other OECD Countries
Source: Organization for Economic Co-operation and Development
Methodology: Numbers are per capita for 2013 or nearest year: Data not available for New Zealand, Turkey, and the United Kingdom.

You should care because even if you're not a regular customer at the pharmacy counter, you're paying for the millions of other Americans who are, through taxes and health insurance premiums that are going up every year because drug companies have so many politicians, Democrats and Republicans alike, in their corner.

According to Express Scripts' prescription price index, a branded drug that cost $100 in 2008 had almost doubled in price six years later. This rapid increase in drug prices is one of the reasons why health insurers and employers that offer coverage to their workers are constantly raising not only the premiums we have to pay but also our out-of-pocket costs through higher deductibles and coinsurance rates.

And if you do get sick enough to need meds that aren't yet available in generic form, your insurer will make you pay much more for them than you would have just a few years ago. Since 2000, the average copayment for such drugs has doubled, according to the Kaiser Family Foundation. And coinsurance rates for people who have to pay a percentage of their prescription drug costs instead of a fixed copayment have risen even faster. The average coinsurance rate for drugs was 14 percent in 2008. The rate had jumped to 32 percent by 2013, according to the consulting firm Towers Watson.

The Cagey Cajun

It's worth taking a closer look at Tauzin's life, both to understand the power a single industry wields over Capitol Hill and to witness the ways in which Washington's revolving door works.

Born into a working-class French-speaking Cajun family in Lafourche Parish, Louisiana, Wilbert Joseph Tauzin II might have settled into the life of a construction worker—his father taught him how to wire houses and install air conditioners—had he not been bitten by the political bug even before college.

The "Cagey Cajun," as he would later be called in Washington, was audacious enough to throw his hat in the ring for student council president of Thibodaux High School when he was just a sophomore. It was the first of many political campaigns he would win.

After graduation, he enrolled in Nicholls State University, which is just two and a half miles from his high school. Not being able to count on his family for much financial support, he worked, at various times, as an electrician's helper, an oil rigger, and a pipefitter to cover his tuition.

While in college, Tauzin realized that remaining loyal to a single political party has its drawbacks. Campus politics when he was a student was dominated by a party system. At the time, Tauzin, who later would be known as a conservative lawmaker, considered himself a Liberal. But when he sought the Liberal Party's nomination for student body vice president, he came up a few votes short. Instead of supporting the Liberal candidate who beat him, however, the young Tauzin decided to stay in the race as an independent. He went on to victory.

He was a Democrat when the voters in Louisiana's Third Congressional District elected him to Congress in 1980. Within a few years he had become one of his party's assistant majority whips. He also would play a key role in bringing together a group of his conservative and moderate colleagues who came to be called Blue Dog Democrats, a name inspired by Cajun artist George Rodrigue's famous Blue Dog paintings, one of which graced a wall of the congressman's office.

But after the Gingrich Revolution of 1994, which put Republicans in charge of Congress, Representative Tauzin crossed the aisle and soon became the deputy majority whip for House Republicans. Thus he became the first member of Congress to have served in leadership positions of both parties. He's "as wily as any alligator in the swamp," former Tennessee congressman Jim Cooper, a Democrat, told the *New York Times* during the debate on what would ultimately become the Affordable Care Act.[4]

For many years, Tauzin was one of the pharmaceutical industry's most important allies in Congress, especially from 2001 to 2004, when he chaired the House Energy and Commerce Committee, which oversees the Food and Drug Administration. While he held that chairmanship, drug companies and insurance and health professionals contributed nearly $1 million to Tauzin's congressional campaigns, according to the Center for Responsive Politics.[5] That's chump change, though, compared to what the pharmaceutical industry paid him as its top lobbyist when he left Congress in 2005. His salary increased more than twelvefold—from $162,100 to $2 million—the minute he signed on as president and CEO of the Pharmaceutical Research and Manufacturers of America (PhRMA), the industry's powerful trade group.[6]

PhRMA spent $26 million on lobbying in 2009, during the debate over the Affordable Care Act, to shape the law to its satisfaction. Individual companies within the pharmaceutical and health products industry spent millions more on top of that. In fact, at $275 million, the industry's federal lobbying expenditures in 2009 stand as the greatest amount ever spent on lobbying by one industry in a single year, according to the Center for Responsive Politics.[7] The total swelled to $558 million when lobbying expenditures from hospitals, medical device manufacturers, and other health care companies and organizations were included. The industry also doled out millions of dollars in campaign contributions in 2008 and 2009, much of it to Democrats who ostensibly were in charge of writing the reform legislation.

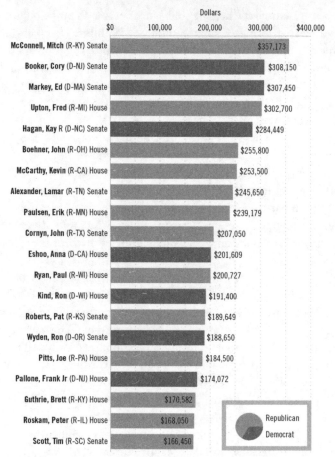

Top 20 Recipients of Pharmaecutical and Health Sector Contributions
Source: Center for Responsive Politics (opensecrets.org)
Methodology: The numbers above are based on contributions from PACs and individuals giving $200 or more. All donations took place during the 2013–2014 election cycle and were released by the Federal Election Commission on March 09, 2015.

PhRMA's ability to influence elections and public policy has made it the envy of most other corporate advocacy groups in Washington. Not only is PhRMA consistently among the top spenders on lobbying activities every year[8], it is widely considered to be the most effective. The PR and consulting firm APCO Worldwide asked hundreds of the city's movers and shakers in 2013 which of approximately fifty leading trade associations had the most clout. PhRMA came out on top, garnering the most wins in the most categories. It was voted the best at lobbying, the most effective at having a local and federal presence, and the group whose members most frequently "mobilize to contact policymakers."[9] In other words, what PhRMA wants, PhRMA is very likely to get.

PhRMA, Clinton, Bush, Obama

Although Tauzin's five-year reign at PhRMA proved extremely successful, the group has been a major force in Washington for more than twenty years. One of the industry's most important victories came in 1994, when it teamed up with lobbyists for doctors, hospitals, medical device manufacturers, and insurers to defeat President Clinton's health care reform proposal. Clinton wanted to give Medicare the ability to negotiate with drug companies and to make it legal for medications made in the United States and exported to Canada and other countries to be imported back into the States and sold at lower prices. Both of those policy changes undoubtedly would have cut into drug company profit margins. But the Clinton reform legislation never made it to the floor of either the House or Senate for a vote. Industry lobbyists were able to kill it in committee.

Lawmakers of both parties tried to put those proposals back on the table nearly ten years later, when President George W. Bush, looking to shore up his support among older voters, pledged to work with Congress to add a voluntary prescription drug benefit—which came to be known as Part D—to the Medicare program. Not wanting to risk losing generous campaign contributions from the pharmaceutical industry, however, Bush and congressional leaders, including Tauzin, who by then chaired the House Energy and Commerce Committee, Republican House Speaker Dennis Hastert of Illinois, and House Majority Leader Tom DeLay of Texas, invited drug company lobbyists to help shape what would become the Medicare Prescription Drug Improvement and Modernization Act of 2003. Also invited to the table were lobbyists for health insurers. They made certain that Medicare beneficiaries who wanted drug coverage would have to buy it from private insurers.

As Bruce Bartlett, who served as domestic policy adviser to President Ronald Reagan, wrote in the *New York Times* ten years later, enacting a new drug benefit—written by lobbyists without cost containment provisions—had Bush's full support.[10] "Looking ahead to a close reelection in

2004, he thought a new government giveaway to the elderly would increase his vote share among this group," Bartlett wrote.

As it turned out, it would take all of Tauzin's charm and wiliness as well as unprecedented flouting of House rules and procedures to pull off what Bush—and the lobbyists—wanted.

Early in the morning of Friday, November 21, 2003, just before the Thanksgiving break and after months of negotiations with drug companies and other special interests, a thousand-page bill finally landed on House members' desks. To their astonishment, they were told they would have only a few hours to review it before having to vote on it.

Many Republicans were just as angry and upset as many Democrats, not only about the unrealistically short amount of time available to read and understand the bill but also about the fact that it would add hundreds of billions of dollars to the deficit while padding drug companies' bottom lines. "The pharmaceutical lobbyists wrote the bill," a disgusted Republican Representative Walter Jones of North Carolina's Third Congressional District later told *60 Minutes* after voting against the measure.

The timing of the vote was in itself unusual. What came next, however, was something that had never happened before in the history of the country. Jones said it was the "ugliest night" he had ever witnessed in more than two decades as a member of Congress.

Tauzin, Hastert, and DeLay, who had received hundreds of thousands of dollars from drug companies during their political careers, knew it wouldn't be easy to pass the legislation without a plan to pay for the costly new entitlement other than through permanent deficit spending. But they believed they had the support they needed when they called for a vote at three A.M. on Saturday.

When asked why he thought House leaders had scheduled the vote long after most Americans had gone to bed, Representative Dan Burton (R-IN), who also voted against the bill, said "a lot of shenanigans were going on that night (that) they didn't want on national television." Among the shenanigans, reportedly sanctioned by House leaders: freezing C-SPAN cameras and allowing lobbyists on the House floor as the vote was being taken. (Lobbyists who previously served in Congress had floor privileges until the enactment of the Honest Leadership and Open Government Act of 2007, which was passed in the aftermath of the Jack Abramoff lobbying scandal.)

Despite the arm twisting, the bill was still short of the 218 votes needed for passage after the standard fifteen-minute voting period. Rather than accept defeat, however, Hastert added two minutes to the voting clock. When that wasn't enough, Hastert decided to keep the vote open indefinitely to give the pharmaceutical lobbyists more time to change minds.

Meanwhile, Thomas Scully, the former hospital industry lobbyist whom Bush had appointed to head the Centers for Medicare and Medicaid Services (CMS) and who had been the White House's lead negotiator for the bill, waited nervously for the result. Scully had a personal as well as a political stake in the outcome of the vote. A few weeks before Congress had started debate on the bill, Scully had asked for—and been granted—a federal government ethics waiver from Health and Human Services Secretary Tommy Thompson, who also had a hand in writing the legislation. The waiver allowed Scully to ignore regulations that barred him from negotiating for future employment with anyone who might be affected financially by his work at CMS.[11] It would be learned later that Scully was in talks with five firms whose financial interests would be affected by the legislation he would soon help to pass. He subsequently joined two of those firms. There were no repercussions.

As Scully knew, and as Bruce Bartlett noted in his *New York Times* op-ed, many House Republicans had said they would not vote for the Medicare drug bill if it cost taxpayers more than $400 billion over the first ten years. "Thus," Bartlett wrote, "it was a huge problem for Republicans when the chief actuary of the Medicare system, Richard S. Foster, concluded during the summer of 2003 that Part D would actually cost $530 billion over its first ten years."

It turned out not to be a problem at all, however, because Scully made sure Foster's estimate would not see the light of day before the vote. Foster later wrote that Scully "ordered me to cease responding directly to congressional requests for actuarial assistance. Instead, I was directed to provide the responses to him for his review, approval and ultimate disposition. Following several vigorous discussions, the administrator made it clear that this was a direct order and that if I failed to follow it, 'the consequences of insubordination are extremely severe.' I understood this statement to mean that I would be fired if I provided the requested information to Congress."[12] An investigation into allegations against Scully, conducted a year later by the Office of Inspector General for the Department of Health and Human Services, substantiated Foster's story and concluded that Scully had indeed threatened to sanction Foster if he released any information that Scully didn't want members of Congress to see.

If Foster's estimate—which turned out to be higher than the actual cost of Part D over the first ten years—had been made public, the bill would never have passed. In fact, it probably wouldn't have passed had House leaders not allowed drug company lobbyists to pressure members directly on the House floor for hours.

As four A.M. approached, the industry was still three votes short, but House leaders and the industry's platoon of lobbyists were not yet ready to concede. Their persistence finally paid off when Republican representative Ernest Istook of Oklahoma switched his vote. Seven other Republicans eventually followed Istook's lead. When the "yeas" reached 220 at five fifty-three A.M., almost three hours after the vote began, Hastert declared the bill passed. It was the longest electronic vote in congressional history.

Writing in the conservative *National Review* ten years later, Noah Glyn described the law as "perhaps the most prominent example of big-government Republicanism during the Bush years."[13] Norman Ornstein of the conservative American Enterprise Institute called it a "huge trophy" for the Bush reelection team.[14]

Indeed. Although his margin of victory over Senator John Kerry of Massachusetts in the 2004 general election was the slimmest in American history for an incumbent president, Bush received just enough additional votes from Medicare beneficiaries, especially in Florida with its 27 electoral votes, to make the difference.

Two days after the election, the *New York Times* reporter Robert Pear wrote that pharmaceutical and insurance company executives "were pleased and immensely relieved at the election results."[15] Bush's reelection meant the Medicare prescription drug program would be implemented as those executives—and their lobbyists—envisioned (and helped write), and that any future proposals to add profit-limiting cost containment provisions would go nowhere. Even if legislation the drug companies and insurers didn't like somehow made it through Congress, Bush could be counted on to veto it.

Also pleased and immensely relieved, with both the election and the bill Bush had signed into law, were many of the government employees, including members of Congress, who had worked on the legislation and were hoping it might lead to better-paying jobs. Within three years after Bush signed the bill into law, according to *60 Minutes*, at least fifteen members of Congress, congressional staffers, and administration officials who had played a role in the bill's passage had left office and joined the pharmaceutical industry.[16]

Among them were Tom Scully and Billy Tauzin. Ten days after Bush signed the bill, Scully signed on with Alston & Bird, a large law and lobbying firm with numerous pharmaceutical clients, and Welsh, Carson, Anderson & Stowe, a private equity firm that invests in health care and information technology companies. Both were among the potential employers Scully was able to negotiate with thanks to his ethics waiver.

Tauzin, meanwhile, had to decide whether to accept a lucrative job offer from PhRMA right away or serve out the remainder of his term and avoid a potential conflict of interest investigation. He chose to wait and continued to serve as chairman of the committee that has jurisdiction over matters pertaining to the pharmaceutical industry. His spokesman repeatedly denied that PhRMA had offered Tauzin a job while the Medicare drug benefit legislation was being considered. Regardless of when the job offer was made, PhRMA waited for him. In January 2005, within days of his retirement from the House, Tauzin started drawing his $2 million salary as the organization's CEO and chief lobbyist.

"To Trump Good Policy and the Will of the American People"

Three years later, after Democrats had regained control of both houses of Congress in the 2006 midterm elections, bills to control the cost of prescription medicines were introduced in both chambers. The House made the most progress when it passed a bill that would have permitted the reimportation of cheaper drugs. But over in the Senate, PhRMA, now led by Tauzin, was able to kill not only the reimportation bill but also the measure that would have given Medicare the ability to negotiate with drug companies. The industry's massive lobbying effort and its generous campaign contributions to senators on both sides of the political aisle had paid off yet again.

Barack Obama, who was still the junior senator from Illinois, had supported both reform proposals. After the Medicare negotiation bill failed, he took to the floor of the Senate to express contempt for the way drug companies were able to call the shots on Capitol Hill. "Once again, a minority of the Senate has allowed the power and the profits of the pharmaceutical industry to trump good policy and the will of the American people," he said. "Drug negotiation," he added, "is the smart thing to do and the right thing to do, and it is unconscionable that we were not able to take up this bill today."[17]

Obama carried those sentiments into his bid for the presidency. His campaign even ran an ad depicting Tauzin as an example of what was wrong with politics. "The pharmaceutical industry wrote into the prescription drug plan that Medicare could not negotiate with drug companies," Obama was shown telling a group of voters at a town-hall-type meeting. "And you know what, the chairman of the committee, who pushed the law through, went to work for the pharmaceutical industry making $2 million a year." That, he said, was an example of "the same old game playing in Washington." He ended the ad with this: "You know, I don't want to learn how to play the game better. I want to put an end to the game playing."[18]

That turned out to be just rhetoric, once the White House decided it would make health care reform a signature accomplishment of the Obama presidency. Obama's top aides—including his chief of staff, the former congressional representative Rahm Emanuel of Illinois, and his deputy chief of staff, Jim Messina, who had worked for Senate Finance Committee chairman Max Baucus of Montana—were tasked with making sure PhRMA was kept happy in the ramp-up to the Affordable Care Act debate, and Baucus would become PhRMA's main contact on Capitol Hill as the legislation was being crafted.[19] The industry's lobbyists made it clear to the White House that if the president was serious about enacting health care reform, drug companies and their cash could help him succeed—so long as he gave up on drug reimportation and Medicare negotiation and any other price control ideas he and congressional leaders might have in mind.

The Sunlight Foundation, a nonprofit transparency group, chronicled the deals the administration and congressional Democrats felt they had to cut to move ahead with the legislation. PhRMA dispatched 165 lobbyists—some of whom focused on the White House while the others worked the Capitol—to ensure that nothing would wind up in the legislation that drug makers couldn't live with. As the Sunlight's Paul Blumenthal wrote, many of those lobbyists, including Tauzin himself, would meet with top White House aides dozens of times "to hammer out a deal that would secure industry support for the administration's health care reform agenda in exchange for the White House abandoning key elements of the president's promises to reform the pharmaceutical industry."[20] If the White House agreed to the industry's demands, drug companies would finance a $150 million ad campaign in support of what by then was begin-ning to be called Obamacare. It probably didn't have to be said what would happen if the White House refused to accept the industry's terms—drug companies would spend whatever it would take to kill reform, as they had done when the Clintons were in the White House.

A few months later, Baucus and Tauzin reached an agreement that Baucus would announce in a press release. Baucus said the pharmaceutical industry had agreed to "accept" $80 billion in cost-cutting measures over ten years—primarily by providing assistance to Medicare beneficiaries who were struggling with the out-of-pocket costs associated with the Part D prescription drug program. By contrast, Medicare beneficiaries could save almost $50 billion *a year* if the government could negotiate with drug companies in the same way that some European countries do, says economist Dean Baker of the Center for Economic and Policy Research.[21] Or even the same way as the U.S. Veterans Administration, which has long had the ability to negotiate with drug companies. The VA pays an estimated 40 percent less than what Medicare pays for many of the same medications.

Much of the $80 billion Tauzin and Baucus settled on would be used to help close a big gap—called the "doughnut hole"—in the Medicare prescription drug program. One of the ways lawmakers and lobbyists were able to keep the ten-year deficit expansion figure of the Medicare Part D law below $400 billion back in 2003 was through a confusing and much-vilified gimmick to limit coverage—Part D enrollees would get coverage for the first $2,250 worth of medications, but after that they would fall into the so-called doughnut hole, as their coverage would not kick back in until they had paid a total of $3,600 out of their own pockets for their prescriptions. Under the Affordable Care Act, the gap will gradually shrink and finally disappear in 2020.

Although the *Wall Street Journal*'s editorial writers accused Tauzin of selling out PhRMA's member companies by cutting the deal with the Democrats,[22] the former congressman was betting that the drug makers would do just fine when millions of newly insured Americans under Obamacare would be finally be able to fill their prescriptions. It was a good bet.

When the details of the deal Baucus and the White House struck with PhRMA became known, it became clear to patient and consumer advocates that their hopes of getting significant relief from skyrocketing prescription drug costs had once again been dashed by politicians more beholden to drug company lobbyists than to the people who voted for them. And this time those hopes had been dashed by a Democrat in the

White House who had won many of their votes by promising to end the game playing in Washington.

One of the longtime champions of legalizing the reimportation of prescription drugs, ironically, is Senator John McCain of Arizona, the Republican presidential nominee Obama defeated in the 2008 election. In 2012, two years after Obama signed the Affordable Care Act into law, McCain and Democratic senator Sherrod Brown of Ohio teamed up as cosponsors of a new reimportation bill. When he realized the drug companies would win once again through a combination of arm twisting by their phalanx of lobbyists and their strategic campaign contributions, McCain made no attempt to hide his disgust. "What you're about to see is the reason for the cynicism that the American people have about the way we do business here in Washington," McCain said as voting was about to begin. "PhRMA, one of the most powerful lobbies in Washington, will exert its influence again at the expense of low-income Americans who will again have to choose between medication and eating."

PhRMA did indeed prevail yet again. McCain and Brown's measure failed 43–54. The Senate's Democratic leaders showed no interest in extending the voting period beyond the standard fifteen minutes to give McCain and Brown additional time to persuade some of their colleagues to switch their votes.

Public Research, Private Profits

In between these big legislative moments, PhRMA does the routine work of persuading policymakers of both parties that any proposed legislation or regulation that might hurt their bottom lines would most certainly inhibit the research and development of new drugs. People who are sick, they essentially claim, will just have to stay sick. Their talking points are carefully crafted to create a fear factor with lawmakers while also appealing to a distinctly American free market ideology.

Yet the profit margins at these companies would indicate that they have plenty of extra cash on hand for R&D. Pfizer, one of the world's largest drug companies as measured by pharmaceutical revenue, for example, recorded a profit margin of 42 percent in 2013. Even without the $10 billion the company made from the spinoff of a subsidiary, Pfizer's profit margin would still have been 24 percent that year.[23] It fell to 18.69 percent in 2014, trailing Merck's 26.98 percent and Novartis's 38.41 percent. Gilead Sciences's profit margin stood at a stunning 51.69 percent.[24]

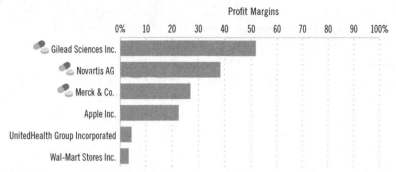

2014 *Company Profit Margins: Drug companies are among the most profitable of any sector*
Source: Yahoo! Finance

To put these numbers in perspective, the profit margin of the country's largest health insurer, UnitedHealth Group, was 4.41 percent in 2014. Walmart's was 3.32 percent, Apple's was 22.53 percent.[25]

It's also worth pointing out that much of the R&D that goes into drug development is funded by us, the taxpayers. The industry's often-cited cost for producing a drug is $1.3 billion over ten to fifteen years. But as the Harvard professor and former editor of the *New England Journal of Medicine* Marcia Angell notes in her 2004 book, *The Truth About Drug Companies*,[26] most original research is done at universities and government agencies such as the National Institutes of Health. And many "new" drugs are slight variations of existing products with patents that are about to expire. Making such "me-too" drugs is just one of the ways pharmaceutical companies are able to extend their patents, a process known as "evergreening."

Pharmaceutical companies do not disclose their exact research and development costs. Instead, they lump them in with other administrative costs that make it nearly impossible to fact-check their claims. But as Angell points out, drug makers spend far more on sales and marketing than on research.

This process—of profiting from publicly funded medical research—brings us back to the Wildricks. Gilead Sciences Inc. makes Sovaldi, the thousand-dollar-a-day hepatitis C pill that Bill Wildrick began taking in 2014. According to an analysis published in *Clinical Infectious Diseases* in January 2014, it likely costs no more than $136 to make a twelve-week course of Sovaldi.[27] That's $83,864 less than what the California-based company decided to charge for a twelve-week course in the United States.

No one else in the world pays nearly as much for Sovaldi as Americans do. In England, for example, the National Health Service was able to get the price down to $57,000—still incredibly expensive but 33 percent less than what the company was able to charge customers in the United States, including the U.S. Medicare program. The Indian government was able to negotiate an even better deal. As a result of Gilead's willingness to give deep discounts to developing countries, the price per pill in India is $10—a mere 1 percent of the cost in the United States.

Even at that price, though, the medication is beyond the reach of most of the 12 million people in India who the World Health Organization estimates have hepatitis C. Worldwide, as many as 150 million people, most of whom live in developing countries, may have hepatitis C, a chronic viral infection that often leads to cirrhosis of the liver or liver cancer.[28]

Pharmasset Inc., a Georgia-based company that grew out of a lab at Emory University, developed Sovaldi, but much of the hepatitis C research that led to the drug was actually funded by taxpayers. As *Modern Healthcare* editor Merrill Goozner wrote in May 2014, the federal government invested heavily over more than two decades in university-based scientists "to understand the genetic weak points" of hepatitis C.[29] Among the scientists the government invested in was Raymond Schinazi, the director of the Laboratory of Biochemical Pharmacology at the Emory School of Medicine who founded Pharmasset at Emory. (Emory received Pharmasset stock as partial consideration for licensing various technologies to the company.)[30] His lab received at least $7.7 million over the past twenty years from the National Institute of Allergy and Infectious Diseases, according to government filings. As Goozner put it, Pharmasset and Schinazi "hit the jackpot" when Gilead, seeing the profit potential of Sovaldi, paid $11.2 billion for the company in 2012. Schinazi reportedly walked away from the deal with $400 million.

Because there were no constraints on what Gilead could charge for the drug, Gilead and its CEO, John Martin, would also hit the jackpot. Sales of Sovaldi exceeded $10.3 billion in 2014, the first year it was on the market. Gilead's board was so pleased with the company's revenues and resulting profit—net earnings for the year totaled $12.1 billion, compared to $3.1 billion in 2013—that it awarded Martin $187.4 million in total compensation in 2014. "It's not fair to ask public and private insurers and patients through their co-pays to be the only parties at risk in the nation's search for miracle breakthroughs," wrote Goozner, author of *The $800 Million*

Pill: The Truth Behind the Cost of Drugs. "The long history of taxpayer-financed involvement in the development of Sovaldi only adds insult to the financial injury."[31]

An analysis published in February 2015 by the National Institutes of Health's National Center for Biotechnology Information confirms Goozner's assertions. It showed that more than half of the most transformative drugs—defined as pharmaceuticals that are both "innovative and have groundbreaking effects on patient care"—that were developed in recent decades had their origins in publicly funded research at nonprofit, university-affiliated centers.[32]

As many critics have noted, the $1,000 Gilead charges for every Sovaldi pill it sold in the United States seems completely arbitrary, with no bearing on either the cost to produce the drug or the overall value of it. The company maintains that in the long run, Sovaldi, in combination with other drugs, is more cost effective than previous treatments for hepatitis C, in part because patients taking Sovaldi are less likely to be hospitalized. Possibly so, but Medicare spent $4.5 billion in 2014 on expensive hepatitis C medications like Sovaldi, which was more than fifteen times the $286 million it spent the year before on older treatments for the disease, according to federal data. And a recent study published in the *Annals of Internal Medicine* suggested that only about one fourth of the money spent on the costly new hepatitis C medications would be offset by avoiding hospitalizations and other treatment costs.[33]

So why does Gilead charge us Americans so much? "The answer is because it can," Steve Miller, chief medical officer of Express Scripts, the large St. Louis–based pharmacy benefit management company, told the *Financial Times*.[34] "Other countries have come up with frameworks to make drugs affordable for people," said Miller, "whereas in the U.S. it has always been a case of what the market will bear. We think the market is no longer bearing up."

Those "frameworks" are another term for laws constructed on behalf of the common good—the kinds of laws that, because of the power of the pharmaceutical industry over Congress, we seem incapable of passing. And it is the lack of such lawmaking that forces Bill and Faith Wildrick to live paycheck to paycheck and give up many of the things they used to do that they can no longer afford.

Bill and Faith both worked at MCS Industries, which has grown since its founding in 1980 to be one of the country's largest suppliers of wall and poster frames. It has also become one of the biggest employers in

Easton, Pennsylvania, which is about sixty miles north of Philadelphia. Faith Wildrick, who packs boxes of frames to send to customers around the world, joined the company in 1993. Bill joined the company two years earlier and was there for more than twenty years, until he got so sick and weak from hepatitis C that he could no longer work.

Bill is one of an estimated 3.2 million Americans who have hepatitis C, although most of them don't know it because symptoms often don't develop until decades after infection. But the virus, which attacks the liver, can be a killer. The Centers for Disease Control and Prevention (CDC) estimates that as many as ten thousand Americans die every year from liver cancer and cirrhosis caused by hepatitis C. Bill believes he was infected in the 1970s, during a time of his life when he occasionally used drugs. The most common way to get hepatitis is by sharing needles, although some people can become infected through sexual contact. (Prior to 1992, many people also got hepatitis C through blood transfusions, but since then, all donated blood and organs are screened for the virus.) Bill said he remembers sharing a needle only one time. But one time was all it took.

It's not just Baby Boomers like Bill who are infected and facing enormous health care costs, by the way. In May 2015, the CDC reported a huge increase in rates of hepatitis C infections among people under thirty, especially in rural areas. The biggest increases were in four Appalachian states—Kentucky, Tennessee, Virginia, and West Virginia—where infection rates jumped 364 percent between 2006 and 2012. Three fourths of the new cases were the result of young people sharing needles to inject prescription drugs.

When Bill's health began to deteriorate a few years ago, he was tested for the virus and told that not only did he have it, it had already begun to damage his liver. His doctor put him on interferon, the most prevalent treatment for acute hepatitis C at the time. After six months on the drug, which is notorious for its debilitating side effects, Bill still had the virus. He was then prescribed Pegasys, another drug with similar side effects.

When tests showed that Bill still had the virus after six months on Pegasys, his doctor told him about a new drug that the FDA had approved just a few months earlier (in December 2013) and that clinical trials had shown had a 90 percent cure rate if taken every day for twelve weeks in combination with other drugs. The new drug was called Sovaldi.

Bill said his heart sank when he was told that Gilead Sciences, which owned the patent on the drug, had priced it at a thousand dollars a pill.

He would also have to take another drug, ribavirin, which would make the daily cost even higher. But he was in luck. Both he and Faith were covered under a Blue Cross health plan Faith had enrolled them in at MCS. After confirming that the policy would cover the drugs, Bill started treatment in April 2014.

Unfortunately, Bill was one of the 10 percent who still had the hepatitis C virus at the end of twelve weeks. His doctor said he needed to keep taking the drugs. Many more weeks went by. By the time his doctor said he could stop taking them, in October 2014, he had been on the medications for six months. Six months at more than a thousand dollars a day.

Although Blue Cross covered most of the costs associated with his treatment, the Wildricks still had to pay several thousand dollars out of their own pockets because they were in a high-deductible plan. Faith said their out-of-pocket costs in 2014 totaled more than $4,000 for Bill's medications alone. "Not only do I constantly worry about Bill," Faith said, "I worry every time he goes to the doctor about whether our insurance will cover it." She said she dreads checking the mail when she gets home from work because of all the bills they get from Bill's doctors and the Philadelphia hospital where he had to go on a frequent basis for testing. "Now that Bill can't work, our income has gone way down," Faith said. "So things have gotten a lot tighter. We've had to cut down on a lot of things. We used to try to go on a vacation every year, but we can't afford to do that anymore. You have to think about everything you spend. You can only stretch your paycheck so far."

Faith said she also can't help but worry about what would happen to them if she got sick and couldn't work or lost her job. "I'm the main source of income, and if I got sick, it would be devastating. I have no idea what we would do."

The Wildricks are not the only ones who are paying dearly for the high cost of Bill's medications. So is MCS. Richard Master, the company's CEO, said the amount of money MCS had to pay for drugs for the 320 employees and dependents who were enrolled in the company's health plan in 2014 was far more than in any previous year. That probably would have been the case had Bill Wildrick been the only one covered under the company health plan who was being treated for hepatitis C. Unfortunately, there were two, the other being an employee in his fifties who was on Sovaldi and ribavirin for twelve weeks. Altogether, the cost of the hepatitis C drugs the two men took in 2014 was more than $260,000. Master said that that was more than 15 percent of MCS's total health plan expenditure for the year.

MCS's experience would come as no surprise to Brian Klepper, CEO of the National Business Coalition on Health, a nonprofit organization comprising more than four thousand employers that offer health benefits to their workers. As he knows all too well, a growing number of employers across the country are experiencing similar rate increases as a result of ballooning specialty drug costs.

"The possibility of specialty drug pricing financially overwhelming business and union health plans is real," Klepper wrote in a May 28, 2015, commentary for *Employee Benefit News*. His prediction for the future of employer-sponsored health benefits was dire:

> Purchasers will be alarmed to find that their drug costs are growing much faster than other, already exorbitant health care spending. CFOs and benefits managers will watch their specialty drug spending, and calculate. To their minds, excessive specialty drug costs could capsize their plans, making it untenable to maintain good health coverage without compromising some other important health plan benefit. Just as worrisome, these costs will substantially increase their already heavy health care burdens, eating into the bottom line.

Klepper added, "Unless something changes, in just another five years we'll likely spend more on specialty than nonspecialty drugs. Or, for that matter, on doctors."

The sharp and unexpected spike in drug costs at MCS didn't go unnoticed by the company's insurer, Blue Cross, which hit MCS with a 14 percent premium increase for 2015. That was the biggest rate hike in the company's recent history. Master's insurance broker recommended that MCS switch to Cigna, which was willing to cover the company's workers at a rate that was still considerably higher than what MCS had paid Blue Cross in 2013. Even with the change, employees saw their premiums increase, and some of the hospitals that were in the Blue Cross network were not in Cigna's. That was bad news for Bill Wildrick, who was told by Cigna that if he didn't switch to a different hospital for his regular testing, he would have to pay much more out of his own pocket.

He also got more bad news in early 2015: even after six months on Sovaldi, he still had the hepatitis C virus. The good news was that Gilead had just released a new drug that might work better. The drug, Harvoni, is actually a combination of Sovaldi and the other drug that Bill had been taking, ribavirin. The catch: the wholesale price of Harvoni is $1,125 per pill. A three-month supply costs $94,500.

It's Not Just Sovaldi

Billy Tauzin's January 2005 announcement that he had decided to take PhRMA up on its two-million-dollar-a-year job offer came ten months after another big announcement from his office: he had cancer.

On March 10, 2004, the congressman's spokesman, Ken Johnson, said his boss would have surgery the following week at Johns Hopkins Hospital in Baltimore, where he had been diagnosed a few days earlier with cancer of the duodenum, a part of the small intestine. "His doctors have assured him he'll live a long, healthy and productive life," Johnson told CNN at the time. That's not at all how Tauzin later characterized what he had been told at Johns Hopkins. After the surgery, he said in a 2009 interview, "The doctor told me very frankly that I was going to die."[35]

"My doctor reviewed my options with me," Tauzin said in the interview. "I could undergo another surgery, but that would probably kill me and would be unlikely to cure the cancer. They had no approved protocol for people in my position, but there was a drug (Avastin) that had been successful in treating colon cancer but was not yet approved for duodenal adenocarcinoma. The drug works by cutting off the blood supply to tumors, which meant that the drug could either damage my healing process or kill the cancer. My wife and I decided to take the risk because we had very little to lose. It was really a choice between 'going to die'—my current situation—and 'might die'—Avastin could cure me. It's a good thing we tried Avastin because it worked like a miracle. By the end of my first round of chemotherapy, the radiologist couldn't even find the tumor on my CT scans. It was gone. I completed several courses of chemo and radiation and I've been cancer-free for over five years now."

He said it was his wife who suggested after his recovery that he take the PhRMA job. "'You know, Billy,'" he said she told him, "'you really ought to go to work for the people who saved your life.' And I thought, 'If there's a meaning in why I'm alive today, then surely it must be to use my experience to help patients like me across the world.'"

As he has told the story about his recovery, Tauzin has made no mention of how much Avastin and many other cancer drugs now cost.

There is no question that many of the products pharmaceutical companies sell save thousands of lives every day. But how long will patients—and the nation as a whole—be able to afford those products?

Like Sovaldi, Avastin, one of the most widely used cancer drugs in the world, is incredibly expensive. It's not unusual for patients—or their insurers or Medicare—to be charged $9,000 a month for Avastin. But as the *New York Times* has reported, studies have shown that for most patients, Avastin prolongs life for only a few months at best. Nevertheless, sales of Avastin, marketed by the biotech firm Genentech, reached $6.6 billion in 2013.

The next year, Genentech implemented a scheme to make even more money from the drug. In a widely criticized move, the company, which became a subsidiary of Swiss-based Roche Holding, notified U.S. hospitals in 2014 that they could no longer buy Avastin from the wholesalers they had been buying it from for years. Going forward, they would have to buy Avastin and two of the company's other cancer drugs through Genentech-approved specialty distributors.[36] That shift, as *Time* reported, meant that hospitals would no longer get an estimated $300 million in discounts they'd been getting from the wholesalers. Instead, Genentech and the specialty distributors would be able to pocket the money.

Pharmaceutical companies have also been repricing their cancer drugs on a regular basis to boost profits. Prior to 2000, the price of cancer drugs for one year of treatment typically ranged between $5,000 and $10,000. By 2012, the average had risen to $120,000.[37]

Another way of looking at it is the cost per additional year of life made possible by the drugs. In 1995, a group of fifty-eight leading cancer drugs cost on average about $54,100 for each year of life they were estimated to add. By 2013, those drugs cost about $207,000 for each additional year of life.

The rapid increase in costs, coupled with the aging of the U.S. population, led the National Institutes of Health to project in 2011 that medical expenditures for cancer in 2020 will reach at least $158 billion—27 percent more than in 2010—and could go as high as $207 billion. Speaking at the annual meeting of the American Society of Clinical Oncology in Chicago on May 31, 2015, Dr. Leonard Saltz, chief of gastrointestinal oncology at Memorial Sloan Kettering Cancer Center in New York, called the rapid cost of cancer drugs "unsustainable." He said the median monthly price for new cancer drugs in the United States had more than doubled over the past decade—from $4,716 in the period from 2000 through 2004 to $9,900 from 2010 through 2014.[38] That increase, he said, could only be explained by the desire of pharmaceutical companies to boost profits. "Cancer-drug prices are not related to the value of the drug," he said. "Prices are based on what has come before and what the seller believes the market will bear."

At the same time, many patients—including cancer patients—are finding that drug companies are not making adequate amounts of some lifesaving medications because they're not as profitable as they once were. The *Wall Street Journal* reported in May 2015 that BCG, a drug used to treat bladder cancer, is now in short supply because the twenty-five-year-old drug is no longer protected by patent. BCG sells for $145 a vial, a fraction of the $2,700 Genentech charges for a vial of Avastin. As the *Journal* noted, there has been no shortage of Avastin.[39]

If anything, spending will go even higher. In 2014, total prescription drug spending in the United States rose to $374 billion, an increase of 13.1 percent in just one year, according to the IMS Institute for Healthcare Informatics.[40] Driving the big increase were the emergence of Sovaldi and other new expensive specialty drugs and pharmaceutical companies' decision to slap new price tags on their older medications, their older specialty drugs in particular. Indeed, spending on specialty medicines, not just for hepatitis C and cancer but also for other diseases such as multiple sclerosis, jumped an unprecedented 31 percent, according to an analysis by Express Scripts, the pharmacy benefit management firm. The company noted in an earlier report that while specialty drugs accounted for less than 1 percent of all U.S. prescriptions, they accounted for 27.7 percent of the country's total spending on medications in 2013. It projected spending on specialty drugs would increase 63 percent between 2014 and 2016.

Not only are brand-name drugs being priced at unprecedented levels, so are generics, which until recent years had been decreasing in price. A survey conducted by AARP and published in May 2015 showed that one in four generic medicines used widely by older Americans increased in 2013.[41] "This is the beginning of a shift," Leigh Purvis, AARP's director of health services research, told the Associated Press. "What we used to get from generics in the way of savings is going away at the same time that the prices of brand-name drugs are extremely high, and they're going even higher." She called some of the price increases "stratospheric." Among them were two generics used for treating infections whose retail prices increased more than 1,000 percent in 2013.

In his 2015 State of the Union address, President Obama stressed the importance of committing taxpayer dollars to help finance the development of "precision medicine"—personalized therapies to treat a broad range of illnesses. He asked Congress to allocate $215 million to get the initiative under way.

"The possibilities are boundless," he said at a subsequent White House event. "It [precision medicine] gives us one of the greatest opportunities for new medical breakthroughs that we have ever seen." Obama mentioned cystic fibrosis in particular, noting that people with certain mutations in a particular gene are now being treated successfully with a new precision drug called Kalydeco. As the *New York Times* later noted, Obama did not mention that the list price for a one-year supply of the drug is $311,000.[42]

The cost of Kalydeco and other specialty drugs is fueling a huge increase in government spending on the Medicare Part D program. The Obama administration's budget proposal for 2016 had this stunning projection: Part D benefits were expected to increase 30 percent in one year's time—from $63.3 billion in 2015 to $82.5 billion in 2016. Deep inside his $3.99 billion budget request to Congress for 2016, Obama once again proposed giving Medicare the ability to negotiate prices for expensive drugs. But as long as Washington's revolving door keeps spinning, and industries can spend hundreds of millions of dollars to finance the political campaigns of the politicians who are supposed to be regulating them, PhRMA almost certainly will continue to rule Capitol Hill.

CHAPTER 6

Fuel Follies

The United States lacks a clearly defined national energy policy. While Congress has passed laws that purport to create comprehensive goals and accompanying strategies leading to energy independence, each attempt has fallen flat as implementation was resisted by entrenched interests committed to preserving the status quo.

The three energy bills that have passed through Congress in recent years (1992, 2005, and 2007) are known as "Christmas tree" bills, festooned with tax breaks for industries such as solar and wind (in the two most recent bills), conservation incentives like the Energy Star program, and a reiteration of the panoply of allowances for extraction of oil and gas.

But none of them approached the topic from the broader perspective of setting forth guidelines for domestic energy development using legislative carrots, such as tax incentives and federal grants, for research and development while meeting consistent environmental regulation. As a result, our current national energy policy is a hodgepodge of special interest favors granted to companies, and sometimes whole industries, paying homage to lobbying efforts and political contributions as surrogates for sound, decisive policy.

But there are respected voices urging a better approach to a national energy policy. One is James Woolsey, who held a number of positions under Jimmy Carter, Ronald Reagan, and George H. W. Bush before finishing his government career as Director of Central Intelligence under Bill Clinton from 1977 to 1979. Woolsey was known as a neoconservative, a hawk on foreign policy and national defense issues.

After leaving government service he started a conservative think tank called the Foundation for Defense of Democracies in response to the terrorist attacks of September 11, 2001. Since then, he has ascended the bully pulpit to become one of the leading voices elaborating a national security argument for a comprehensive energy policy. Reflecting on the tragedies in New York City, Washington, D.C., and Pennsylvania ten years later, he wrote: "Apart from the heartfelt honoring of those lost—on that day and since—what seemed most striking is our seeming passivity and indifference toward the well from which our enemies draw their political strength and financial power: the strategic importance of oil." He goes on to bemoan the fact that "for 35 years we have engaged in self-delusion."[1]

Woolsey's crusade is echoed by business leaders. The Pew Charitable Trusts gathered a group of experts and executives in 2012 to examine replacing the "patchwork of state policies and cyclical tax incentives, such as the production and investment tax credits" that constitute America's excuse for energy policy with a clear plan that businesses can use to make long-term decisions.[2] Businesses need some degree of certainty and stability to plan for future expansion, without which they tend to be cautious about long-term investment in capital goods and hiring people.

At the Pew meeting was former senator John Warner (R-VA), who had served as secretary of the Navy under Richard Nixon. His summation: "We are hopeful that Congress will formulate a national energy policy that will provide not only economic benefits but strengthen our national security and reduce our dependence on foreign oil."[3]

Woolsey and Warner are talking about oil, which is necessary for the American military's ships, aircraft, and land vehicles. But they are making a more important and less obvious point: Every major energy source in this country—petroleum, natural gas, coal, and renewables—is part of a larger consortium or trade group. Each has a serious and robust statement of national policy promoting the future of that business, but there is no overall melding into a national policy.

To dig more deeply into how special interests are deeply rooted in our moribund energy policy, this chapter will examine how an entrenched industry, coal, has fought tooth and nail to protect its position despite issues clearly affecting the health of our country. As evidence of environmental degradation piled up, the industry turned increasingly to buying influence and political contributions as a way to preserve its declining business.

We'll then shift to the relatively new technology called hydraulic fracturing. When "fracking" began to take the stage, the price of generating electricity using natural gas dropped well below the price of using coal. To protect profits, the new industry did everything within its power to mimic the efforts of Big Coal by frustrating oversight of groundwater contamination and obscuring transparency in identifying toxic chemicals used in the drilling process.

As an example, we will then turn to the state of Pennsylvania, where coal and natural gas coexist in abundant quantities, to show how political contributions have been used to direct energy policy and how the revolving door between government and private industry works to thwart the development of a coherent policy.

Old King Coal

Coal is truly a remarkable substance. Holding a piece of the black, burnished mineral in your hand can be almost mesmerizing. After all, it's the stuff that diamonds are made of. Much of it was formed hundreds of millions of years ago, before the dinosaurs roamed.

Coal has powered the modernization of human civilization, from fueling train engines to electrifying the world. But, as we all know, coal mining and coal burning also have some significant downsides. They contribute to public health problems, global climate change, and the destruction of countless mountains, valleys, and streams. And although the industry is cleaner today than it was fifty or a hundred years ago, that's in part because lawmakers occasionally have been able to overcome industry resistance to pass legislation on behalf of the public interest.

In 1990, for example, President George H. W. Bush signed into law sweeping improvements to the Clean Air Act. He was fulfilling a campaign promise to deal with the problem of acid rain, and the bill mandated dramatic action to reduce the amount of sulfur dioxide spewing into the air from coal-fired power plants. U.S. Environmental Protection Agency studies showed that pollutants generated by Midwestern plants were causing havoc to the Northeast's ecosystems, turning the region's streams, lakes, and forests into spotty wastelands. The legislation had broad bipartisan support, passing the House 401–21 and the Senate 89–11. By 2011 both sulfur dioxide and nitrous oxide emissions had declined to well below the targets established by the new law and, despite howls of protest and dire warnings in the late 1980s and early 1990s from the coal industry, the average price per kilowatt hour of electricity nationwide had not risen one penny for either residential or industrial users.

The 1990 amendments worked because they were based upon sound science and had strong bipartisan support, passing the message to the industry that the nation's elected leadership was committed to solving the problem. Yet, although we can celebrate a reduction in acid rain, two major problems related to coal still needed to be fully addressed: mercury and carbon dioxide emissions.

Coal's Mercury Problem

The EPA estimated that in 1997, about 50 tons of mercury was being released annually by coal-fired utility plants. When combined with organisms that live in oceans, lakes, wetlands, and streams, airborne mercury becomes highly toxic and makes its way into the human food chain, mainly through the consumption of fish.

Several studies have shown a causal relationship between high levels of methylmercury in pregnant women and developmental problems such as diminished language skills and impaired memory function in their offspring. As a result, pregnant women were advised in 2001 by the EPA, the U.S. Food and Drug Administration, and forty-four states to limit their intake of certain fish, particularly higher-level predators such as tuna and swordfish that consume other species, to limit the toxic effects on their unborn children. A later study done for the EPA on methylmercury effects in the United States linked the chemical to diminished IQ and attention deficit disorders in young children.[4]

As bad as it is in the United States, the problem of mercury exposure is much worse in other parts of the world, Asia in particular. Studies done after mercury-laden industrial waste was dumped in two Japanese cities showed children whose prenatal mothers were exposed had severe mental retardation and neurological impairment.

The good news is, as shown on the chart opposite, mercury can be controlled.

So, while the technology exists, the political will has been sidetracked. Scientific and medical studies targeting human health consequences by the National Academy of Sciences, the National Institutes of Health, the FDA, and the EPA have been constantly challenged—by King Coal and utility money shoveled into the political process. Here, in part, is how.

MACT Attack

When President Bill Clinton took office in 1993, it was widely assumed in Washington that dramatic reductions in sulfur dioxide and nitrogen oxide, as a result of the 1990 amendments to the Clean Air Act, were accompanied by diminished amounts of mercury being released into the atmosphere through the installation of scrubbers in coal-fired power plants.

However, according to a study submitted to Congress by the EPA, the nation was being blanketed by about 158 tons of airborne mercury a year from anthropogenic (human-caused) sources, a third of which came from burning coal.[5] In the last month of his presidency, Clinton decided it was time to press for full implementation of the Clean Air Act and regulate mercury emissions from coal-fired power plants. The EPA ruled that power plants would be required to install equipment to meet "maximum achievable control technology"—known as MACT—which, in simple terms, meant that coal-burning electric generating facilities had to meet a standard calculated by averaging the emissions from the best-performing plants across the country.

Bush Retreat

After George W. Bush was elected, aided by $20 million in campaign contributions from King Coal and electric utilities, he took dead aim at the Clinton EPA's MACT rule by appointing a lawyer from the Washington firm of Latham & Watkins, which represented coal-burning utility Cinergy Corporation, to be an assistant administrator at the EPA. His name was Jeffrey Holmstead, and he would be in charge of regulating air and radiation pollution.

Holmstead was well known to the Bush family. As an associate counsel in George H. W. Bush's administration, he had worked on the Clean Air Act amendments of 1990 and become familiar with the concept of cap-and-trade, a system that would allow companies not meeting emission caps to buy pollution credits from companies that were meeting or exceeding emissions goals.

One of Holmstead's principal efforts as Bush's point man on the Clinton MACT standards was to avoid the requirement to set health-protective standards for mercury. He did, by ruling that those emissions would no longer be regulated under Section 112 of the Clean Air Act, but rather under the less stringent Section 111 and by ordering his staff to begin drafting alternatives to MACT.

The process was fraught with problems. The *New York Times* found that Holmstead's office had either altered or deleted information from a National Academy of Sciences report to Congress on mercury and human health, and a large chunk of the alternatives language being drafted—as much as twelve paragraphs—was reported to be lifted directly from Latham & Watkins memos.[6]

After two years, the crowning achievement of Holmstead's brief sojourn at EPA was issued on March 15, 2005: the Clean Air Mercury Rule. Under this alternative proposal, mercury would be regulated in two steps. The first, a nationwide cap of 38 tons (remarkably close to the industry group's recommendation), would be accomplished as a by-product of existing pollution control devices designed to reduce sulfur dioxide and nitrogen. The rule attempted to establish a cap and trade market for polluters to buy credits beginning in 2010 under the assumption that "the ability to bank unused allowances for future use can lead to early reductions of mercury."[7] The second step, to take effect in 2018, had a 15-ton cap "upon full implementation."[8]

Jeff Holmstead resigned from EPA, took a year off, and moving smoothly between government and the private sector, joined the lobbying firm of Bracewell & Giuliani, cofounded by former New York City Mayor Rudy Giuliani. Research by a group called Environment America, based on a review of disclosed lobbying records, showed that by 2011, nine of the twenty-five top mercury-polluting companies in the United States were represented by Jeff Holmstead.[9] We point to his story, specifically, to provide an example of the ease with which the political class in Washington toggles in between representing the narrow desires of special interests and working for the government, where they are employed by us taxpayers to stand for the long-term public interest. Unfortunately, though, for too many in D.C., they see their time in government as just another means of advancing the typically narrow objectives they worked for in the private sector.

Holmstead's successor at the EPA was his personal counsel, Bill Wehrum, again courtesy of the revolving door at Latham & Watkins.

Wehrum did his best to establish a single cap of 34 tons of mercury, but he had to contend with a lawsuit filed by the National Resources Defense Council arguing that Holmstead and the EPA had improperly attempted to regulate mercury under the Clean Air Act's less-demanding Section 111. In December 2009, the U.S. Court of Appeals in Washington agreed with the NRDC and ordered the EPA to create hard and fast rules requiring coal-fired plants to install equipment that would bring emissions down to the MACT standards. The case was one of twenty-six brought by the NRDC against the Bush administration.

Fits and Starts Under Obama

Barack Obama was elected to be an agent of change. It was clear that the nation's courts wanted action on reducing sources of airborne toxins and pollutants despite the continuing pushback from lawmakers representing coal-producing states, and on the campaign trail, Obama had promised to deal with the problem.

Following through during his first year in office, he persuaded congressional representatives Henry Waxman (D-CA) and Ed Markey (D-MA) to introduce legislation to reduce airborne toxins from coal-fired power plants and reduce carbon emissions 80 percent by the year 2050. It was classic market-based cap-and-trade, providing certainty on a nationwide basis as to emissions reduction by allowing flexibility among states and without forcing the controversial issue of a carbon tax.

The bill passed the Democrat-controlled House but languished in the Senate as Republicans joined with coal-state Democrats to slow it down. When Republicans regained control of the U.S. House after the 2010 midterm elections, the new majority introduced a measure to significantly deregulate the coal industry. Their Stop the War on Coal Act picked up support from nineteen Democrats and was eventually passed 233–175 in the House. Part of the reason: Coal state legislators of both parties were lobbied heavily by groups like the Heartland Institute, which got its initial funding from oil and extraction companies. The Institute claimed to have made contact with government officials 291,989 times in 2011. According to the Center for Responsive Politics, in 2011 mining companies spent $16.5 million and electric utilities $74.8 million to affect legislation.[10]

That's, in part, why the Senate never took up Waxman and Markey's bill.

During the 2012 presidential campaign, the industry spent $35 million on ads attacking Obama, alleging that his energy proposals would kill jobs and stifle economic growth. In total, during Obama's first term, the coal industry and its surrogate, the American Coalition for Clean Coal Electricity, more than tripled political contributions, with 90 percent going to Republicans.

By 2014, the Obama White House, having lost both the House and Senate to Republican control, was left only with rulemaking as a path to cleaning up problems created by the coal industry. In July 2015, U.S. Secretary of the Interior Sally Jewell announced new regulations, and a clarification of water quality standards, for mountaintop removal and surface-mining operations called the Stream Protection Rule.

For the first time in thirty years, coal companies would be responsible for monitoring water quality in streams and rivers adjacent to their mines to ensure that drinking water supplies were not affected. Companies would be required to post a financial bond for cleanup as a result of environmental pollution, relieving taxpayers of the financial burden.

The rulemaking was greeted with derision by Big Coal. "This is a rule in search of a problem," said National Mining Association president Hal Quinn. As of the writing of this book, the new regulations were still under mandated review.

The Decline of Coal

The coal industry may have won some key fights in the last decade, but it's down to its last pile of chips and is betting some on carbon capture and sequestration (CCS), a technology that would store carbon dioxide in both natural and constructed underground cavities. A second approach to cleaner coal suffered a major setback in May 2015 when the South Mississippi Electric Power Association pulled its $600 million investment out of the Southern Company's $6.2 billion coal-gasification experiment, forcing a reevaluation of the entire project. According to one source in 2010, the four largest publicly traded coal companies in the United States were worth a total of $21.7 billion, but by 2015 those same four companies had a combined stock market value of only $1.2 billion.[11] Part of the reason for the drop: the price of natural gas, coal's main competitor for electric utility generating plants, had dropped through the floor with the advent of a new technology called hydraulic fracturing. And politics

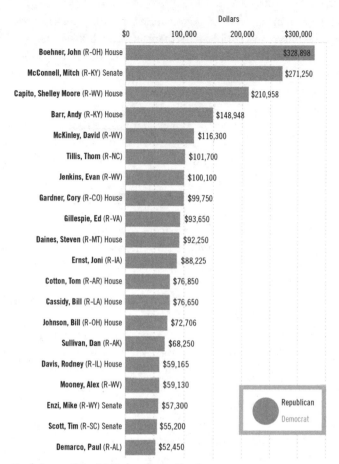

Dollars

| | $0 | 100,000 | 200,000 | $300,000 |

Boehner, John (R-OH) House — $328,898
McConnell, Mitch (R-KY) Senate — $271,250
Capito, Shelley Moore (R-WV) House — $210,958
Barr, Andy (R-KY) House — $148,948
McKinley, David (R-WV) — $116,300
Tillis, Thom (R-NC) — $101,700
Jenkins, Evan (R-WV) — $100,100
Gardner, Cory (R-CO) House — $99,750
Gillespie, Ed (R-VA) — $93,650
Daines, Steven (R-MT) House — $92,250
Ernst, Joni (R-IA) — $88,225
Cotton, Tom (R-AR) House — $76,850
Cassidy, Bill (R-LA) House — $76,650
Johnson, Bill (R-OH) House — $72,706
Sullivan, Dan (R-AK) — $68,250
Davis, Rodney (R-IL) House — $59,165
Mooney, Alex (R-WV) — $59,130
Enzi, Mike (R-WY) Senate — $57,300
Scott, Tim (R-SC) Senate — $55,200
Demarco, Paul (R-AL) — $52,450

Republican
Democrat

Top 20 Recipients of Coal Mining Contributions 2013–2014
Source: Center for Responsive Politics (opensecrets.org)
Methodology: The numbers above are based on contributions from PACs and individuals giving $200 or more. All donations took place during the 2013–2014 election cycle and were released by the Federal Election Commission on March 09, 2015.

would inevitably play a part as domestic gas drillers flexed their newly acquired muscle, as we shall see now.

Fracking Right

Many of the stories in this book detail shadow relationships, money influencing policy decisions, and crony capitalism at the federal level.

But there is another level of government, and it is as susceptible—in many ways more susceptible—to manipulation by moneyed interests than it is to what goes down in the cloakrooms of the U.S. Capitol and the restaurants of K Street. What follows is the story of one of America's earliest coal-producing states, where the lines become blurred between the revolving doors of public and private interest and where another fossil fuel industry, eager to replace coal, replicated King Coal's playbook with campaign contributions, industry-funded studies, and manipulation of regulations and regulatory bodies to achieve its business objectives.

This story actually began over a century ago, when the state of Pennsylvania provided 80 percent of the coal to fuel the steel mills and railroads that opened up the American West after the Civil War. The state's waterways ended up polluted by the mining of its vast deposits, and cities like Pittsburgh and Philadelphia were enveloped by soot from coal-burning furnaces.

In 1890 the first oil well in the United States was drilled near the town of Titusville in western Pennsylvania, a new find that would lubricate and power smaller engines throughout the world. For the last 150 years, the state has consistently ranked among America's top five producers of hydrocarbons, and by the turn of the twenty-first century it was sitting atop a newer and cleaner source of energy than coal or crude oil: natural gas. Much of it, though, was embedded in rock far below the earth's surface, in some cases almost four miles below. The challenge was how to tap it. The solution was hydraulic fracturing.

The process commonly known as fracking breaks up compressed subsurface rock by high-pressure injection of a combination of water, sand, and chemicals into deep geologic formations to create cracks through which gas and petroleum can flow and accumulate. The hydrocarbons are then captured and brought to the surface. About 50 percent of the chemical soup used in the fracking process is recycled; the other half remains underground, where it sometimes migrates into subsurficial wells and aquifers.

In 2005 a well drilled in Washington County, Pennsylvania, using fracking technology, came in, and came in big—much bigger than expected—setting off a wild boom in six states, all sitting on top of a giant formation called the Marcellus Shale. By 2008, a respected geological survey estimated that the Marcellus held as much as 500 trillion cubic feet of natural gas[12] Pennsylvania's share was estimated to be worth over $500 billion, and getting the gas out of the deep rocks was projected to create 75,000 jobs by 2020.[13]

Big Ed

Ed Rendell is a large, robust man as equally at ease in front of a group of heavy-hitter donors as a television camera. A liberal Democrat in a purple state, he swept into the Pennsylvania governor's office in November 2002 with the support of normally Republican strongholds in suburban Philadelphia, where he had been a well-liked and effective mayor for eight years.

Rendell's years as governor were marked by a number of challenges, and at the end of his first term came one from an unexpected source. Working with his Department of Environmental Protection secretary, Kathleen McGinty, Rendell had been keeping an eye on the developing fracking industry, but it remained a background issue until 2008, when he appointed John Hanger to succeed McGinty. Drilling was picking up, and Rendell told Hanger that the state was woefully unprepared for the boom that had already arrived. Hanger's best bet was to update existing laws like the Oil and Gas Act, but legislation on the books failed to address issues of water contamination and the disposal of the toxic chemical cocktails associated with hydraulic fracturing.

Rendell was on the horns of another dilemma. Although he favored continued growth of the extraction industry with the jobs it brought to his state and the energy independence it promised for the country, he also knew that regulation was critical in order to preserve Pennsylvania's lakes, streams, and drinking water sources; but the banking crisis of 2007–2009 had precipitated a brutal economic recession. Rendell was facing a $4 billion deficit due to lower tax receipts, and he salivated over the stream of potential revenue generated by other states that were successfully levying a tax averaging 5 percent of receipts on gas extraction.

Rendell and Hanger appealed to the legislature for immediate help in both regulating and taxing the burgeoning drilling boom, but the well-paid (fifth-highest in the nation) and well-staffed (first in the nation) Republican-controlled Senate and Democrat-controlled House could not agree on a course of action. With the legislature in paralysis, the state's Department of Environmental Protection, under Hanger's leadership, established a set of enhanced executive regulations to cover both the design and construction of new wells. Rendell pressed the legislature to pass a tax during his last year in office, but the state's lawmakers, many of whom were by then on the receiving end of generous campaign contributions from fracking companies, refused to go along.

Part of the reason was a Pennsylvania State University study released in 2009, funded in part, to the tune of $100,000, by the Marcellus Shale Coalition, the lobbying front for a large group of companies with a direct financial interest. The study's conclusion: energy companies would flee Pennsylvania if a tax was imposed. Hotly debated, the issue became central to the 2010 governor's race pitting Republican Tom Corbett against Democrat Dan Onorato.

Buying the Governor's Office

With the tax on drillers on the campaign's front burner, and Onorato openly favoring it, Pennsylvania's oil and gas industry went all in for Corbett, who opposed any form of levy on oil and gas producers, giving him $1.3 million compared to $130,000 for Onorato. Corbett prevailed by a nine-point margin.

Among Corbett's contributors were a select group of oil and gas executives. The top three were Terry Pegula, founder of East Resources, and his wife ($280,000); Alan C. Walker, former president of Bradford Energy ($112,782); and Ray Walker, senior vice president of Range Resources ($16,800). They joined eleven other campaign donors on Corbett's newly created Marcellus Shale Advisory Commission (MSAC), ten of whom were either lobbyists or executives for oil and gas companies.

MSAC and the gas industry didn't limit 2010 giving to the governor's race, kicking in more than $4.3 million to assorted legislators including Senate president pro tem Joe Scarnati, who got $373,384—nearly 30 percent of the total collected for his upcoming campaign—even though he wasn't on the ballot until 2012.[14]

According to public records, acquired by the Pennsylvania Land Trust, Corbett donor Pegula's company, East Resources, violated environmental regulations 106 times between 2008 and 2010, the third most in the state.[15] Pegula sold part of East Resources to Royal Dutch Shell in May 2010 for $4.7 billion and the balance to American Energy in August, using the proceeds to purchase the NFL's Buffalo Bills and to help Tom Corbett get elected.

Alan Walker, a former board member of the Pennsylvania Coal Association, was rewarded for his support by being named secretary of the

Pennsylvania Department of Community and Economic Development. It was Corbett's first major appointment.

Ray Walker's company, Range Resources, was the largest driller in Pennsylvania. The company had experienced a number of problems, beginning with a wastewater pipe breaking and killing fish in a thousand-yard stretch of stream in a state park. It was also in court with problems in Washington County.

Another of Corbett's first appointments was Michael Krancer, an attorney from the Philadelphia revolving door law firm (as we'll see later) of Blank Rome, to become secretary of DEP. Krancer asserted greater jurisdiction over review of any notices of oil and gas regulatory violations citing companies drilling in the Marcellus Shale. Issuance of a citation would require his, or his deputy's, personal approval.[16] Citations were problematic to begin with, because at the time, the state had only thirty-one inspectors and 125,000 active wells.[17] Federal oversight was lax because the federal Clean Water Act exempted oil and gas drilling operations from many of the mandated precautions to control runoff and wastewater disposal from well sites. With Krancer in place asserting personal jurisdiction over violations, and the EPA's hands tied, the industry breathed a sigh of relief, and Governor Corbett's Marcellus Shale Advisory Commission went to work, holding hearings for the next eighteen months.

By February 2012, Republicans controlled both houses of the Pennsylvania legislature, supported heavily by oil and gas money (see chart next page). The nine members of the Senate Environmental Resources and Energy Committee received $540,894 from extraction companies, or 12 per cent of their total contributions received for the 2012 election.[18] In return, compliant legislators passed Act 13, based partly on recommendations from the MASC, mandating drilling in all zoning areas and giving the State Public Utilities Commission absolute power to override local laws passed to regulate drilling in counties and municipalities.

In the same act, the legislature also proposed an impact fee on drilling that would be adjusted for inflation and market conditions (the price of natural gas). The proceeds would be shared only with municipalities that did not have fracking regulations more stringent than the state's. (Pennsylvania's Supreme Court eventually overrode some of the provisions in Act 13 that limited the ability of local governments to control fracking within their respective jurisdictions, asserting that communities had the right to do so).

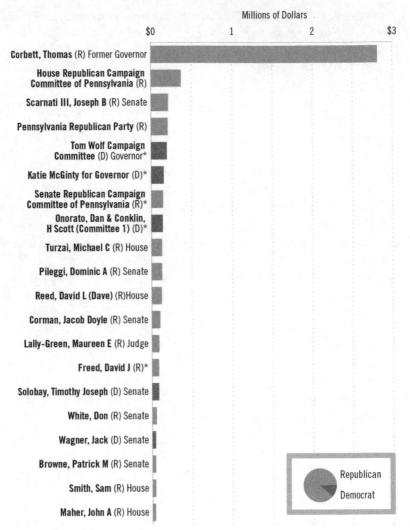

Contributions to Pennsylvania State Candidates and Committees from the Oil and Gas Industry
Source: National Institute on Money in State Politics
Methodology: Contributions made between 2007 and 2014.
Tom Wolf was elected governor in 2014; Katie McGinty was candidate for governor in 2014; Dan Onorato and Scott Conklin were candidates for governor and lieutenant governor in 2010; David Freed was a candidate for attorney general in 2012.

In May 2012, Tim Considine, the author of the 2009 study at Penn State, came out with a second paper from SUNY–Buffalo University claiming that Pennsylvania had achieved a satisfactory level of safety with its new regulatory structure. But that conclusion was questioned when a blogger discovered that the author's department had received nearly $6 million from the oil and gas industry.[19] The blogger's allegation was later corroborated by faculty, who forced cancellation of another Penn State study that was to have been funded by the Marcellus Shale Coalition.[20]

Michael Krancer left DEP in the middle of Corbett's term and was replaced by Christopher Abruzzo, one of the governor's deputy chiefs of staff. Then, in November 2012, two whistleblower employees complained that DEP groundwater test results in Washington County failed to include volatile organic compounds and certain heavy metals including chromium. Later tests showed that seven residents living within one mile of Range's Amwell County drill site and wastewater facility were found to have arsenic, benzene, and toluene—which when inhaled can cause neurological damage—in their systems.[21] The evidence was overwhelming, and the Corbett administration was forced to pursue the matter, finally fining Range Resources, campaign donor Ray Walker's company, $4.15 million for failing to obtain DEP permits to construct six holding ponds that had spilled the fracking fluids. It was the largest fine ever levied on a natural gas driller in Pennsylvania.

Despite the Range Resources settlement, Corbett's coziness with the fracking industry didn't sit well with a lot of Pennsylvania voters. At least partly because of voters' concerns about real and potential environmental hazards, Corbett became a one-term governor. Tom Wolf, a Democrat and wealthy businessman from York, beat him soundly in the 2014 election, despite Corbett's overwhelming advantage in campaign funds raised from energy companies: $1,148,351 to $192,985.[22] Heavy hitter Terry Pegula, former executive of East Resources, contributed $250,000 to the Corbett campaign.

By 2014 Marcellus Shale companies increased their overall political spending in Pennsylvania to over $9 million, as compared to $1.7 million when the boom began in 2007.[23]

One of Wolf's first acts as governor was to ban fracking in Pennsylvania's state parks, and his 2015 budget included a tax on natural gas—making good on a campaign promise. House Speaker Mike Turzai, a Republican from Alleghany County, was in no mood to see the tax implemented. As of the writing of this book, Turzai has refused to allow the tax bill to come

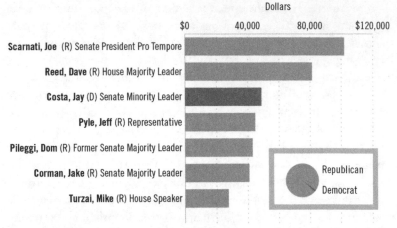

Top Political Contributions to Legislators in Pennsylvania by Natural Gas Interests 2013–2014
Source: Marcellus Money (marcellusmoney.org)
Methodology: Contributions made between 2013 and 2014.

to floor of the House, arguing that it would lead to a loss of jobs. Turzai receved $27,500 from the gas industry in his 2014 bid for reelection.[24]

The Keystone State's Revolving Door

There is no better example of the revolving door between elected officials, appointees to regulatory positions, and the fossil fuel extraction industry than the State of Pennsylvania. Ed Rendell returned, within a week of leaving office, to his Philadelphia law firm, Ballard Spahr, one of the top five energy practice law firms in the United States.[25] In addition to his law practice, Rendell had also been hired as an operating partner of Element Partners for a tidy $30,000 fee. Element Partners, billing itself as providing "Growth Equity for Energy & Industrial Technology,"[26] was financially involved in a number of energy companies including 212 Resources, a company that provided fracking fluid systems to drillers. And to go full circle, another adviser to Element Partners was none other than Rendell's first DEP secretary, Kathleen McGinty. Not an unusual situation in Pennsylvania, as every single secretary of the state's DEP, since its inception, had connections or employment with the natural gas or coal mining industry.

Michael Krancer, the DEP secretary in the Corbett administration, left office in 2012 to return to the law firm Blank Rome, where he was named head of the energy, petrochemical, and natural resources practice representing the industries he was purported to regulate when holding public office. Blank Rome is a member of the Marcellus Shale Coalition. According to Pennsylvania's National Public Radio, the aptly named public relations firm Greentarget put out an email stating that "Michael offers access to regional policymakers that other firms do not have."[27] Pennsylvania state law prohibits former government officials from appearing before the body they worked for, but attorneys are exempted from that section of the ethics code, allowing Krancer full access to state regulatory bodies.

After former Pennsylvania governor Tom Ridge left Washington as George W. Bush's head of Homeland Security, he went into business. He founded Ridge Global, an international consulting and lobbying company specializing in security issues, and joined the board of the nuclear power company Exelon. According to the Public Accountability Initiative, his firms received nearly $900,000 in fees from the Marcellus Shale Coalition.[28]

Today's Postscript is Tomorrow's Promise

We've provided just a few examples of how one state fell into the vacuum created by the lack of a coherent national energy policy. But another state, a thousand miles south of Pennsylvania, is experiencing the same battle. An entrenched and influential industry is using the same techniques of disinformation, industry-funded studies, and lobbying power to defeat a citizens' initiative to bring solar-generated electricity to the Sunshine State.

That is happening because the cost per kilowatt hour (kwH) of solar generation has fallen below ten cents—below electric utility retail prices.[29]

The electric utility industry, however, is doing its best to frustrate the movement to solar by consumers. In Florida, which ranks third in sunshine but thirteenth in solar installations, a compliant legislature has eliminated third-party leasing of solar installations. They have mandated that only utilities can sell electricity to retail customers by banning what are known as power purchase agreements. Florida is only one of four states with a ban on sales by providers other than utilities. Moving the upfront cost to a leasing company would relieve the homeowner or small businessman of the large initial investment, amortization of which would be built into the leasing fee.

According to former state legislators, NextEra, (owner of Florida

Power & Light or FPL) and Duke Energy, the state's two largest electric utilities, have aggressively opposed this option.[30] And the two companies, along with Tampa Electric and Gulf Power, have backed up their opposition with $12 million in campaign contributions to state legislators since 2010.[31]

A group called Floridians for Solar Choice is collecting signatures for a November 2016 ballot initiative to amend the state's constitution to allow citizens to purchase solar-generated electricity from a third party. The group claims that 74 percent of the state's voters support the amendment.[32] Tea party activists have joined Christian conservatives and environmental advocates in support of this measure, claiming it is a matter of free choice. "What's happening now in Florida is really blocking the free market," according to Conservatives for Energy Freedom state director Tory Perfetti.[33] But the Heartland Institute, supported by electric utilities, is cautioning the Florida Tea Party, saying that "tremendously expensive solar power could not compete against more affordable conventional energy alternatives."[34] Heartland is the same organization that lobbied so hard for the Stop the War on Coal Act.

The monopoly utilities in the state have taken a first step in openly opposing the ballot initiative by creating a front group called Consumers for Smart Solar. With a budget in the seven-figure range, the organization is preparing a campaign of disinformation by arguing that solar choice will increase rates to consumers.

The sad tale of Florida's ability to mandate monopoly pricing only happens because of the absence of a comprehensive national policy that would encourage competition to reduce expenses to the consumer as the cost per kwH of solar-generated power continues to decline. The solution appears to be citizen engagement, fueled by outrage at limited available options, pushing back against entrenched interests, sometimes regulated monopolies, willing to spend whatever it takes to preserve the status quo.

Jim Woolsey believes that by freeing the market from the power of foreign cartels, by gradually reducing tax incentives and subsidies, and by having Congress mandate alternative fuels in new cars and trucks, America's competitive spirit will discover new and cost-efficient ways to fuel our needs in the future.

He spoke to the point before the Senate Finance Committee on April 19, 2007: "I would only conclude by noting that I continually find it interesting that there seems to be so much more consensus on what needs to be done in moving decisively to reduce oil dependence than on reasons for doing so. In broad terms the approach suggested above—using a combination of regulatory and market mechanisms to remove barriers to the use of oil alternatives, including electricity, and to promote the development of such renewable technologies—can obtain, I believe, substantial support from a rather wide coalition."

Nine years later, little has been done.

CHAPTER 7

Fat Wallets, Expanding Waistlines

America is one of the fattest countries on earth. More than one third of American adults are obese—roughly defined as thirty pounds above a healthy norm. Another third are overweight.[1] Perhaps most concerning is that 17 percent of children and adolescents are obese.[2] Certain groups are impacted more than others: an astonishing 48 percent of African Americans and 43 percent of Hispanics are afflicted by obesity.

This epidemic has been building for years. Over three decades through the early 2000s, the obesity rate more than doubled for preschoolers and adolescents as it tripled for young children, according to the Institute of Medicine (IOM), a scientific organization the government relies on for advice on health issues.[3]

It is an undisputed fact that corpulence increases the risk of diabetes, heart disease, sleep respiratory disorders, gallbladder disease, and osteo-arthritis, as well as some cancers.[4] So the current crop of American kids may be the first to experience a decrease in life expectancy—by as much as five years—unless we undertake "aggressive efforts" to stem the problem, a 2005 study by the National Institutes of Health found.[5] A more recent study says that excessive heftiness can shorten a lifespan by up to eight years.[6]

We already know what "aggressive strategies" are necessary to shrink waistlines. This is not rocket science. Among the main recommendations from the Institute of Medicine to prevent childhood obesity: a varied and nutritious diet, increased physical activity, infant breast-feeding, and reducing the amount of time kids spend staring at screens.[7]

There is reason to believe that increasing numbers of Americans have started following this kind of advice: obesity among low-income preschool children in several states actually decreased by about 1 percent from 2008 to 2011.[8] The Centers for Disease Control and Prevention (CDC) says it's not exactly sure what's behind the improvement, cautioning that cultural factors differ across the country. But it offers some possibilities: publicity leading to greater awareness, state and national initiatives such as First Lady Michelle Obama's Let's Move! campaign (a big push to get kids exercising and eating right), and policy reforms such the 2009 changes made to the federal nutrition program for Women, Infants, and Children, known as WIC, to conform more closely to national dietary guidelines.

Nonetheless, as made clear by a 2013 IOM study, investments in anti-obesity efforts have been sporadic at best. The IOM suggested a solution: the creation of a national "obesity evaluation task force" that would establish common standards to measure our progress on obesity prevention and track goals at national and community levels.[9]

Americans recognize the seriousness of the problem more than ever, according to a 2012 Gallup poll. For the first time, they saw obesity as a more serious societal problem than cigarette smoking. Gallup had been polling on that question since 2003. And 81 percent of Americans said our collective weight was a very serious or extremely serious problem, up more than 20 percentage points from a 2004 poll. More than half think it's very important to have federal programs to address the concern.[10]

But most Americans still eat a shockingly unhealthful diet, with little improvement in consumer choices in recent decades, according to a 2015 Dietary Guidelines Advisory Committee report.[11] We have a school lunch program that is beset by Washington partisan bickering, making it more difficult for kids to get nutritious food at a reasonable price.[12]

We know what "aggressive strategies" need to be implemented. Eight in ten Americans understand we need to take action, and—as is the case with other public health crises—the public believes our government should be playing a role in addressing the crisis. Yet . . .

Enter Big Food

One enormous force distorting the debate on healthy eating is Big Food. The food and beverage industry, along with crop and food producing, processing, and sales companies, spent close to $92 million lobbying Washington in 2014 alone.[13] That figure does not include the U.S. Chamber of Commerce, the lobbying behemoth that often joins Big Food and many other industries in lobbying battles.

On the other side, the most prominent organization lobbying for healthier eating—the Center for Science in the Public Interest (CSPI)—spent $82,000 in 2014. That's less than 1 percent of the lobbying budget for just one company, Coca-Cola, which reported spending $9.3 million lobbying Washington that same year.

Here's another way to look at this David vs. Goliath battle: in 2011, CSPI spent about $70,000 on lobbying. The coalition of companies opposed to new federal guidelines on the marketing of food and beverages—guidelines that would only have been voluntary—spent that much *every thirteen hours* in 2011, according to an analysis by Reuters.

On just one contentious issue we will examine in this chapter—whether the government should establish optional guidelines for how companies can market food to children—the industry and its allies outspent opponents by at least a 17-to-1 margin, according to our own analysis. On this issue, we could find only a dozen groups lobbying on the side of child nutrition, including CSPI, the American Cancer Society, the Environmental Working Group, and associations of dentists, pediatricians, and dietitians. Lobbying against them were more than three dozen food, beverage, and media companies.

Soft Drinks, Too

In recent years, beverage makers have succeeded at another tactic to keep kids and adults alike gulping down their products: spend tens of millions of dollars on misleading public relations campaigns to defeat city and state ballot initiatives to levy a small tax—typically a penny per ounce—on sodas and other sugary beverages.

The trade associations for the beverage makers have one of the biggest PR budgets of any industry. Collectively, they spent $105 million on various PR campaigns between 2008 and 2012. Leading those campaigns has been the American Beverage Association, which along with its state and local affiliates has bankrolled the anti-soda-tax campaigns in cities and states from coast to coast.[14]

It's worth noting that the industry, in reaction to the ballot initiatives and other attacks, has voluntarily taken some steps to keep Americans' waistlines from growing even bigger. The ABA announced in 2010 that as part of a joint initiative with the American Heart Association and the William J. Clinton Foundation, beverage makers had cut 88 percent of the calories from drinks shipped to schools since 2004. (It is ironic that the agency the beverage industry hired to develop and implement its ongoing anti-soda-tax campaign, Goddard Gunster—formerly Goddard Claussen—is the very same firm the health insurance industry hired to create the "Harry and Louise" ad campaign that played a major role in turning the public against the Clinton health care reform proposal in 1993 and 1994.)

Again and again, we have seen sound public health policies backed by expert research fail at the hands of special interests with large sums of money to spend. As Reuters noted in its 2012 report "the food and beverage industries won fight after fight during the last decade. They have never lost a significant political battle in the United States."

Before turning to sugar, both fructose and processed, let's take a hard look at Big Food and how it manipulates dietary guidelines at the federal level.

Big Food and America's "Lunch Ladies"

On the heels of the First Lady's Let's Move! campaign, Congress passed the Healthy, Hunger-Free Kids Act of 2010, a historic law that included a significant increase in federal funding for the school lunch program as well as incentives for schools to provide more nutritious food to an estimated 32 million kids.[15] In exchange for six cents a meal in additional funding for each lunch ($4.5 billion in total federal funding), lunches would have to be more healthful. The specific standards required by the law were unveiled in 2011 by the U.S. Department of Agriculture, which consulted academics, industry representatives, and health care professionals and relied on expert recommendations from the IOM and the Dietary Guidelines for Americans. The USDA would ultimately rule that school meals had to be richer in fruits, vegetables, and whole grains and include less sugar and sodium.

From the moment the bill was introduced in early 2010 by Senator

Blanche Lincoln (D-AR), the food and beverage industry viewed it as a potential threat to profits and began mobilizing to weaken it if necessary. The year before, in response to Congress's exploration of a national soda tax, the food and beverage industry began devoting far more money to influence lawmakers than it had during the Bush years. The industry's spending on lobbying increased 250 percent—from $22 million to $58 million—between 2008 and 2009. Over the next half dozen years, as food and beverage companies perceived a threat to its school district revenues, the industry's lobbying ballooned by more than 140 percent, when you compare lobbying numbers from the first six years under Obama to the first six under Bush.[16]

The increase in lobbying expenditures has been matched by increases in campaign contributions. Food and beverage companies contributed approximately 30 percent more to federal campaigns during the first six Obama years than they did during the last six Bush years.[17]

Although the food and beverage companies had the most to lose—at least in terms of profits—if the rules developed by the USDA forced significant changes in the nutritional value of school lunches, tens of thousands of schools and their lunchroom workers would also be affected. As the legislation was working its way through Congress, the School Nutrition Association (SNA), which represents more than 55,000 workers

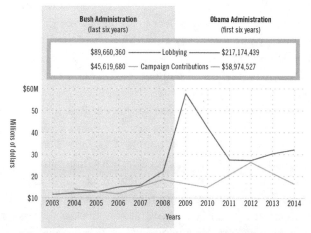

Influence of the Food and Beverage Industry: Lobbying spending and campaign contributions during the Bush and Obama administrations
Source: Center for Responsive Politics (opensecrets.org)

running school cafeterias, initially embraced it. But after the lobbyists for food companies that help fund the SNA came out vehemently against it, and it became clearer how the USDA's rules would change the way the "lunch ladies," as SNA members are often called, ran their school programs, they began to push back. They would soon find themselves allied with Big Food in a pitched battle to keep several of the USDA's school nutrition rules from being implemented.

Once the USDA started unveiling those rules in 2011, both cafeteria food suppliers and the lunch ladies' association had many objections. They didn't like the requirements that sodium levels would have to be halved, fruits and veggies doubled, and fewer calories could come from potatoes.[18]

While the SNA's complaints were making headlines, the food companies were already working behind the scenes in Washington—on Capitol Hill as well as at the Department of Agriculture's offices on Independence Avenue—to keep their bottom lines from taking a hit. The industry's strategy would be to lobby on each part of the lunch tray—from pizza to French fries to pasta—to weaken the rules.

Pizza as a Vegetable

The first big battle between the USDA and industry was over pizza. A loophole in the old rules had made the tomato paste in pizza count as a serving of tomatoes. (During the Reagan years, even ketchup was briefly considered a vegetable.) The USDA's new rules closed the tomato-paste loophole, which meant that pizza could no longer get credit for containing a vegetable. Among the USDA's concerns was the high sodium content—and in some brands, high sugar content—of tomato paste.

The Schwan Food Company, a privately held company with about $3 billion in annual sales and the biggest supplier of frozen pizza to schools, was especially upset with the tomato-paste ruling. In a letter to the USDA, the company, whose brands include Red Baron, Tony's Pizza, and Freschetta, made the case that its products were important because they appeal to kids and keep them buying school lunches.[19] In addition to the letter, Schwan began spending more than it ever had on lobbying. Along with the American Frozen Food Institute, the industry's trade group, it spent about $600,000 on lobbying in 2011, an all-time high.

Another part of Schwan's strategy was to appeal directly to members of Congress from its home state of Minnesota. The company succeeded in getting eight of the ten members of the Minnesota congressional delegation—including its two Democratic senators, Al Franken and Amy Klobuchar—to go to bat for it.[20] Those efforts paid off after Klobuchar pressured Secretary of Agriculture Tom Vilsack to relax the rules. In a June 2011 letter to Vilsack, Senator Klobuchar touted the benefits of tomato paste, criticized the whole-grains mandate as far too tough and called the proposed decrease in sodium unattainable, especially "when serving a dairy based center-of-the-plate item, such as pizza." As Minnesota Public Radio pointed out later, at least one sentence of Klobuchar's letter was identical to the written testimony Schwan would soon provide to a congressional committee that was holding a hearing on the issue.[21]

Neither Schwan nor the American Frozen Food Institute had donated to Klobuchar's campaign before 2009. That was soon to change. By 2013, they had donated thousands of dollars to her reelection campaign.[22] In all, nineteen food and beverage groups gave Klobuchar's campaign $160,000 between 2009 and 2011, double what they'd given her the three prior years. Her office told Reuters there was no connection between the money and her efforts on behalf of the industry.

Once Klobuchar got involved, several other Democrats joined what came to be called the pizza-as-a-veggie campaign, greatly increasing the chances that Schwan and the industry would be able to declare victory.

There was protest from the potato lobby, too, despite a Harvard report that found overconsumption of potatoes contributes to obesity. After pressure from the National Potato Council, Senators Susan Collins (R-ME) and Mark Udall (D-CO) intervened to fight limits on starchy vegetables so that French fries could remain a staple on school lunch menus.[23]

The result of all the lobbying and campaign contributions: House and Senate lawmakers came together in November 2011 to pass a big spending bill that included a rider preventing the implementation of the tomato paste and potato rules.[24]

The Industry's Lunch Ladies Strategy

Part of Big Food's strategy to mobilize against the law, beginning in 2011, appeared to include a push to create a rift within the SNA. It succeeded. In fact, as the *New York Times* reported, food companies like Schwan and ConAgra Foods enlisted dozens of school lunch directors to join an industry-created and -funded group in 2011 called the Coalition for Sustainable School Meals Programs.[25] The new front group was headed by the lobbyist Barry Sackin, a former SNA official. Stanley C. Garnett, the former director of the USDA's Child Nutrition Division who was once an SNA member, was dismayed when several school lunch directors joined the coalition. "They sold their souls to the devil," he told the *New York Times.*[26]

SNA members' willingness to front for the industry should have come as no surprise, however. About half of the organization's budget —$11.2 million in 2013—comes from the industry.[27] The food and beverage companies pay to exhibit their products at the group's annual conference, buy advertising in the group's publications, and provide grants.

In addition, the companies fund the SNA's School Nutrition Foundation. Since 2009 Schwan has provided more than $200,000 in education scholarships for SNA members. The National Dairy Council has provided about $75,000 in grants to the organization since 2008.

The USDA issued more rules in 2012 and 2013, ranging from limits on junky snack foods to a requirement that calories must come from many different food groups. Kids were not happy. In the 2012–2013 school year, participation in the federal school lunch program declined for the first time in more than two decades.

Some of the school lunch directors were not happy, either, and they turned to the industry's friends in Congress to allow them to apply for a waiver from some of the USDA's rules. They found a champion in GOP congressional representative Robert Aderholt of Alabama, who in 2013 became chair of the House Appropriations Committee's Subcommittee on Agriculture. At the time, Alabama ranked eighth-highest in the nation in adult obesity, with 32.4 percent of the adult population carrying too many pounds (up from 11.2 percent in 1990),[28] and led the nation in Type 2 diabetes.[29] A member of the Tea Party caucus, Aderholt said during a meeting of the House Appropriations Committee that, "[The USDA's rules] is where the heavy hand of government is coming down and trying to dictate to local school systems."[30]

Sharing that point of view was Senate Agriculture Committee member John Hoeven (R-ND). Hoeven's state is home to American Crystal Sugar, the nation's largest processor of sugar beets and the industry's largest political contributor.[31] Aderholt, who was first elected in 1996, has received almost $900,000 in campaign contributions from agribusiness during his career, more than from any other sector. Hoeven, who was elected to the Senate in 2010, had received approximately $300,000 from the agribusiness sector by 2014, far more than from any other sector.

Aderholt and Hoeven came through. In late 2014, Congress approved a measure allowing schools to apply for a waiver from the rules requiring the use of whole grains exclusively. It also eased salt restrictions. The SNA issued a press release to thank Aderholt and Hoeven.

Many former SNA presidents were outraged by the changes, however. Nineteen of the former presidents sent a letter to members of Congress reminding them of broad public support for the law, which they called a "strong response to the nation's obesity epidemic," and urging them to oppose efforts to undermine the healthful lunch program. They added: "We must not reverse the progress that was sought by school leaders and is well on its way to success in most schools."[32]

Soon after that letter was made public, the SNA issued a press release saying that while it "supports many of the law's regulatory requirements," its members wanted "greater funding and flexibility to address the financial consequences of overly restrictive regulations."[33] An SNA spokesperson told us in an email that the organization supports calorie limits on school meals, balanced lunches, and caps on saturated and trans fats but wanted more flexible rules on sodium and whole grains. The waiver gave school lunch directors that flexibility, at least temporarily.

Despite the protests over the new rules the USDA reported that more than 90 percent of the nation's schools were able to meet them by 2014. In a fact sheet touting the success of the program, the USDA wrote that "despite concerns raised about the impact of the new standards on participation and costs"—a subtle jab at the SNA—school revenue had actually increased by about $200 million nationwide in the program's first year. The fact sheet cited a Harvard study that concluded that under the new standards, school children were eating 23 percent more fruit and 16 percent more vegetables at lunch.[34]

The relationship between the White House and the SNA had become pretty toxic by 2014. When Sam Kass, a former White House chef, who at the time was the executive director of the Let's Move! campaign, asked to speak at the SNA's annual conference, he was turned down. And while the USDA had a presence at the conference, the event also featured booths, presentations, and speakers from Domino's Pizza, General Mills, ConAgra, Sara Lee, Smuckers, and Sunny Delight, among others. A Cheetos mascot even put in an appearance.

The Big Gulp

As noted earlier, another food fight has been popping up in recent years as states and cities as well as the federal government have sought to reduce obesity-related health care costs. More precisely, it's a drink fight. From Congress to state capitals and city halls, measures have been proposed to tax sugary beverages, which are strongly linked to obesity.

Medical research on the effects of sugar began in the late 1970s with the introduction of high fructose corn syrup into soft drinks. By the year 2000 there was sufficient data (twenty years or more) for scientists to identify the long-term effects of sugar consumption on human health. A 2001 article published in *The Lancet*, a venerable and respected peer-reviewed journal, related sugary drinks to the growing epidemic of childhood obesity.[35] Despite growing evidence, the sugar industry chose to ignore the connection.

But when the World Health Organization (WHO) recommended in 2003 that no more than 10 percent of daily calories should come from sugar, the industry went ballistic. The Sugar Association attacked WHO funding by Congress and even demanded that the secretary of health and human services, Tommy Thompson, force the WHO to withdraw its report. As Kelly Brownell, an internationally renowned expert on obesity and Dean of the Sanford School of Public Policy at Duke University, commented, "This is the WHO that deals with AIDS, malnutrition, infectious disease, bioterrorism, and more, threatened because of its stance on sugar."[36]

The next blow was struck by a U.S.-government-issued report linking sugar-loaded drinks with obesity. The U.S. Department of Health and Human Services and Department of Agriculture, normally tight with the sugar industry, recommended consumption guidelines even lower than WHO's—no more than eight teaspoons per day. The American Heart Association (AHA) followed with a recommendation that women should consume no more than six teaspoons a day and men no more than nine teaspoons, far below the consumption rate of 22 teaspoons per day in 2005. (For comparative purposes, one 16-ounce soft drink contains about 12 teaspoons of sugar.)

A 2009 *New England Journal of Medicine* article suggested that sodas and other sugary beverages "may be the single largest driver of the obesity epidemic."[37] A Yale study concluded that they're "high in calories, deliver little or no nutrition," and increase the "risk for obesity, diabetes, and a number of other serious health problems."[38]

On a second front, medical research began to seek a causal relationship between diabetes and the consumption of added sugars. For years, obesity was believed to be the main cause of type 2 diabetes, but new studies related excess sugar consumption directly to the disease. In March 2013, the open-access scientific journal *PLoS ONE* published a peer-reviewed study from the University of California, San Francisco, isolating the link between high sugar consumption and type 2 diabetes (after adjusting for other factors such as obesity).

Enter the Beverage Lobby

Those and numerous other studies have convinced many health experts and policymakers that efforts need to be made to reduce consumption of drinks that are loaded with sugar, or to reduce the amount of sugar in those drinks, or both. Standing in the way of progress, however, are beverage companies and sugar growers that want nothing to do with initiatives that might have an adverse effect on profits. To supplement their lobbying efforts, they have spent millions of dollars on PR and advertising campaigns to scare voters—and lawmakers—away from any proposal that would make Americans pay even a few pennies more for their products.

A 2015 investigation by the Center for Public Integrity into the world of high-stakes spin found that many trade associations—including the American Beverage Association—frequently have bigger advertising and PR budgets than lobbying budgets. It also found that among trade associations in Washington, few devote more resources to PR and advertising than the ABA, which spent at least $98 million hiring PR firms to influence public opinion and public policy between 2008 and 2012.[39]

It was during those years that the industry was under siege on several fronts. Not only were several states and cities considering a tax on sugar-sweetened beverages, so was Congress. The ABA was so alarmed by proposals for a national soda tax that it increased its Washington lobbying budget of less than $700,000 in 2008 to about $19 million in 2009. To supplement that, Coca-Cola increased its spending from $2.5 million to $9.4 million. Pepsi's lobbying budget went from $1.2 million to $9.4 million. The reason: during the health care reform debate in 2009, some members of Congress proposed an excise tax on sugar-sweetened soft drinks as a means to help pay for reform. But intense lobbying by sugar and soft drink companies stopped the idea dead in its tracks.

Top 20 Recipients of Food & Beverage Contributions
Source: Center for Responsive Politics (opensecrets.org)
Methodology: The numbers above are based on contributions from PACs and individuals giving $200 or more. All donations took place during the 2013–2014 election cycle and were released by the Federal Election Commission on March 09, 2015.

The idea appeared again when a tax on sugar-loaded soft drinks was proposed by Democrat Rosa DeLauro of Connecticut in 2014. Backed by the Center for Science in the Public Interest and several other advocacy groups, DeLauro's Sugar-Sweetened Beverage Tax (SWEET) Act would impose a one-cent-per-teaspoon tax on sugary drinks and raise $10 billion a year. But after intense lobbying from sugar beet and cane growers and producers, beverage companies and the high fructose corn and sucrose sugar industry, the excise tax effort failed.[40]

Local Governments Step Up to the Plate
(but Usually Strike Out)

The ABA and its member companies and local bottlers also poured millions more into lobbying efforts in several states and cities. It has been money well spent. Across the country, soda tax initiatives have failed or been overturned in at least thirty states and cities since the mid-2000s. The ABA's first defeat came during the 2014 elections, when Berkeley, California, became the first city in the United States to approve a soda tax. The one-cent-per-ounce tax on sugar-sweetened beverages, charged to retailers, brought in $116,000 during its first month. The industry had better luck across the bay in San Francisco, where voters rejected a two-cents-per-ounce soda tax measure on the same day that Berkeley residents approved their city's tax. The beverage industry reportedly spent more than $10 million fighting the two measures.

There are factors other than the PR and lobbying campaigns that have contributed to the industry's success: the broad appeal and iconography of Coke and Pepsi, the soda industry's seamless marketing in our everyday lives, and the fact that Americans just don't like being taxed. But it could be argued that the industry's deception-based PR strategy has made the biggest difference.

One of the beverage industry's key tactics has been to hire PR firms to create front groups with misleading names to obscure the industry's involvement, especially its massive funding. The idea is to make voters believe that the front groups are grassroots organizations made up of concerned citizens.

One such group is Americans Against Food Taxes (AAFT), which registered its tax documents at the same address as the American Beverage Association and shared the same president. The group, which also received support from the U.S. Chamber of Commerce, raised about $25 million between 2009 and 2011.[41] One of the ads it ran in Washington— aimed, of course, at members of Congress—featured a young mother saying she couldn't afford the proposed soda tax because "those pennies add up when you're trying to feed a family."[42] The apparent goal was to mislead people into thinking that the tax would apply to all grocery items.

Aiding the beverage industry in its opposition to the national tax were the corn and sugar lobbies, which have big operations in the states of senators that led the tax-writing Senate Finance Committee at the time (Iowa, home to Republican Chuck Grassley, the committee's ranking member, and Montana, home to Democrat Max Baucus, the committee's chairman). The tax "ran into a committee with a lot of farm members," Chuck Marr, director of federal tax policy at the nonpartisan Center on Budget and Policy Priorities, told the Center for Public Integrity.[43]

The AAFT advertised itself as "a coalition of concerned individuals, working families, and large and small businesses" and reported that more than 95,000 individuals had signed its petition. Analysts at the Rudd Center for Food Policy and Obesity at Yale checked that claim and found that 73 percent of the group's member organizations were in the food and beverage industry and just 7 percent were community organizations. Of the community groups where sponsors could be identified, 83 percent were sponsored by Coca-Cola, and 94 percent of them marketed their services to African American or Hispanic populations.[44]

Similar front groups have appeared out of nowhere whenever a city or state has proposed a soda tax. In New York, the beverage industry spent approximately $13 million on lobbying and PR to kill a one-cent-per-ounce tax that then governor David Paterson proposed to offset costs related to diabetes and other obesity-linked diseases. Much of the money went to the firm Goddard Gunster, which set up the front group New Yorkers Against Unfair Taxes.[45,46,47] After the proposal died in the legislature, Paterson compared the soda lobby to a Mack truck. "We got smashed," he said."[48,49]

Goddard Gunster also helped create the California version of Americans Against Food Taxes when El Monte, a Los Angeles suburb, and Richmond in the Bay Area put a one-cent-per-ounce soda tax on their ballots in 2012.[50] The industry's front group in Richmond—the Community Coalition Against Beverage Taxes (CCABT)—even sued the city when the council passed an ordinance requiring special interest groups to disclose their sources of funding on campaign mailers. CCABT claimed the ordinance violated the group's First Amendment rights.[51] According to public disclosure documents made available later, the coalition received 95 percent of its $2.5 million budget from Washington lobbying firms. Just $4,778, or 0.0019 percent, came from local groups. CCABT never mentioned the ABA's support on its website during the campaign.

In all, Big Soda spent more than $4 million opposing the tax proposals in El Monte and Richmond, while advocates spent just $114,000, according to the Berkeley Media Group, which analyzes public health campaigns in the media.[52] Both cities were blitzed. "The conversation here is dominated by the ABA," El Monte mayor Andre Quintero said at the time. "Billboards, cable television ads, events, mailers, canvassing teams, phone banks, legal maneuvers, constant polling . . . We are under siege." He added: "It's a domination by corporate interests that's similar to the early 1900s, when the railroad barons rode roughshod on the state." Between the El Monte and Richmond campaigns, it was estimated that the beverage industry spent at least $115 for every vote it got.[53] When all the votes were counted, the tax had been soundly defeated in both cities.

Undoubtedly one of the reasons the industry has spent so much money to defeat the soda tax initiatives is what happened in Mexico after lawmakers there passed a bill that added one peso (about 7 cents) to the price of a liter of sugary beverages. The increase went into effect January 1, 2014. According to Mexico's National Institute of Public Health, purchases of sugary drinks dropped by 10 percent during the first three months of the year compared to the same period in 2013, while consumption of healthier beverages—including water—increased.

A University of California, San Francisco study suggested that a national penny-per-ounce tax in the United States would reduce sugar-sweetened beverage consumption here by 10 to 15 percent. The researchers predicted that would lead to modest weight loss and a significant reduction in diabetes. Over ten years, they estimated there would be 26,000 fewer premature deaths, 95,000 fewer instances of heart disease, and 8,000 fewer strokes.

Guaranteed Profits

There are two kinds of sugar in America's diet, and they are largely undifferentiated and interchangeable: high fructose corn syrup and sucrose. The big difference between the two is how the beet and cane sugar industries (sucrose) approach the marketplace—with a guarantee of profit no matter what the world price.

Sugar (sucrose) is one of our country's oldest crops, highly adapted to the Caribbean and southern United States. It is likely that Columbus brought sugar plants on one of his three voyages to the West Indies. States abutting the Gulf of Mexico provided a hospitable climate and good transportation for the harvest; today, Florida, Louisiana, and Texas are the main cane-producing states. Cane, a perennial crop, can be produced year-round.

Beet (as opposed to cane) sugar can be grown in more temperate climates. It was a staple of the American colonies, particularly those in the Northeast who saw beet sugar as a way of striking an economic blow against the slave-produced cane sugar from southern states and the West Indies. Today it is grown in the northern tier of inland states including Montana, North Dakota, Idaho, Minnesota, and Utah. Beet sugar is an annual crop, harvested before the ground freezes. Together, cane and beet growers form one of Washington's most powerful—and oldest—lobbies.

Protection of the domestic sugar industry goes back to the eighteenth century, when a tariff was established to protect the nascent republic's small sugar farmers. In 1842 a special act of Congress expanded the tariff to protect sugar refineries. The first comprehensive price support program was begun in 1934 under President Franklin Roosevelt. That legislation, the Jones-Costigan Act, remained in place until a 1974 bubble when the world price of sugar went through the roof.[54]

Commodity prices collapsed to more normal levels in 1976, and the sugar industry began hounding Washington to once again protect domestic producers from both the world market and a new product, high fructose corn syrup, which was making inroads into the soft drink industry. Secretary of Agriculture Robert Berglund, a farmer from the beet sugar state of Minnesota, used powers granted him under the Agricultural Act of 1949 to create a complicated interim program that was institutionalized in the Food and Agriculture Act of 1977. The program underwent a major revision with the Farm Bill of 1990 by establishing a quota system to further restrict sugar imports. That act is the basis of the current sugar support policy. It has been modified slightly since then, but the basic structure remains.

In simplified terms, here is how the program works. The secretary of agriculture sets a country-by-country quota system with a two-tiered tariff scheme. Imports up to the quota are allowed; over the limit they are subjected to a punitive tariff. Beet and cane growers in the United States are given crop allotments to try to balance supply and demand. Congress (via farm bills) establishes a minimum price for domestic sugar. Refined and raw sugar are given two separate price floors. For a recent example, in 2013 the price floor for beet sugar was 22.9 cents per pound and for cane sugar 18.75 cents per pound. Based on 2013 prices, domestic beet sugar was pegged at 88 percent and cane sugar at 73 percent above the world market price respectively, and in that year, U.S. consumers paid $1.3 billion more than they otherwise would have for sugar products.

A second element is a complex loan system begun with Berglund's 1977 order. Loans are available to processors who agree to pay the price floor to farmers (provided they meet federal minimum wage requirements for field workers). The lender (the federal government) accepts sugar as collateral, and no interest is charged if the principal is repaid. If market prices are not high enough for farmers to make a profit, as was the case in 1977 and 1978, the loans go into default and the collateral (sugar) becomes the property of the federal Commodity Credit Corporation, which then sells it at a loss, generally for ethanol.

Loans made to processors rather than farmers might lead one to believe that cane and beet growers are disadvantaged. But an examination of the industry belies this conclusion. Cane sugar, as mentioned earlier, is becoming increasingly concentrated and vertically integrated. The biggest producer is the privately owned U.S. Sugar Corporation, founded in 1931 by Charles Stewart Mott, which produces 700,000 tons of cane sugar grown on almost 190,000 acres between Lake Okeechobee and the Everglades in Florida. It even operates its own short line railroad, the South Central Florida Express, which connects its cane-growing and processing operations with larger rail systems to the north and south.

The government's loan program is little more than a pass-through for U.S. Sugar and other big companies, and a guarantee of profit. In 2013, 55 percent of the $1.1 billion in federal loans went to just three companies, according to the *Wall Street Journal*, which obtained documents on the loan program after filing a Freedom of Information Act request. Although the companies—Amalgamated Sugar Co., Michigan Sugar Co., and Western Sugar Cooperative—borrowed more than half of the funds, at interest rates ranging from just 1.125 percent to 1.25 percent, they produce only about 20 percent of the country's sugar. In addition to the cheap loans that year, the USDA announced that it would buy $38 million worth of sugar "in a bid to raise prices," the *Journal* reported.[55]

If this arrangement seems overly complex, it is designed that way. The only people who understand convoluted programs like the U.S. sugar subsidy are the lawyers and lobbyists who wrote the 1990 bill and the sugar barons for whose benefit the bill was written.

Sugar Daddies in Politics

Once the 1990 bill became law, the industry maintained an annual level of around $3 million in direct lobbying expenses. This jumped to $7 million in 2005 when alarm bells went off. The U.S. Commerce Department was studying the loss of confectionery manufacturing jobs. The department reported the next year that for every job created in cultivating and harvesting, three jobs were lost in the United States due to the high price of raw and refined sugar. Sensing increased scrutiny of their guaranteed profit scheme, the beet and cane growers and processors were forking over nearly $8 million to lobbyists by 2008.

The Heritage Foundation found that by 2013, sugar represented 2 percent of the value of domestic crop production but 40 percent of crop industries' lobbying money. The following year, sugar chipped in 35 percent of agribusiness's campaign contributions to candidates.[56] Sugar lobby expenses were at an all-time high of nearly $10 million. It was a big boys' game, with beet producer American Crystal Sugar popping $2.0 million for lobbying and $2.2 million in widely sprinkled campaign contributions, with 55 percent going to Democrats to assure bipartisan support for the subsidy program. Heritage concluded that more than $50 million was spent between 2009 and 2013 to preserve the federally mandated profit margins of the sugar barons.

So why the dramatic increase of sugar money into the politicians' pockets?

Jelly Belly Jobs Go Abroad

Arrayed against sugar's protectionist program are the American Enterprise Institute, the Heritage Foundation, the Koch-brothers-funded Competitive Enterprise Institute, the U.S. Chamber of Commerce, and even the *Wall Street Journal*. But their arguments have little to do with human health and everything to do with the functioning of a free-market economy.

Writing in *American Boondoggle: A Project of the American Enterprise Institute* in a paper entitled "Sweets for the Sweet: The Costly Benefits of the US Sugar Program," Michael Wohlgenant is very blunt: "The only reasonable policy is no policy: the sugar program should be repealed."[57] Wohlgenant, a professor at North Carolina State University, did an exhaustive study of the direct and indirect costs of sugar subsidies, concluding that in 2009, while producers benefited to the tune of $1.43

billion, American consumers paid $2.44 billion more than they should have as a result of higher prices.

Aside from costs to the consumer, the sugar quota, tariff, and subsidy program wrecks another part of the economy. Confirming the Commerce Department's earlier report, U.S. Census Bureau statistics showed that confectionery manufacturing jobs in the United States dropped from around 70,000 to 55,000 between 1998 and 2011. During that same time span, the average price of domestic sugar was twice the world price. To maintain the disparity, sugar's lobbying expenses rocketed from $2.8 million to $7.5 million annually.

Jelly Belly has been a family-owned company for six generations. It sells 20 percent of the jelly beans consumed in the United States, but it is moving operations out of this country while expanding in Thailand, where sugar and labor prices are significantly lower than in the United States. "You can't compete shipping finished U.S. goods," commented CEO Bob Simpson, explaining why Jelly Belly has been forced to raise prices in recent years due to the high cost of domestic sugar.[58]

In another example, "Atkinson Candy Co. has moved 80 percent of its peppermint-candy production to a factory in Guatemala that opened in 2010. That means it can sell bite-sized Mint Twists for 10 percent to 20 percent less. We did it for survival reasons . . . There are 60 jobs down there . . . that could be in the U.S. . . . it's a damn shame," the company's president, Eric Atkinson, told the *Wall Street Journal*.[59]

One of sugar's most organized opponents is the Coalition for Sugar Reform. Its members include an odd assortment of bedfellows: the Club for Growth, Grover Norquist's Americans for Tax Reform, the National Association of Manufacturers, Kraft Foods, the American Beverage Association, and the Everglades Trust. In 2013, Senator Richard Lugar (R-IN) introduced a bill to end the program. The U.S. Chamber of Commerce, in a letter supporting the Sugar Reform Act of 2013, estimated that tens of thousands of jobs were lost in the "sugar-using industry" between 1997 and 2011, a number plucked out of a U.S. Commerce Department report.

Despite carefully documented economic arguments, the bill went down to defeat. In a rare demonstration of bipartisanship, Florida's two senators, Democrat Bill Nelson and Republican Marco Rubio, who is now running for the presidency, voted against reform. As a reward, Nelson received $42,000 from sugar growers. Rubio, who regularly campaigns against government intervention in the economy, was the beneficiary of a New York fundraiser hosted by sugar magnates Pepe and Alfonso Fanjul that raised more than $100,000.

The Competitive Enterprise Institute summed up the defeat: "The sugar lobby's sweet contributions and their day-in-day-out lobbying means broad bipartisan support for continuing the U.S. sugar program in the 2013 Farm Bill . . . Numerous attempts have been made to rein in this egregious program but the sugar industry's intense and consistent lobbying and the huge contributions they make on both sides of the aisle almost guarantee them the program's continuation."[60]

Aside from dollars spent to buy votes in Congress, the clout of the industry is perhaps best illustrated by a moment during Bill Clinton's term in office. The president was in the middle of an *entre nous* with a young White House intern named Monica Lewinsky when the phone rang. According to testimony given to independent counsel Kenneth Starr, Lewinsky recalled that the call came from someone named "Fanuli." In reality, it was Alfonso Fanjul, co-owner of Florida Crystals, the largest cane sugar processing operation in the world. Clinton interrupted the proceedings with his intern and took the call.

Hooking Our Kids

If Jennifer Harris could raise her kids all over again, she says she probably wouldn't have a TV. And she says she definitely wouldn't serve them products that are marketed to kids on TV. Harris says that although Big Food and Big Sugar claim that their marketing leads merely to brand preferences, not necessarily to an increase in consumption, research shows that if you market sugary drinks to kids, they'll consume more of them.

Before going to Yale for a PhD in how companies market food to children, Harris assumed that letting her kids have some sugary cereals wasn't so bad. What she learned as she was getting that degree, however, changed her mind—so much so that she went to work for the University of Connecticut–based Rudd Center for Food Policy, a nonprofit research and public policy organization whose mission is to "improve the world's diet, prevent obesity, and reduce weight stigma." She is now director of the center's food marketing initiative. "As I was learning more about the psychology of [marketing to kids], it just made me realize how really unfair it is to . . . spend all this money to shape kids' minds so it makes them love all these products that are damaging to their health," she told us.

One of the things Harris said she has come to understand is that, with the billions of dollars food companies spend marketing their often-unhealthful products to kids every year, it's a misconception that parents can control what their children eat. "Once they go to elementary school, parents have very little control over what their kids eat, other than at the dinner table," she said.

Big Food spends about $2 billion per year marketing directly to children, and 90 percent of that money promotes foods that are unhealthful, according to Harris. As a consequence, say food marketing experts, kids become "brand-conscious" when they're two years old.[61] By age three, they can start understanding what the brand can say about their personality, and by first grade, they are typically loyal to their favorite soda, cereal, or candy. That loyalty often sticks through adulthood.

Children watch an average of forty thousand ads every year, mostly for toys, cereals, candy, and fast food, according to Dale Kunkel, a University of Southern California professor specializing in the media's effect on children.[62] Kids are also targeted online, particularly through "advergames" that push product while they play, like a "build your own Fruit Loops" game, or a Capri Sun activity that requires access to the computer's webcam but doesn't verify the player's age.[63]

In 2009, in response to rising concern from the health sector and parental advocates, a bipartisan team of senators, Tom Harkin (D-IA) and Sam Brownback (R-KS), asked the government to set some voluntary guidelines for companies marketing to children. In response, a "working group" of officials from the Federal Trade Commission, the Centers for Disease Control and Prevention, the USDA, and the Food and Drug Administration was formed to develop the guidelines, and in 2011, the group submitted its proposals, which were based on well-established research, for public review. Among the group's recommendations was that marketed food should make a meaningful contribution to a healthy diet and should meet specific limits on salt, added sugar, and certain fats.[64]

Of the 29,000 comments the group received, the vast majority were favorable. Many public health organizations also weighed in with praise. "Everyone was pretty much 100 percent behind those guidelines," said Harris.

Industry groups, on the other hand, which submitted about a hundred comments, were not happy. They claimed the proposed standards—

even though they were completely optional—would be unworkable and were not even needed. Food and beverage companies, they said, could be trusted to regulate themselves. The companies then went to work to make sure the proposals would go nowhere. In short order, they teamed up with big media companies, including Viacom and Time Warner, to form the Sensible Food Policy Coalition. The U.S. Chamber of Commerce joined the lobbying effort, too. The companies hired former Obama communications aide turned public messaging expert Anita Dunn to manage the effort.

The main coalition members had already spent nearly $60 million lobbying during the Obama administration through mid-2011, according to the *Washington Post*.[65] The companies would supplement their lobbying budgets with a generous PR and advertising budget to finance the activities of their front group. One of the first orders of business was to commission a study that warned that the guidelines would kill 75,000 jobs and eliminate more than $28 billion in revenue to companies. The coalition also released a list of 88 products it said would be banned under the guidelines, including Cheerios.[66]

On Capitol Hill, the companies focused attention on Senator Dick Durbin, Democrat of Illinois, and Representative Jo Ann Emerson, a Missouri Republican. Both served on committees overseeing FTC funding. Emerson, a former director of state relations and government programs at the National Restaurant Association, which lobbied against the proposal, told Reuters at the time that she feared that even though the guidelines would be voluntary, they would eventually become mandatory. Contributions from food and beverage companies and crop producers poured into Emerson's 2012 campaign. Among the donors was American Crystal Sugar, which was especially worried about the guidelines. Other big contributors to her campaign were cereal maker General Mills and the Dairy Farmers of America.

Dick Durbin had previously received $11,000 from Kraft Foods, based in his home state. The company gave him another $3,000 in 2011. Kraft also lobbied on the marketing guidelines as part of its $2.8 million 2011 lobbying budget.[67]

Tom Harkin, on the other hand, who had once been an industry favorite, became persona non grata after suggesting the guidelines. In the two years prior to his push for them, food and beverage companies had donated more than $75,000 to his campaigns. In 2010 and 2011, they contributed just $3,000.

Industry lobbyists were able to persuade 176 members of the House and almost a third of the Senate, Democrats as well as Republicans, to send letters to the working group opposing the recommendations. The Sunlight Foundation later noticed that Democrats who signed letters critical of the guidelines had received about twice as much campaign money from food lobbying interests as those who didn't.

It was Emerson who would kill the guidelines in the House by inserting a fifty-five-word sentence into a 130-page budget bill in December 2011. Her sentence required the various agencies involved in the guidelines to do a cost-benefit analysis of their recommendations before finalizing them. The effect of Emerson's language was to make it too costly for the agencies to move forward with the guidelines. On the other side of the Capitol, Durbin agreed to go along with Emerson's language. An aide told Reuters that Durbin did so because he believed the industry was moving toward self-regulation. The final recommendations were never released.

Harris said the FTC, one of the working group participants, might have decided to back off from pursuing the guidelines because of a bad case of déjà vu, from when the FTC's authority was neutered by Congress more than twenty-five years earlier after intense pressure from industry lobbyists. The FTC was attempting to ban TV ads aimed at young children, on the basis that the ads were "unfair and deceptive," but broadcasters, ad agencies, and food and toy companies fought back. They tried to stop the agency from holding hearings and lobbied Congress to cut off funding for the agency's initiative. The companies' lobbyists succeeded in getting Congress to pass a law in 1980 preventing the FTC from issuing industry-wide rules on advertising to children.[68,69] "Ever since then, they're still too scared to stick their neck out too far," says Harris.

So we're left with self-regulation. Eighteen big companies, representing most of the food and drink advertising market, have now signed an agreement with the Better Business Bureau pledging either not to directly target its advertising at kids under twelve or to market only what the companies call "better-for-you" foods to them.[70] The companies say progress has been made. Some advocates agree. The Rudd Center found that by 2013, children were watching about 40 percent fewer TV ads for sugary drinks than they did in 2010. But Harris says this self-regulation has many holes. For one thing, the industry classifies children as eleven and younger, and it really covers only TV programming designed for children, not other programs that many children watch.

Why It Matters

When Big Food reaches into its deep pockets, and Big Sugar moves its protectionist-gained taxpayer dollars into lobbying, both can not only halt or move legislation in Washington and state houses across America, but they can also prevent us from acting on the mounting public health problem that is obesity.

Our annual economic productivity loss due to obesity by 2030 is projected to be between $390 billion, according to a study commissioned by the American Public Health Association,[71] and $580 billion, according to the Robert Wood Johnson Foundation, the largest private funder of anti-obesity efforts in the United States.[72]

One out of every five dollars spent on health care goes toward treating obesity-related illnesses, according to research in the *Journal of Health Economics*, and direct medical costs are even greater than those associated with smoking.[73,74,75] Medicare and Medicaid spend nearly $62 billion annually to treat obesity-related diseases.[76] The medical costs for obese people already are $1,429 higher than nonobese people annually, and their prescription drugs are 105 percent more expensive.[77,78]

Costs will only go up if obesity rates rise as they have in the past. According to research by Duke University professor Eric A. Finkelstein and others, 42 percent of the U.S. population could be obese by 2030. If, however, we could keep obesity rates at 2010 levels, we would save about $550 billion in medical spending.

Other nonmedical costs include an estimated $4 billion in increased fuel costs per year attributed to heavy passengers in cars, buses, and planes.[79] Bus manufacturers have to upgrade components of their vehicles to comply with Federal Transit Authority requirements drafted after concerns that additional passenger weight poses a safety threat.[80] New York City is considering upgrading its subway cars with sturdier seats; Blue Bird, maker of the ubiquitous yellow school bus, is widening the front doors on newer models so bigger children can get through them; baseball stadiums, theaters, and airplanes are adding wider seats. Some military leaders have even called this epidemic a national security threat, as one in four young people cannot qualify for service because of their weight and the military spends more than $1 billion a year on obesity-related medical care.[81]

Efforts to tackle this problem, particularly by nonprofits and health care professionals, have had their impact blunted by the food and beverage

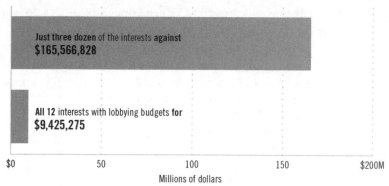

Lobbying Budgets for & Against Nutrition Guidelines
Source: Comments received by the FTC in response to issuing nutrition guidelines and federal lobbying disclosures.

industries. It's commendable that the Robert Wood Johnson Foundation has promised to spend more than $1 billion on various anti-obesity efforts by 2025.

But the groups fighting obesity are far outgunned in Washington by industry lobbyists. As we mentioned, the companies and groups against the optional marketing guidelines had a combined annual lobbying budget of about $166 million, compared to $9.6 million for the groups advocating for them.[82] And that discrepancy leaves out PR budgets, all of the undisclosed resources used to support their lobbying efforts, and millions in campaign contributions.

Just as is the case with the other issues we report on in this book—banking, energy, medicine, toxins—it is difficult to imagine how we can make meaningful progress as long as so many of our lawmakers and regulators are in the deep pockets of a few big companies.

The Institute of Medicine released a report in 2012 outlining what it would take to solve America's weight problem.[83] It included some obvious suggestions: encouraging people to get more exercise; getting employers, doctors and nurses, schools, and marketers to encourage healthy living; making nutritious foods accessible to people at all income levels; and "strengthen schools as the heart of health." But lobbying and campaign contributions have halted progress on many of the suggestions.

Of course, government intervention and public programs designed to curb obesity rates will always face some level of disapproval, and they may not always be the best course of action. Any public health campaign must balance outcomes with freedom of choice, recognizing people's individual responsibility for their own health. But in a democracy, we, the citizens, should have the power to enact legislation to tackle a public health crisis—especially one we know so much about solving. It almost seems silly to have to write such a sentence in a nation dedicated to the project of self-government. Yet over and over again, we have seen how special interests with seemingly unlimited funds have been able to shut down our collective ability to act.

CHAPTER 8

Enough to Make You Sick

Soon after installing new flooring in her home, breast cancer survivor Casandra Barrett of Dorr, Michigan, started feeling sick. Her husband, Steve, was having the same symptoms: frequent headaches and a chronic runny nose. The Barretts both suffer from allergies and try to avoid bringing anything into their home that might be toxic. They are especially concerned about Mrs. Barrett, who developed a weakened immune system after undergoing chemotherapy and radiation to treat her breast cancer several years ago. They searched their house to try to identify the source but found nothing obvious.

Then came a blockbuster news segment on CBS's *60 Minutes* in March 2015, reporting that Lumber Liquidators, which manufactured the Barretts' laminate flooring, appeared to be selling a Chinese-made product that was emitting unsafe levels of a known carcinogen, formaldehyde, while labeling it as safe.[1] Formaldehyde helps bind the glues that keep composite wood particles together in laminate flooring. Many Americans turn to this kind of flooring as a cheaper alternative to hardwood.

In the *60 Minutes* segment, one independent lab said the levels of formaldehyde in the Chinese-made flooring tested so high that lab employees thought the instruments were broken. One product registered at thirteen times the limit in California, the only state with a formaldehyde emissions standard for laminate flooring. The Barretts had even checked Lumber Liquidators' website before buying the flooring to make sure it was safe and compliant with California standards.

The Barretts' story is detailed in a class-action lawsuit filed by the law firm Hagens Berman alleging that Lumber Liquidators, which sells more than a hundred million square feet of relatively low-cost laminated flooring every year, defrauded its customers.[2] The company insisted its flooring was safe and sought to prove it by sending free air testing kits to its customers. The lawsuit claimed, however, that the kits were "inherently unreliable" and were actually designed to underreport the formaldehyde levels. With the litigation and negative publicity came a big drop in Lumber Liquidators' stock price. The company eventually pulled the Chinese-made flooring from its shelves.

The bigger picture here is that after years of delays pushed for by the chemical, manufacturing, and furniture industries and their business and political allies, no federal standard for a safe level of formaldehyde exposure for humans exists. That standard would put us all in a safer place, says Tom Neltner, the chemicals policy director at the Environmental Defense Fund. He told us that for starters, state agencies could base enforceable rules on it.

The industry has been so successful that, as of 2015, the Environmental Protection Agency had not finalized its latest scientific assessment, which it began in 1998, of how dangerous formaldehyde is, even after a growing body of research has called it a carcinogen linked to leukemia. The most recent delays, in 2009 and 2011, are significantly due to the power of chemical industry lobbyists and campaign contributors to paralyze our government from taking action.

We also detail the story of how the connections of one deep-pocketed lobbyist can have a big impact on regulations affecting public health. This Washington lobbyist, Charlie Grizzle, gave thousands of dollars in campaign contributions over the years to Senator David Vitter of Louisiana and Representative Mike Simpson of Idaho. The lawmakers led the charge in getting the EPA to delay its assessments, an investigation by the Center for Public Integrity revealed.[3] In Vitter's case, the delay was aimed at formaldehyde. In Simpson's, the scientific assessment of another chemical toxic in high doses—arsenic—was put on hold.

The federal regulation that could have helped prohibit high levels of formaldehyde in flooring was supposed to have been in place by 2013 after Congress passed a law in 2010 mandating formaldehyde emissions standards in that type of flooring. But by 2015, the rule still had not been completed by the EPA. So the agency was left watching from the sidelines when Americans were made aware by *60 Minutes* that dangerously high levels of formaldehyde could be in their homes. On its website, the EPA addressed their concern with this less than comforting statement: "Because national formaldehyde emissions standards will not take effect until after EPA issues its final implementing regulations, EPA is not yet doing any enforcement investigations relating to the formaldehyde emissions standards for composite wood products."[4]

Sowing Seeds of Doubt

Formaldehyde is big business. Nearly 4 billion pounds of it was produced in or imported to the United States in 2011.

It is present in many products—carpets, plywood, nail polish, paper, and pesticides, to name a few—and, as it is a naturally occurring compound, has been thought to be safe at lower levels. A gas that can be condensed into liquid form, formaldehyde is now used primarily in the production of industrial resins. It was a key ingredient in a foam used extensively for home insulation until U.S. Consumer Product Safety Commission banned the foam in 1982. Wood flooring companies sell billions of dollars' worth of products containing formaldehyde every year. In defense of the use of formaldehyde in building materials and many other products, the American Chemistry Council notes that the chemical exists naturally in our bodies.[5] In the past, the council sought to create doubt about the reliability of research linking formaldehyde to leukemia.[6] As Tom Neltner points out, however, "While the industry will tell you that formaldehyde is natural, it's also used to embalm people. They lack a little context."

At higher levels, formaldehyde can cause cancer, according to the National Cancer Institute. An NCI study that followed 25,000 workers for 42 years and was published in 2009 found that workers with the highest exposure to the chemical were 37 percent more likely to die from lymphatic or blood cancer and 78 percent more like to die from myeloid leukemia, a cancer that inhibits the production of normal blood cells.[7]

Less serious but nonetheless troubling, at the levels contained in some of Lumber Liquidators' flooring, formaldehyde can trigger asthma, burning eyes, and nosebleeds as it seeps into the air, the EPA has reported.

Upper respiratory problems were found among the thousands of people who said they suffered from formaldehyde exposure after Hurricane Katrina. All of them had lived at least for a while in trailers the Federal Emergency Management Agency had bought to house displaced residents.

Soon after the families moved into their trailers in late 2005, some started complaining of burning eyes, trouble breathing, and rashes, among other symptoms. Becky Gillette, an Arkansas volunteer with the Sierra Club, became suspicious of materials used in the trailers and bought $39 kits to test for formaldehyde levels. She told us that of the 120 trailers she tested over the years, about nine out of ten exceeded 0.1 parts per million of formaldehyde, the exposure at which the National Cancer Institute says it can have adverse health effects.[8,9] The CDC later confirmed that many occupied trailers had formaldehyde levels above that norm.

Her discoveries helped lead to a class action lawsuit against the manufacturers of the trailers on behalf of 55,000 Gulf Coast residents. In 2012, more than six years after the hurricane, U.S. District Judge Kurt Engelhardt in New Orleans approved a settlement requiring the manufacturers and FEMA contractors who set up and maintained the trailers to pay the plaintiffs $42.6 million. One Mississippi woman, Agnes Mauldin, told Judge Engelhardt that her sixty-six-year-old-mother died of leukemia in 2008 after living in a FEMA trailer.[10] Several other people reported that they or relatives who lived in the trailers were later diagnosed with leukemia.

Gillette doggedly took on bureaucrats in Washington who preferred to deny the problem, and she did not let up. She and Lindsay Huckabee, a Mississippi mother of five whose family fell victim to a toxic trailer, even testified before Congress.[11] Gillette's crusade clearly had an effect on lawmakers. The legislation they passed in 2010 calls for limiting the amount of formaldehyde that can be used in certain wood products, such as the ones used in the trailers. But to Gillette's chagrin, the industry's objections over the specifics of regulations proposed by the EPA continue to delay the law's implementation.

Ubiquitous

At least 2 million Americans are exposed to formaldehyde in the workplace every year, according to the Occupational Safety and Health Administration.[12] It's one of the most common chemicals we encounter. Elizabeth Ward of the American Cancer Society told USA Today in 2009 that it has become "ubiquitous."[13] Two workplaces of particular risk are nail and hair salons. Several hair salon workers have become sick from exposure to a formaldehyde-laced hair straightening product used in so-called Brazilian blowouts. A *New York Times* investigation in 2015 found scores of nail salon employees who complained of nosebleeds and breathing problems.

Many products in our bathroom cabinets contain formaldehyde. And even if it isn't listed as an ingredient, you could still be exposed to the chemical. For example, the ingredient list on a bottle of a popular face wash—one of the commonly used exfoliating scrubs found on pharmacy shelves—doesn't list formaldehyde, but it did contain several other chemicals, including DMDM hydantoin, which the Occupational Safety & Health Administration lists as a chemical that can release formaldehyde.[14] Philip Landrigan, the dean for global health at Mount Sinai Hospital and an expert on toxins, says children, pregnant women, and the elderly are more likely to be sensitive to the chemical's effects, although he added that he doesn't think home testing for formaldehyde is probably necessary unless symptoms develop.

Most Chemicals Go Untested

In addition to formaldehyde, Landrigan says federal limits on exposure to arsenic, which can cause developmental and neurological problems, are past due for an upgrade. An estimated 730 out of 100,000 women get cancer annually as a result of exposure to arsenic—present in water and pesticides—at current maximum exposure levels. High levels of manganese, present in stainless steel utensils and soda cans and also our water supply, has been linked to Parkinson's disease. These are chemicals we *know* can be unsafe. "The great fear is always that there might be other chemicals out there that have never been tested but to which children are exposed," Landrigan said.

Indeed, most of the eighty thousand chemicals in products we use have not been tested. Still, as of 2015, most were not required to be.

And Americans are not exactly happy with that. Three quarters of the people polled in 2012 by Public Opinion Strategies for the Natural Resources Defense Council think the threat posed to people's health by exposure to toxic chemicals is serious. More than two thirds support stricter regulation of chemicals, including a majority of conservatives and Tea Party supporters.[15] In a separate 2012 poll conducted by Lake Research

Partners for the American Sustainable Business Council, three fourths of small business owners support stricter regulation of toxins in everyday products.[16]

Formaldehyde companies have successfully blocked regulation at the federal level for years by presenting studies by industry-funded scientists, by objecting to the EPA's process, and, most important, by persuading members of Congress to write letters and pass legislation that delays the EPA's work. All of this can be hazardous to our health, to say the least. Commenting on the willingness of some members of Congress to go to bat for the chemical companies, the Government Accountability Office noted in 2009 that the EPA assessments that have "been in progress the longest cover key chemicals likely to cause cancer."[17] Advocates say the GAO was referring to the political involvement of Senator Jim Inhofe, Republican of Oklahoma and a member of the Senate Environment and Public Works Committee. In 2004, Inhofe, who now chairs the committee, persuaded the EPA to delay its assessment of formaldehyde until another scientific study was completed. That study was finally published five years later and was unequivocal in calling formaldehyde a carcinogen. The industry also discredited that study, saying it wasn't definitive.

The chemical industry's lobbying effort is well funded. Just ten of the biggest chemical interests that support a new industry-friendly chemical safety bill spent more than $150 million on lobbying in Washington in 2013 and 2014, according to MapLight, a nonpartisan money-in-politics research organization.[18] In contrast, all of the public interest, environmental, and medical associations that lobbied on the bill spent a combined $17.6 million in 2013 and 2014.

The most frequent Washington mouthpiece for the industry is the American Chemistry Council, a trade association with $130 million in assets, and a CEO with a total annual compensation package worth $3.6 million in 2013. The American Chemistry Council is behind another group called the Formaldehyde Panel, a network of more than 150 companies, ranging from small wood manufacturers and the National Funeral Directors Association to big corporate players such as DuPont, 3M, BASF, ExxonMobil, and Chevron.

The American Chemistry Council's toolbox goes beyond lobbying. The group spent $38 million to mount a PR campaign to counter the public's worries about phthalates, a family of chemicals used in plastics that has been linked to development problems in children.[19] The PR firm, Ogilvy, won a coveted industry CLIO award for shifting public opinion against banning the chemicals.

Unlike the chemical industry, environmental and public health groups lack the resources to fund swarms of scientists and consultants to attend every relevant EPA meeting and become intellectual resources for officials, all of which puts them at a disadvantage, Jennifer Sass, senior scientist in the health and environment program at the Natural Resources Defense Council, told us.

The Name of the Game: Delay, Delay, Delay

Charlie Grizzle was an assistant administrator at the EPA during the George H. W. Bush administration. He was appointed to the next Bush president's transition team and then became a "pioneer" for George W. Bush's reelection, a designation for folks bundling in the six figures, the Center for Public Integrity reported.[20,21] He opened his own lobbying firm soon after leaving his post at the EPA and took in well over $1 million in recent years from companies in the chemical and mining industries, among others. From 2004 to 2010, his firm was paid more than $600,000 to work for the Formaldehyde Council, an industry group formed in the face of a regulation threat in 2004.

The Formaldehyde Council members included Georgia-Pacific, a subsidiary of Koch Industries (owned by two of the biggest political donors in recent years, Charles and David Koch), and DuPont, one of the oldest and most successful public companies in the world. It also had furniture and composite wood manufacturers and the National Funeral Directors Association as members. It disbanded in 2010.

More recently, the American Chemistry Council has formed another front group that it named, creatively, the Formaldehyde Panel, and which lists more than 150 companies as members. Most of the companies and organizations comprising the panel are the same ones the Formaldehyde Council claimed. Like the Formaldehyde Council, the Formaldehyde Panel is not required to disclose how much it spends on the effort to resist regulation, and an ACC spokesperson didn't respond when we asked.

In 2009, after the EPA released a draft assessment report concluding that formaldehyde was indeed a known carcinogen, a more dangerous classification than it had previously given the chemical, the Formaldehyde Council issued a statement slamming the study and said the EPA's proposals should be reviewed by the National Academy of Sciences, an independent research organization established by Congress. Such a review could take four years.[22] The Grizzle Company worked to make that happen.

Grizzle's connections helped the formaldehyde makers get the time they wanted. On his website, Grizzle touts his ability to use his "strong Republican credentials" to "bring a client's interests to the immediate attention of the most influential leaders in the White House or Congress." To maintain those strong credentials in Washington, Grizzle has opened his checkbook frequently. He has made more than five hundred individual contributions to candidates and committees since 1989, totaling nearly $400,000, almost all of it to Republicans. (Although he was never elected to public office, he even referred to himself as "the Honorable Charles Grizzle" in at least two disclosures.)

One of the beneficiaries of Grizzle's cash is David Vitter, the senator from Louisiana. Around the time in May 2009 that the National Cancer Institute released its study,[23] Grizzle gave Vitter a $2,400 donation, reports show, part of the $15,000 he and members of his firm have given to Vitter since 2000, most of it since 2008. Campaign contribution reports show that Vitter became a favorite of the chemical industry: he was the second-biggest recipient of campaign money among senators from the chemical manufacturing business in 2010, a reelection year for him, with donations of about $76,000.[24]

In 2009, Vitter used his power in the Senate to block the nomination of an EPA official in an unrelated office until the agency acquiesced to sending the EPA's formaldehyde assessment to the National Academy of Sciences, as the Formaldehyde Council had requested. For lobbyists, kicking a study to the NAS is not a new strategy. "The standard playbook that industry uses first begins with questioning the science, and they can question the science in any one of a number of different forms," Charles Fox, a former EPA administrator, told the Center for Public Integrity. "There is a scientific advisory board at EPA. There's the National Academy of Sciences."

The Natural Resources Defense Council warned that kicking the study to the NAS would mean at least a two-year delay before the EPA could issue a final assessment.[25] That turned out to be wishful thinking. Six years later, the EPA's formaldehyde regulations still had not been made final. "Delay means money," James Huff, associate director for chemical carcinogenesis at the National Institute for Environmental Health

Sciences in the Department of Health and Human Services, told ProPublica in April 2010. "The longer they can delay labeling something a known carcinogen, the more money they can make."

Vitter's rationale for the holdup, his office's spokesman told a reporter at the time, was that "because of the FEMA trailer debacle, we need to get absolutely reliable information to the public about formaldehyde risk as soon as possible." In response to questions we submitted to Vitter's office, his spokesman replied in an email, "During his tenure as Ranking Member of the Environment and Public Works Committee, Senator Vitter had concerns that EPA was failing to utilize strong scientific standards, not using accurate cost benefit analysis, and not adequately regulating. His position on the committee offered him a unique opportunity to provide additional oversight over the standards EPA was employing when making regulations."

The EPA pushed back against Vitter's demands; EPA administrator Lisa Jackson even met personally with Vitter to ask him to stop blocking the nomination of a key official. The EPA said it was "not time for delay."[26]

At least three House Democrats also wrote to Jackson to request a review by the Academy because, they said, it is important for the assessment to be "thorough and accurate." They wrote that since "formaldehyde is found in so many applications from building and construction materials to consumer goods and medications, we are concerned that the public needs the certainty of an NAS review to support broad acceptance" of formaldehyde's "potential health effects." In December 2009, the Society of the Plastics Industry, a trade group representing formaldehyde manufacturers DuPont and BASF, held a fundraiser for Vitter, suggesting donations of $1,000 per person. Later that month, in a letter to the Formaldehyde Council, Jackson acquiesced, writing that she would send the EPA's findings to the National Academy of Sciences for review.

The industry heaped praise on Vitter for his help. "Overcoming the agency's intransigence in engaging NAS on formaldehyde would have been impossible without the timely intervention of U.S. Senator David Vitter," Betsy Natz, the Formaldehyde Council's director, told ProPublica in April 2010. In March 2010, Grizzle cohosted another $1,000-per-plate fundraiser for Vitter, records show, at the exclusive Republicans-only Capitol Hill Club.[27]

In 2011, the National Academy of Sciences completed its review, which criticized the EPA's work on formaldehyde for being disorganized. But its scientists wholeheartedly agreed with the conclusion of the EPA report—

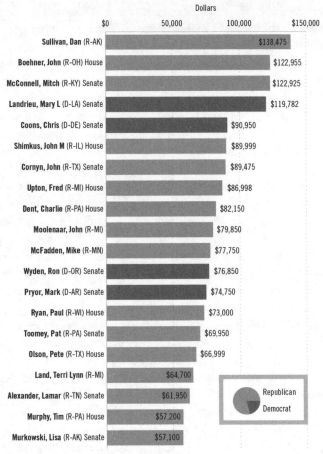

Top 20 Recipients of Chemical Industry Contributions
Source: Center for Responsive Politics (opensecrets.org)
Methodology: The numbers above are based on contributions from PACs and individuals giving $200 or more. All donations took place during the 2013–2014 election cycle and were released by the Federal Election Commission on March 09, 2015.

that formaldehyde can cause cancer. On that point, 51 out of 52 NAS scientists agreed.[28] The NAS also said the issuance of new formaldehyde regulations should not be delayed.[29]

Nevertheless, the chemical lobby continued to have its way in Washington. A few months after the Academy report was issued, an unnamed member of the House Appropriations Committee added a few lines to a 2012 appropriations measure that had the effect of delaying a final assessment not only on formaldehyde, but also on forty-six other chemicals it was in the process of assessing, according to an investigation by the Center for Public Integrity.[30]

Speculation as to the identity of the lawmaker who authored that language has centered on Mike Simpson, the Idaho Republican. Although Simpson, chair of the subcommittee that oversees EPA funding, has not confirmed that he did it, Grizzle admitted lobbying him for it.[31] By that time, Grizzle was working for two pesticide makers whose products contain arsenic, which the EPA was also in the process of evaluating.[32] When the Center for Public Integrity reporter David Heath asked Grizzle if the donations were made to influence the delay, Grizzle replied, "I don't see a connection. I've been a friend and supporter of Congressman Simpson for a long time."

Regardless of which lawmaker wrote the legislation, the result was to almost completely halt the EPA's evaluations of chemicals for three years as the agency was directed to overhaul and improve its scientific process.

The American Chemistry Council has continued to be helpful to Vitter, who decided to run for governor of Louisiana in 2015. The council became the first donor at the over-$100,000 level to a super PAC backing his election.[33] At the time, Vitter was also one of the main point men in Congress in shaping a Chemical Safety Act, which ostensibly would toughen standards for testing and enforcement of the industry. Not surprisingly, it was written in consultation with the council.

Jennifer Sass told us it's hard to blame Jackson for eventually giving in. "When Congress tells you to do something, I'm not sure what you can do," she said.

Floored

Even after the publicity surrounding the FEMA-supplied toxic trailers and the almost $43 million the trailer makers were ordered to pay victims, and even after Congress passed a law to restrict formaldehyde levels in certain wood products, the EPA has yet to issue final regulations. Thanks, of course, to the formidable power and influence of the chemical industry and its friends in business and politics.

In 2015, the *New York Times* reporters Eric Lipton and Rachel Abrams documented the many steps the industry and its allies can take to shape regulations after a law is passed.[34] Those allies in this case include furniture makers and retailers. They joined forces with the chemical companies because the EPA's proposed regulations would affect not only flooring products and cabinetmakers but also lamination facilities that employ a process that adds more formaldehyde to the final product.

The furniture industry, in particular, fumed and used one of the most common tactics of industries under attack: they claimed that new legislation or regulations affecting them would lead to massive layoffs. It's part of a playbook, detailed in *Deadly Spin*,[35] that goes back to efforts by public health officials and consumer advocates to protect people from the harmful effects of cigarette smoke. Formaldehyde producers and users seized on it. The furniture makers said the rule would cost manufacturers up to $200 million per year to implement, considerably more than the tens of millions of dollars estimated by the EPA, the *Times* reported. The chief lobbyist for the American Home Furnishings Alliance, or AHFA, warned the EPA that if the proposal was not fixed, over a million manufacturing jobs might be impacted.[36]

Executives from La-Z-Boy, Ashley Furniture, and other companies met with House Speaker John Boehner and ten rank-and-file Republicans and Democrats to request that they sign on to a letter pressuring the EPA to fold.[37] They got what they wanted. Members of the House who sent letters included Doris Matsui, a California Democrat, and Alan Nunnelee, a Mississippi Republican. Senate Republicans Roger Wicker of Mississippi, Ron Johnson of Wisconsin, and Roy Blunt of Missouri and Democrats Mark Warner and Tim Kaine of Virginia also sent letters. The furniture executives and lobbyists had reported meeting with all of them except Kaine. All the correspondence echoed the industry's concern that requiring the companies doing the final wood lacquering to test their products would be redundant. They maintain that tests show the lamination process seals in the formaldehyde.

Hundreds of comments were sent to the EPA on the topic from, among others, IKEA, wood products associations, a trade group for mobile home makers, and lobbying powerhouses such as the American Chemistry Council and the U.S. Chamber of Commerce. A few state regulatory agencies, medical associations, and environmental groups sent comments supporting the rule.

All of the influencing and delays has left Becky Gillette demoralized and disgusted with the process. Some members of Congress wanted the rule issued in three years, she told us in the spring of 2015. "It's been five and we've got at least another year to go."

In fairness, Tom Neltner, who negotiated with the industry to help pass the 2010 law, said the EPA's initial proposal may well have been unnecessarily burdensome on hardwood laminators. Another factor, he said, is the EPA's inadequate funding. Still, he added, the chemical industry's well-funded campaign also delayed the process.

The EPA declined to answer many of our questions about those delays. A spokesperson replied only in an email that "since we are looking to revise the standards, all we can say" is "EPA plans to finalize the proposed standards before the end of [2015]."

Is the EPA Its Own Worst Enemy?

The preponderance of resources that the industry can bring to bear and, ironically, the open process that the agency has created to listen to various stakeholders, have further tilted the balance against environmental groups. These factors have also contributed to delays in making rules, the green groups claim.

Advocates such as Richard Denison, a scientist at the Environmental Defense Fund, believes it's a systemic problem. At one of EPA's "stakeholder panels" in 2012, he got up to say so, noting that the average completion time of the assessments is 7.5 years, almost four times the EPA's goal.[38]

On one meeting's agenda, Denison found that as many as six industry representatives from the same consulting firm were scheduled to speak on the same issue. The Center for Public Integrity, analyzing the meetings in recent years, found that 85 percent of the speakers were industry-funded scientists.

This all brings to mind Lee Drutman's book *The Business of America Is Lobbying*. As K Street has drawn the best talent from Congress (with money), Congress has become a kind of "farm system" for lobbying firms, Drutman wrote. "This contributes to a declining government capacity, which means that government policymakers must increasingly rely on lobbyists to help them to develop, pass, and implement policy."[39]

There are other factors pushing the demand up for lobbyists. One is the lobbyists themselves. "More lobbying also makes legislation more complex [in order to accommodate all the lobbying interests]," Drutman wrote.[40] The U.S. Code of Federal Regulations—all requiring specialized knowledge—is now more than 174,000 pages long, he noted, more than doubling since 1975.

That environment, combined with the fact that lobbying itself has become much more competitive and costly, yields a big advantage to trade associations and businesses over public interest groups. They can afford to wield an everything-but-the-kitchen-sink strategy—targeting Congress, the White House, independent agencies—hoping that at least one approach works. As Drutman says, "In an ever-more-complex policy environment, the need for expertise becomes greater, but the gap between public sector and private sector expertise is wider. Again, organizations that can supply the expertise are at an advantage."[41] The nonprofit groups just don't have as much firepower—in terms of scientists, lobbyists, or dollars—to be a source of knowledge for regulators or even to respond to each round of comments submitted to regulators by industry-funded consultants. "A lot of times there are details that I don't have the time to understand," said Tom Neltner of the Environmental Defense Fund. He added: "The public interest community is always outgunned."

Arsenic and Old Science

Arsenic, like formaldehyde, can cause health and developmental problems and at high levels is linked to certain cancers. Columbia University professor Joseph Graziano jokes, darkly, that arsenic makes lead look like a vitamin. That's because, as he told the Center for Public Integrity's David Heath, it "sweeps across the body and impact[s] everything that's going on, every organ system."[42] It's in weed killers marketed to fight your lawn's crabgrass, and, in many places, it's in the water we drink.

A 2008 draft assessment by the EPA estimated that arsenic was seventeen times more potent than previously thought.[43] In assessing the impact of arsenic on women in particular, the agency estimated that if a hundred thousand women were to consume the legal limit of arsenic currently permitted, 730 would get bladder or lung cancer.

After seeing the draft assessment, the producers of arsenic-based pesticides that hired Charlie Grizzle to lobby for them, Drexel Chemical Co. and Luxembourg-Pamol, began to take action, as did mining companies like Rio Tinto, which also would have been affected by the regulation. As the Center for Public Integrity's David Heath reported, a group of lobbyists, including Grizzle, set up a meeting with Representative Mike Simpson, the Republican from Idaho, who by 2015 had received a total of $8,000 in campaign donations from Grizzle, according to data compiled and analyzed by the Sunlight Foundation and the Center for Responsive Politics.

All it took to send the EPA's draft assessment to the National Academy of Sciences for a review was for a congressman to slip one paragraph into in a 221-page spending bill. When Heath asked Simpson about the paragraph, he said he worried about small communities not being able to meet drinking water standards.

Such stealth maneuvers are not uncommon in Congress. A senator, for example, can anonymously put a hold on legislation, completely blocking it. Committee members can insert language written by lobbyists directly into a large spending bill before anyone has adequate time to review it. As Chellie Pingree, a Democrat from Maine, bemoaned to Center for Public Integrity reporter David Heath in June 2014: "It's happening more and more in this Congress that we see less and less of what goes on behind the scenes, that members aren't informed until the last minute. So things like this, major policy changes like this, can happen somewhat in the dark of the night with very little information to the public."

When confronted by a reporter, Simpson said he didn't know that the paragraph inserted into the spending bill kept a weed killer containing arsenic on the market, and he said he had "no idea" that Grizzle had donated to his campaigns.

Delays continued in subsequent years as industry-funded scientists presented their views to the Academy, sometimes without disclosing their financial ties. (The Center for Public Integrity reported that one such scientist suggested that an arsenic dose even higher than the current drinking water standard doesn't cause cancer.) The result: in 2015, seven years after the EPA's draft assessment that arsenic is considerably more dangerous than previously thought, many public health experts said the federal government was continuing to allow too much arsenic in our water and in products like weed killers.

"Nobody's Looking Out for Our Welfare"

"We have a broken Toxic Substance Control Act," says Tom Neltner. That's the big problem that "federal health officials, prominent academics and even many leaders of the chemical industry" agree on, the *Atlantic*'s senior health care editor, Dr. James Hamblin, wrote in 2014.[44]

The obstacles for public health are (1) the vast majority of the eighty thousand industrial chemicals available for use are not regulated or even tested by the government, and (2) companies are not even required to submit most of them for testing.

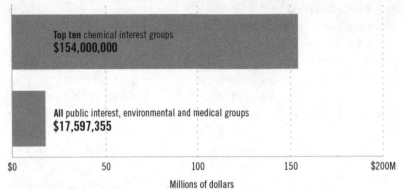

Sources of Lobbying $$$ on Chemical Safety Reform Legislation
Source: MapLight, authors' analysis (maplight.org)
Methodology: Analysis from organizations disclosing that they lobbied on S. 1009 in 2013 or 2014.

"What most Americans don't realize is nobody's looking out for their welfare," Mount Sinai's Philip Landrigan told us. "The great fear is always that there might be other chemicals out there that have never been tested but to which children are exposed."

In addition, the EPA (like the FDA) has to meet a very high standard before it can ban a toxin. The EPA has banned or limited only five.[45] Weak laws even made it difficult to ban asbestos.

There were signs in 2015 that the chemical safety laws might be strengthened when legislation to update the laws for the first time in thirty-nine years received bipartisan support in the Senate. It would, among other things, require more frequent testing at the federal level and make it easier for the government to pull products off the shelves.

Sponsored by industry favorite David Vitter and New Mexico Democrat Tom Udall, who in the past has supported increased environmental protection, the bill even received kudos of sorts from some environmental advocacy groups, including the Environmental Defense Fund, which view the legislation as an improvement over the broken status quo. Other green groups maintained it was much too weak.[46] Senator Barbara Boxer was pushing a separate, more stringent bill that allowed for testing of more chemicals each year.[47]

Vitter's spokesman wrote that the "legislation provides common-sense reforms that are necessary to update the United States' forty year old chemical regulatory program. Senator Vitter has worked with colleagues across this aisle, stakeholders from all sectors, and the EPA to draft this legislation that will drastically increase EPA's ability to ensure the safety of chemicals being used in the United States." It soon became apparent, however, that the bill was being vetted—and possibly even written, at least in part—by industry lobbyists. Using metadata on a Microsoft Word document circulated by Udall, a reporter for Hearst Newspapers found that the document originated at the American Chemistry Council. Senator Boxer said she felt certain the industry wrote it, citing a Senate information technology staffer who investigated the issue.

Udall, who the *New York Times* suggested had formed an "unlikely alliance" with the chemical industry, maintained that the document originated in his office. One of his aides told Hearst that "it was shared with a number of stakeholders including at least one other senator's office. One of those stakeholders was the ACC."[48] But the council did not deny authoring that draft of the bill. "There's no way for anyone to tell," a council spokesperson said. Others, including Udall's office, said anyone could change some metadata. A spokesperson for Udall said the senator has been engaged with all groups on all sides of the issue.

Regardless of who wrote the bill's language, the end product was more than palatable to the chemical industry. The American Chemistry Council called the bill the "culmination of a multi-year effort" to secure "compromise, common-sense" legislation that it characterized as "a balanced, science-driven solution that reassured the public that our products are safe and that keeps our economy growing."[49]

The ten biggest chemical companies spent $154 million lobbying on the bill over 2013 and 2014, the watchdog group MapLight found. In contrast, public interest, environmental, and medical groups together spent less than $18 million. The environmental groups spent $6.6 million.

Those chemical companies also contributed almost more than $4 million in campaign contributions to several candidates' campaigns in the 2014 election as the sponsors were shepherding the bill through Congress, MapLight found. The ACC also donated $150,000 to a super PAC supporting Vitter's gubernatorial bid in Louisiana.

The ACC also spent $4 million plus on TV and radio advertising in support of the reelection of Udall and the industry's other allies in Congress, the *Times* reported. The ads portrayed Udall as a man who brings "both sides together to get results."[50] According to the *Times*, Udall "emphatically rejects" that he was doing the industry's bidding: "We can't do something that is pie in the sky; we have to deal with reality," he said.

The Price We Pay

In 2007, Lindsay Huckabee of Mississippi, a mother of five whom Becky Gillette called "a real strong mama bear," was invited to testify before Congress. She and her family were among the tens of thousands who had lived in a FEMA trailer after Hurricane Katrina.

Huckabee testified before multiple congressional committees. She told how her son, Michael, was born prematurely, just weeks after she and her family moved into the trailer. She said he had suffered sinus infections and asthmatic bronchitis since he was six days old. Her four-year-old daughter, Leah, had a recurrence of asthma when they moved into the trailer, "more ear infections than I can count," frequent nosebleeds, and several bouts of pneumonia. An ear, nose and throat specialist suggested they move out of the trailer as soon as possible.[51] Lindsay's thirty-year-old husband, a healthy nonsmoker, later developed a mouth tumor that required surgery.[52]

As noted earlier, the prevalence of formaldehyde in a broad range of products and building materials has affected some professions far more than others. Of the 125 nail salon workers interviewed by the *New York Times*, many reported allergies, asthma, and frequent nosebleeds. Others told of worse problems, including miscarriages and children "born special."

Formaldehyde is among a "toxic trio" of ingredients in nail products, including dibutyl phthalate (DBP), which Australia classifies as causing reproductive problems, and toluene, which can lead to developmental problems in fetuses.[53]

There was a bit of good news in 2015. In response to the *Times* article, New York governor Andrew Cuomo signed a bill that would require nail workers to wear gloves and goggles while performing certain tasks and their employers to make respirators available. Still, the health risks for nail and hair salon workers, and consumers of their products, may be even greater than for the rest of us. That's because the U.S. government has even less regulatory power over cosmetics than it has over other consumer products. In fact, except for color additives, the government does not have authority to test what goes into cosmetics before they hit the shelves.[54] The cosmetics industry is self-regulated by an organization that it funds, the Personal Care Products Council, which is also a registered lobbying group.[55] The group insists that the "toxic trio" does not pose a risk to salon workers or their customers.

Researchers have tried to calculate the price we pay for high levels of chemicals. High lead and arsenic exposure has caused neurological problems and are linked to IQ loss. The *Atlantic* reported that "the combined current levels of pesticides, mercury and lead cause IQ losses amounting to around $120 billion annually—or about 3 percent of the annual budget of the U.S. government."[56]

Separately, Philip Landrigan estimated the annual costs of mercury toxicity in children in the United States to be about $5 billion.[57] Researchers writing for *Health Affairs* in 2014 estimated that reducing exposure to BPA, a common chemical in plastics and cans that is linked to childhood obesity and adult heart disease, could save almost $3 billion per year.[58]

There has been progress on some fronts, as Landrigan has noted.[59] The government has made substantial progress in reducing exposure to lead. Every dollar spent to reduce lead hazards produces a benefit between $17 to $220 per person, according to a study by Landrigan and Philippe Grandjean, a Harvard Medical School scientist.[60] Lead-free gasoline alone has generated an economic benefit estimated at $3 trillion since 1980.

Curbing the use of formaldehyde would have measurable health care benefits, according to the Environmental Defense Fund and partner organizations. They maintain that the EPA's proposed rule for wood products would prevent more than twenty-one thousand children from developing asthma each year, resulting in more than $250 million in annual savings.

The cost may also be greater than what current science has shown. Grandjean told the *Atlantic*:

> We don't have the luxury to sit back and wait until science figures out what's really going on, what the mechanisms are, what the doses are, and that sort of thing. We've seen with lead and mercury and other poisons that it takes decades. And during that time we are essentially exposing the next generation to exactly the kind of chemicals that we want to protect them from.

But as long as the vast majority of chemicals that wind up in thousands of consumer products are considered innocent until proven guilty, and as long as the industry and its allies are able to spend whatever it takes to prevent or delay testing and to block legislation and regulation that might affect profits, future generations will be as exposed to poisons as we are today.

PART 3

CHAPTER 9

It's Fixable

You might conclude, at this point in the book, that there's nothing to be done to solve the crisis of money in politics, and that a truly representative republic—a government of, by, and for the people—has become an impossible dream.

You would be wrong.

In fact, the good-government community has spent decades thinking through solutions and creating working models of those solutions at the state and local levels. Such solutions are *technically* easy to implement—establishing a new campaign finance system is a matter of tweaking the tax code and distributing bits of revenue; a new transparency regime is a matter of collecting and sharing data; stronger ethics and lobbying laws are a matter of written words on a page.

Compared to, say, overhauling the ways we produce, distribute, and consume energy in America—which involves hundreds of millions of consumers, thousands of corporations, decades of technological development, trillions of tons of equipment, and a mind-boggling amount of natural resources—campaign finance and ethics laws are remarkably simple to turn into new realities. (And, of course, overhauling our energy infrastructure would be easier if we first reduced the control the energy companies have over politics and policy making.)

Winning back American democracy is not a logistical or technical challenge, it's a matter of political will. That is, our will to make our elected representatives, whose salaries we pay, make it happen.

Remember, we have given ourselves the authority to do it. Look back at the words of the Massachusetts state constitution, which inspired the federal Constitution:

> Government is instituted for the common good; for the protection, safety, prosperity, and happiness of the people; and not for the profit, honor, or private interest of any one man, family, or class of men; therefore, the people alone have an incontestable, unalienable, and indefeasible right to institute government; and to reform, alter, or totally change the same, when their protection, safety, prosperity, and happiness require it.

When we first discussed this quote, in the introduction to this book, we focused on the first part of the sentence—how we've lost government for the common good. But take a look at the last part: *The people alone have an incontestable, unalienable, and indefeasible right to institute government; and to reform, alter, or totally change the same, when their protection, safety, prosperity, and happiness require it.*

Those lines are very reminiscent of the third sentence of the Declaration of Independence:

> That whenever any Form of Government becomes destructive of these ends, it is the Right of the People to alter or to abolish it, and to institute new Government, laying its foundation on such principles and organizing its powers in such form, as to them shall seem most likely to effect their Safety and Happiness.

Democracy requires reinvention and constant vigilance. Like the Founders and the abolitionists, the suffragists and the civil rights activists, when we see a fundamental problem in our system, we fix it. That's the American way. Now we need to fix democracy—before we can fix the other problems we all face.

We also need to define, up front, what winning means. Will we ever "get money out of politics"? No. That phrase is misguiding. Can we limit the amount of coin-operated governing that goes on? Yes. Can we retrain our elected representatives to prioritize our Main Streets over billionaire political donors? Yes. Can we give public-interest legislation a much better shot of winning over the private interests? Yes.

In this respect, maintaining a functioning democracy—which must always include limiting the undue influence of money over politics and policy making—should be seen as a routine function of a civil society. Just as nearly everyone sees schools, libraries, news outlets, green spaces, public health initiatives, hospitals, animal shelters, civic centers, good jobs, secure retirements, public transportation, safe streets, theaters, and art museums as essential components of a thriving community, so should democracy be seen.

Viewing democracy in such a light also helps gauge expectations about what progress means, which then helps reduce the potential for cynicism and resignation. Who among us believes that we can create perfect public health, in which no one is overweight, preventable diseases are eradicated, and everyone is avoiding behaviors that are risky to their health? How about perfect schools, in which all children are achieving their maximum potential? How about a pristine, virginal environment, in which the impacts of human activity are undetectable? How about a 100-percent-efficient and meritocratic economy, in which everyone is justly rewarded for their work and only the best-run businesses flourish?

Goals such as these, of course, are things we would all like to see happen, or most of us would. But we also know that nothing ever reaches a state of perfection. Instead, we keep working on causes and improving systems and pumping money and effort into civic institutions so that they get better over time.

If someone told you they were working on reducing homelessness, would you ever say, "Well, I don't think you'll ever be able to get rid of homelessness, so I don't have time for you." If someone says he or she is the director of an education-reform organization, could you ever imagine saying, "What's the point? There will always be bad students and under-performing teachers, so why bother?" If someone explained to you that they were working on improving air quality, would you ever quip, "It's too late. The air will never be truly clean again because most of the nations on Earth are industrialized." Of course not.

Yet, way too often, when democracy reformers talk about reducing the power of money over politics, many people, especially in Washington, feel perfectly content saying, "Ha! Good luck with that. It'll never happen." It's that very response that has terminally limited the amount of energy and money flowing into the fight for reform. But such a response is appropriate only if the assumption is that the goal is to permanently "get money out of politics." If, instead, the goal, as it is with every other element of a good society, is to keep improving, knowing that a perfect, final destination is unachievable, then we will all be thinking correctly about the challenge ahead.

Which doesn't mean that our task will be easy. This book demonstrates just how powerful Big Money has become. But a movement is building, one that is growing every day, and we'll tell you about it in the next chapter.

One factor that makes our job harder is the current Supreme Court. *Citizens United* was, as we discussed in part 1, a setback. The part of the decision that extended beyond the freedom of the press was naïve and overzealous. Time will show what a mistake it was. The five justices of the majority, without the political experience to understand how the case could warp our democracy, narrowed the ability of legislators to regulate the way money flows to and around the legislative process. But, as you'll learn in the coming pages, those limitations aren't fatal. We can still accomplish 75 percent of what needs to be accomplished to improve the American experiment of self-government.

Also, we should always remind ourselves that the Supreme Court doesn't exist in a vacuum, and like other misguided decisions of yore, like *Plessy v. Ferguson*, which asserted that racial segregation was perfectly constitutional, *Citizens United* will be swept away by the current of time.

Most visible among the efforts to correct the Court's mistake is the movement to overturn *Citizens United* via a constitutional amendment. This strategy has galvanized hundreds of thousands of grassroots activists. A coalition of more than a hundred organizations, called United for the People (united4thepeople.org), is driving the movement, which was sparked more than five years ago by pioneering groups like Free Speech for People. However, amending the Constitution requires approval from two thirds of Congress and then ratification by three quarters of the state legislatures (38 of the 50). Or it requires the calling of a constitutional convention, which means that two thirds of the states (34) would have to agree to do so, and then any amendments that emerge from the convention still need to be ratified by 38 states. So it's a long-term strategy, one that will take many years to accomplish, if indeed it ever succeeds.

More attainable is a three-pronged effort to establish a pro-reform jurisprudence, which groups like the Brennan Center for Justice, the Campaign Legal Center, and Demos are driving.

The first prong of this work is focused on clarifying aspects of the *Citizens United* decision that are demonstrably ill-informed. The most obvious example is one of the central arguments held dear by the five justices: that independent spending is not at all corrupting of candidates and public officials because it is completely unaffiliated with the candidates and their campaigns.

This claim is difficult to square with the current political reality, now that Jeb Bush and Hillary Clinton have super PACs whose "independence" is clearly in name only. All you have to do to prove this lack of independence is search Google for "super PACs and coordination" and you can read hundreds of newspaper articles that document the connections. Jeb raised more than $100 million for his super PAC before he officially filed his candidate paperwork with the government. A nonpartisan group called the Campaign Legal Center has filed complaints against most of the major presidential candidates, on both sides of the aisle, raising the red flag about such coordination.

The second prong of the work is to reassert that Congress has the right—and duty—to make laws preventing corruption or the appearance of corruption. As we mentioned in previous chapters, Fordham University law professor Zephyr Teachout points out in her book, *Corruption in America*, that regulating against systemic corruption is in perfect accord with what the Founders believed, and what served as campaign finance precedent for the hundred years prior to *Citizens United*. The reestablishment of this principle of corruption will require legal scholarship, the shaping of ideas in and around law schools, and the assertion of public opinion—in a 2014 poll, 75 percent of Americans said they believe politicians are "corrupted" by campaign donations and lobbyists.[1]

The third prong of the work is the nominating of judges and Supreme Court justices whose positions on democracy and money in politics are in line with those of the vast majority of the American public. Developing standards for vetting judicial nominees based on their sophistication about the way money and influence manifest themselves in our democracy—the very sophistication that is lacking on the current Court—is necessary to make sure that those on the bench "get it." In the late spring of last year, Vermont Senator Bernie Sanders said, "If elected president, I will have a litmus test in terms of my nominee to be a Supreme Court justice, and that nominee will say that we are all going to overturn this disastrous Supreme Court decision."

Soon after, Hillary Clinton told a group in Iowa: "I will do everything I can to appoint Supreme Court justices who protect the right to vote and do not protect the right of billionaires to buy elections."

As of the writing of this book, no Republican presidential candidates have said they would probe potential justices on their views of money in politics, but there is an increasing amount of discussion among Republicans about taking firmer and clearer stances on the matter. Which is a good sign. If there's a silver lining to *Citizens United*, it's that the decision has ignited an awareness and anxiety about the usurping of our democracy that hasn't existed since Watergate.

So what are the legislative fixes that we can accomplish now, regardless of the Supreme Court?

Broadly speaking, they fall into four categories that embody the principles of a high-functioning democracy: (1) everyone participates, (2) everyone knows, (3) everyone plays by the same commonsense rules, and (4) everyone is held accountable.

Yes, that's four categories. Most people want a single category and ask if there is a silver bullet for this cause—a simple fix that will solve the whole problem. There is not. Most major issues are of such complexity. From public health to education to crime and poverty reduction, it takes all kinds of strategies and policies, applied simultaneously over long periods of time, to make lasting progress. The legislative and judicial fixes we focus on are as varied as the problem. We don't have the space to describe all the efforts to get such fixes enacted and implemented. Instead, we will detail the most promising efforts taking shape across the country.

(1) Everyone Participates

This is the "game changer" category. Unless we create better ways of financing politics in this country, we're never going to be able to rebalance the power dynamic in Washington and the state capitals.

There's no need for us to say anything more about the need to create new ways of financing campaigns than the quote we included in chapter 2 from Representative Jim Himes (D-CT):

> I won't dispute for one second the problems of a system that demands [an] immense amount of fund-raisers by its legislators.

It's appalling, it's disgusting, it's wasteful and it opens the possibility of conflicts of interest and corruption.

This admission is stunning. A sitting member of the United States Congress telling one of the most respected news outlets in the world that the way we finance our politics—and therefore, the baseline for our way of governing—is *appalling, disgusting, wasteful,* and potentially corrupting.

Even when the money isn't given with any transactional intentions—even if the donor has no expectation of bending legislation or pressuring a government official for a favor—the process of raising it marinates the minds of politicians in the concerns of the wealthiest among us. Day after day after day, four to five hours a day, our elected representatives are spending their time begging for money primarily from people who can afford to attend $2,700-a-plate dinners and lunches ($2,700 is the current limit on what an individual can donate directly to a politician's campaign). That includes, of course, the lobbyists and political fundraisers who often "bundle" four-figure checks and then hand over envelopes stuffed with $100,000 or more in contributions.

The fealty we want politicians to have is to their constituents back home on Main Street. We want them obsessing about Jane and John Doe, not David and Charles Koch. We want them spending as little time as possible dialing for dollars from wealthy people, nearly all of whom live outside their districts. We want them to have maximum time to study legislation, attend committee hearings, and reach across the aisle to engage in the high art of compromise.

The one thing that will most engender such a shift of attention, time, and loyalty is what some reformers call "citizen funding" of elections. We prefer the term "citizen funding" rather than "public financing" because the latter seems generic and somewhat bureaucratic. There are public restrooms and pools and beaches. There are public works administrations and public programs. Citizens, though, are human beings. In America, a citizen is an agent of democracy. Such agents—asserting their agency on the system—are what we need more of today.

Citizen funding programs provide the vast majority of Americans, the 99.7 percent of us who can't afford to write significant checks to politicians, with an incentive to participate. Either by limiting the amount and type of fundraising a candidate can do or by providing constituents with funds to contribute as they please, the government is able to redirect a politician's attention to the rest of us.

There are several types of citizen funding programs, dozens of which are already in place at the state and local levels:

- Clean Elections, in which candidates receive a set amount of money to operate their campaigns. Once they do, they are required to cease raising money from other sources. To qualify for the program they must cross a threshold of viability and popularity by collecting a certain amount of low-dollar private donations and signatures from their districts. Connecticut has the best-functioning of such systems.
- Matching Funds. Candidates opt in to these systems. Once they are in, a government fund matches every dollar raised from citizens, by some multiple, up to a certain amount. In some places the match is as much as six dollars for every dollar raised. New York City's matching-fund system has often been heralded as the best in class, and the politicians who participate in it testify that it has turned their gaze back to their districts.
- Tax Incentives. People get a tax credit or deduction for political contributions, up to a certain amount. In some states, the contribution is eligible to be counted for a credit or deduction only if it's made to a candidate who has agreed to limit his or her campaign spending. Oklahoma and Montana have the most generous incentives, at $100.
- Vouchers. The government provides each citizen with a certificate for $50 or $100, which he or she can then contribute to a candidate or party.
- Hybrids, or some combination of the above approaches.

The criticism of such systems is that they provide "taxpayer-funded welfare for politicians." To which our response is: Your tax dollars will be paying their salaries once they're in office, and they will be allocating trillions of your tax dollars through government spending and contracting. So who would you rather they feel beholden to once they're in office: you, or a bunch of special interests and wealthy benefactors? One of the most important prerequisites of a democracy of, by, and for the people is one funded of, by, and for the people.

Take Connecticut, for example. Its Citizens' Election Program (CEP) is financed through a mix of cash receipts received from unclaimed properties reverted to the state; voluntary contributions from individuals and businesses; donations of surplus funds from dissolved candidate campaigns or political committees; and investment earnings on CEP's resources. In 2014, the program reached an all-time high participation rate with 84 percent of winning candidates using the system, and with striking parity between the two major parties.

A study of CEP by the nonprofit think tank Demos demonstrated just how valued the program is by its participants and how effective citizen funding is at meeting its stated goals: "It is clear," the report stated, "that public financing is a fundamental step towards a more representative legislative process that is more responsive to constituents."[2] According to the think tank, which relied on quantitative data analysis and the reflections of elected officials, CEP brings about a much stronger, more representative legislature in several ways.

First, the program eliminates most of the need to fundraise, allowing candidates to spend more time talking with actual voters. A study by a professor at the University of Maryland found that the average legislator in a typical state spends at least 28 percent of their time fundraising;[3] in a state like Connecticut, with its citizen funding program, that percentage decreased to just 11.[4] Said one member of the state House, "I get all my fundraising done early in the summer and then spend the rest of the time door knocking and talking to constituents, which is where I should be spending my time."[5]

Connecticut's system has also expanded the pool of candidates running for office, because personal wealth and connections are a less necessary component of a successful campaign. Plus, the more candidates run for office, the fewer uncontested or noncompetitive seats there are, expanding choice for voters and allowing fresh voices to compete with incumbents. In a similar vein, CEP has increased the number of donors participating in the process, and incumbents have increasingly shifted away from big-money PACs and toward individual donors.

Because legislators no longer rely on their donations, the influence wielded by lobbyists has waned significantly. Former Connecticut representative Juan Figuero described a system of "shakedowns" where "lobbyists and corporate sponsors had events and you ... had to go."[6] Now, power dynamics in the statehouse have shifted, and, as a Republican notes, "people concentrate more on the issues ... the big issues get bipartisan votes."[7] Demos notes, "the actual process of legislating [became] more responsive and substantive." In practice, that means that the policies enacted are more representative of what *all* residents of Connecticut want, not just political donors.

Another Republican legislator explained, "Before public financing, to get donations you had to call people. That would go on. You'd spend half of your time in the election cycle calling up people, raising money instead of going out and knocking on doors. Now, you're getting it from the people and hearing what they want and not from special interests."[8]

In New York City, the effects of the matching funds system have proven to not just remake the way city politics are funded, but also the way politicians think about their constituencies. A data-rich report produced jointly by the Brennan Center for Justice and the Campaign Finance Institute details how politicians who have run on the system said "that by pumping up the value of small contributions, the New York City system gives them an incentive to reach out to their own constituents rather than focusing all their attention on wealthy out-of-district donors, leading them to attract more diverse donors into the political process."[9]

The system has lit up political giving in most of the neighborhoods throughout all of the city's five boroughs. Why? Very simply, because candidates have more incentive to do so than to try to entice wealthy donors to fancy fundraising dinners. Moreover, because the match is six to one, a $100 donor (whose contribution is increased by another $600) all of a sudden starts to look more like a wealthy donor to candidates. As a result, politicians are more inclined to hold large small-dollar fund-raisers and rallies back in their districts that regular people can attend, and to reach out more frequently to their constituents with individual fundraising appeals. All of this has a democratizing effect on elected representatives: "The city's public financing system appears to have achieved one of its key goals—strengthening the connections between public officials and their constituents."[10]

Citizen funding programs exemplify the very best of American democracy: public officials fighting hard to earn your support, whether that's in the form of your vote or your donation. And they back up that support by fairly representing you in the halls of government, because their loyalty is to you, the voter.

These programs are proliferating and have earned the support of all sorts of people: in Maryland, Republican governor Larry Hogan became the first gubernatorial candidate in the state to win using public funds. In 2014, Montgomery County, Maryland, enacted its own county-level fair elections program, and Chicagoans passed a resolution in support of such a system by a 58-point margin. Twenty-five states and many more localities have some kind of financing system in place, and activists are pushing for new or strengthened ones in places including Los Angeles, Albuquerque, Santa Fe, and Arizona. By the time this book gets to your hands, this list will likely be longer.

At the federal level, Representative John Sarbanes (D-MD) is currently at work generating support for a bill that would enact citizen funding for members of Congress. We already have public funding for presidential candidates, but for all intents and purposes, it's no longer being utilized; the system failed to keep pace with the astronomical rise in the cost of elections. Sarbanes's bill, H.R. 20, contains three simple provisions: it provides a $25 tax credit to every American to contribute to candidates; it establishes a 6-to-1 matching fund for low-dollar contributions; and it pushes back against outside spending—"dark money" 501(c)(4)s and super PACs—by providing additional resources to qualifying candidates during the sixty-day "home stretch" before an election. By the summer of 2015, the bill had picked up 151 cosponsors in the House.

(2) Everyone Knows

While citizen funding programs are effective at ensuring that candidates remain beholden to the voters who elect them, they don't have any effect on reducing the massive amounts of radicalized "independent expenditures" that outside groups spend to try to elect and defeat candidates. As you have learned in other sections of this book, thanks to the Supreme Court, and to inaction by the Federal Election Commission and the IRS, super PACs and "dark money" 501(c)(4) groups are on the rise.

The one thing we do know is that darkness encourages bad behavior—more extreme messages, which feed the fires of polarization and keep candidates flinching when special-interest groups mention they have a (c)(4) or a super PAC. That's why it's critical that voters know exactly where the money is coming from. And the information should be available online immediately, presented in an intuitive and easy-to-navigate format to give the public the true transparency they need to make informed decisions.

Supreme Court Justice Antonin Scalia isn't on the side of reformers when it comes to most campaign finance issues. But get him talking about disclosure, and he lights up:

> For my part, I do not look forward to a society which, thanks to the Supreme Court, campaigns anonymously ... and even exercises the direct democracy of initiative and referendum hidden from public scrutiny and protected from the accountability of criticism. This does not resemble the Home of the Brave.

No matter your pet issue or level of partisanship, if you want to participate, you should do so in the public square. There is no uncertainty from the Supreme Court that disclosure is constitutionally sound—and necessary. It was a fundamental premise of the *Citizens United* decision, and everyone from New Jersey governor Chris Christie to *American Idol* contestant turned politician Clay Aiken agrees. That's another benefit: this is an area where the left and the right often find common ground.

A caveat: By themselves, transparency and disclosure will not create truly representative and responsive systems of governing. Those who claim otherwise are engaging in wishful thinking. As Harvard professor Larry Lessig says, recall the BP Deepwater Horizon oil spill of 2010 and the infamous live video stream that broadcast the torrent of oil as it billowed into the Gulf of Mexico: "The point is to stop the guck from pouring into the Gulf, not [just] to see it more clearly."[11]

But sunlight is the baseline for all reform. It's absolutely essential. Thanks to nonprofit groups like the Center for Responsive Politics, MapLight, the Sunlight Foundation, and the National Institute on Money in State Politics, anyone can click around and view much of the political money that's floating around in the system.

At the state level, transparency laws vary significantly, and few states deserve praise. The State Integrity Investigation, a project of several respected good-government groups, is a massive data-driven analysis of how effective states are at deterring corruption and promoting transparency. Each state government is graded based on 330 specific measures. The findings are somewhat chilling.

Connecticut ranks best in the nation, mostly due to components of its clean elections program. Unfortunately, though, it got the only A grade. Six others received a B- or better. Most of the pack was clustered at the failing end of the scale. Dead last is Wyoming, where the legislature exempted itself from open records laws and state officials aren't even required to disclose their investments (critical information for anyone attempting to assess conflicts of interest). The state scored an F, along with twenty others earning a D- or worse.

Of the bright spots, California's transparency requirements, managed by the Fair Political Practices Commission (FPPC), demand reporting on just about everything imaginable, from candidates' stock holdings to money flowing in and out of party committees. There's even a rule specifying the font size of the "paid for by" text on mass mailings.

California has also developed ways to tackle the "dark money" problem. They don't distinguish between entities (super PACs, (c)(4)s, (c)(6)s, etc.) or types of spenders (corporate, union, or individual), instead focusing their rules on one question: Is the organization spending money to influence elections? Groups spending more than $50,000 must reveal the names of their donors.

Montana also has a long history of standing up to big money. Their independent streak continued in 2015 with the passage of a state version of the DISCLOSE Act. The bill, introduced by a Republican and passed with bipartisan support, bans dark money outright. As state representative Bryce Bennett (D-MT) said, "If somebody's shooting at you, you deserve to know who's holding the gun."[12] The Montana legislation came into being because a shadowy pro-coal group was illegally coordinating with candidates while spending millions in local elections. But the only reason we know they were breaking the rules is because a box of incriminating documents turned up in Colorado—in a meth house. Voters shouldn't have to depend on the kindness of strangers, meth addicts or otherwise, to learn about political influence.

At the federal level, the landscape lacks adequate sunlight. The Democracy Is Strengthened by Casting Light on Spending in Elections Act of 2010 (DISCLOSE Act) has been floundering on the Hill for five years. It's a pretty straightforward bill that would, among other things, increase transparency around certain kinds of political giving and spending, and discourage political operatives from setting up unaccountable political attack groups.

DISCLOSE came within a single vote of clearing the Senate in 2010, but it has been shelved since then. That's a problem, because right now, only certain types of spenders are subject to disclosure rules, and those rules are not difficult to get around. Some groups have to report to the FEC, others to the SEC. Still others report only to the IRS and often do so months after their spending has taken place.

This independent spending is the guck that's harder to see. Nonprofit 501(c)(4) groups, exempt from donor disclosure rules, are especially easy conduits for "dark" money, which is simply political dollars that can't be traced to their source.

While the Hill falls into an ever-deeper state of dysfunction, though, federal agencies have the opportunity to make progress. The Securities and Exchange Commission could establish a rule mandating that all publicly traded companies disclose their political spending to their share-holders. The idea is a popular one. Since 2011, the SEC has been flooded with positive feedback from state treasurers, institutional and retail inves-tors, former SEC commissioners of both parties, philanthropic founda-tion leaders, nonprofit advocates, and 1.2 million Americans—the most public comments in the agency's history. A 2014 survey of 1,500 financial analysts found that two thirds support mandatory disclosure of corpo-rate political contributions.[13]

Some businesses already voluntarily disclose this information. The Center for Political Accountability measures the transparency practices of the three hundred largest companies in the S&P 500, and, encouragingly, scores are trending toward more disclosure. Familiar brands such as Capital One, UPS, Aflac, and Microsoft rank strikingly high, and many others have publicly committed to doing even more. But the SEC can, and should, make this reporting mandatory for all.

Another opportunity lies in the hands of the chief executive. With the stroke of his pen, President Obama could sign an executive order mandating that all federal contractors disclose their political activity. These companies receive trillions of taxpayer dollars. We, the taxpayers, have a right to know if and how they are attempting to influence politics and our government. As former Republican senator Larry Pressler (R-SD) wrote in *US News & World Report*, it's a "simple, long-overdue action [that] would go a long way towards restoring a dose of transparency and faith in our democracy."[14]

(3) Everyone Plays by the Same Commonsense Rules

Beyond campaign financing and transparency lies a realm of ideas that is too often overlooked: ethics and lobbying reforms. Many of these involve changing the way lobbyists interact with politicians and government officials.

Americans dislike lobbyists. They dislike them so much that in 2013 the

American League of Lobbyists changed its name to the Association of Government Relations Professionals. As in any industry, there are good lobbyists and bad lobbyists. Some are engaged in the profession because they believe in informing the legislative and regulatory process and in making the best possible arguments for their clients. Others' motives—and means—are less virtuous. They see it as a way to make money, lots of money. And they are willing to pump out endless amounts of false or misleading information to sully and confuse what should ideally be honest policy debates about tough issues.

Earlier in the book, we told you about the political scientist Lee Drutman and his in-depth study of the influence game in his book *The Business of America Is Lobbying*. He found that the balance of lobbying expenditures is vastly tilted toward businesses—80 percent of all reported spending, or $2.6 billion a year—and that the amount of political activity by corporations today is both unprecedented and completely unmatched by environmental, consumer protection, and public interest groups.[15] This inherent imbalance is reflected in the changing culture of Washington. As Demos senior fellow Michael Winship wrote:

> Fifty years ago, people came to Washington drawn by a sense of public service, however they defined it, and they often stayed in the public sector over much of their careers. Now working in government is a brief way station on the road to better things.[16]

Almost all lobbyists claim they get a bad rap. In recent years, though, even the lobbying industry has started to raise red flags about the system within which it is embedded. Jack Quinn, one of D.C.'s most prominent lobbyists and a cofounder of the firm Quinn, Gillespie and Associates, told the website Reddit that political money "has reached the point of being a cancer on our democracy."[17] John Feehery, who, as we noted earlier in the book, was Republican Dennis Hastert's communications director when Hastert was Speaker of the House, wrote in the *Wall Street Journal*, the system is not "just pretty bad. It's really bad." He added:

> If you ask any lobbyist in town about the campaign finance system, they would agree that it is fundamentally broken and needs to be fixed. They would tell you that they don't really want to drain their kid's college fund to give money to political campaigns. They would also tell you that they get hundreds of

requests every month to participate in fundraising efforts, and that they really don't have much of choice but to give in, every once in a while.

So here's our first fix. On behalf of lobbyists' kids' college funds, let's enact at the federal level what many states have in place: bans on campaign contributions from lobbyists. As the former lobbyist Jack Abramoff, who went to jail for crossing the line of influence peddling and is now focusing his energy on fixing the broken system, has said: "If you choose to lobby you need to abstain from campaign contributions. It's your choice either way. But you have to choose one, not both."[18] Twenty-nine states restrict the giving of campaign donations during legislative sessions. South Carolina prohibits lobbyists from making any campaign contributions at any time. The thinking: when an individual has business to do with the government (a registered lobbyist) and then gives money to a politician, it looks like corruption. Let's extend that logic to Washington, D.C., and every state capital in America.

Fix number two: call lobbyists lobbyists. As we reported earlier, 50 percent of politicians and their staff go from Capitol Hill to K Street, often to lobby for the industries they once were regulating, based on their committee assignments. Right now, the "cooling-off" period for former House members and senior Hill staffers is a year; former senators and staff must wait two. Former members of Congress can pass the time during their cooling-off periods by lobbying the executive branch, or state and local officials. And of course they can easily get around the lobbying bans entirely.

So, no more calling these people "policy advisers," or "strategic consultants," or "historians." Any retired congressman or senior staffer who makes contact with the legislative or executive branch for the purpose of influencing official actions is a lobbyist, plain and simple. The Association of Government Relations Professionals agrees. "If you're talking to a lawmaker about an issue or anything, you're lobbying," said AGRP president Dave Wenhold in 2010.[19]

Some members of Congress want to permanently jam the revolving door. In 2014, Senators Michael Bennet (D-CO) and Jon Tester (D-MT) introduced legislation that would institute a lifetime ban on lobbying for former members of Congress. In 2015, Representative Rod Blum (R-IA) introduced similar legislation in the House, observing, "This would be another step in that effort to make Congress more accountable to the people by reducing the incentive for our elected officials to use their position for their own personal gain."[20]

Framing such reform efforts not as campaign-finance-reform initiatives but as ethics and corruption fights can, in some places, help them gain unexpected support. Take Tallahassee, Florida. With the help of the reform group Represent.Us, they started a local campaign to "fight corruption" in their city. What made their strategy so notable, and so successful, was framing the debate around ending conflicts of interest and cronyism. The coalition they formed was a left-right effort including the Tea Party Network, the League of Women Voters, the Florida Alliance of Retired Americans, and Common Cause. And the law they established— with 67 percent of the vote!—requires, as Represent.Us has explained:

> A new, independent cop on the beat policing ethics laws, and ensuring everyone follows them. Lower contribution limits to prevent city candidates from amassing huge war chests from a small handful of special interest donors. And a citizen-funding system that enables anyone with a strong base of supporters to raise significant small contributions from everyday constituents, making city leaders more directly accountable to all voters—not just big donors. That means less cronyism and more efficient use of taxpayer money in the long run.

(4) Everyone Is Held Accountable

All the laws on the books are utterly irrelevant without a strong enforcement mechanism ensuring that everyone is held accountable to the laws.

The most powerful cop on the beat right now, on paper, is the Federal Election Commission, established, as we explained in part 1, after the Watergate scandals in the early 1970s. Unfortunately it's also the most broken regulatory body in Washington.

We'll let the experts diagnose the problems with the FEC in their own words. Current FEC Democratic chairwoman Ann Ravel calls the agency she heads "worse than dysfunctional."[21] Former Republican chairman Trevor Potter says it's "not healthy for our system."[22] Former Republican commissioner Frank Reiche lamented, "[It's] almost doomed to failure."[23] Former FEC general counsel Larry Noble says politicians are blatantly disregarding campaign finance law because "they are unafraid of enforcement."[24] And the verdict of the watchdog group the Center for Public

Integrity after a months-long investigation: "The FEC is rotting from the inside out."[25]

Potter says the central issues are fundamental philosophical differences and a lack of consensus around what the FEC's job actually is. The Democrats push for strong regulatory oversight, and the Republicans fight for "free speech" above everything else. So, instead, we get complete inaction, which, according to Noble, was the whole point: "It's the perfect agency for Congress—it regulates them and it doesn't do anything."[26]

The FEC's dysfunction has reached Comedy Central levels of self-parody. In 2009, the commissioners failed to come to consensus on whether to accept payment of a fine the candidate in question had already paid. At an event in 2015, they couldn't even agree on whether to serve bagels or donuts. Deadlocks are becoming tradition. With three votes each, the Democrats and Republicans are increasingly unable to pass rulings on either routine or critical election issues. These "no decisions" have increased nearly 20 percent since 2010, and by 2013, 41 percent of the cases before the commission could not garner the necessary four votes to be resolved.

As of the writing of this book, four of the six commissioners are serving on expired terms, and President Obama hasn't nominated anyone to take their places. The agency budget remains flat, while staffing levels (and morale) have fallen to a fifteen-year low. Meanwhile, workloads have exploded—analysts who review compliance issues are facing a quarter-million-page backlog.

Must campaigns disclose funding for online ads? Can foreign nationals donate to a ballot initiative? Just how independent does a super PAC truly need to be? No one knows, because the FEC can't decide. And according to Ellen Weintraub, one of the Democratic commissioners, "people feel free to ignore" the few rules that are left.[27] For example, several candidates for president spent 2015 openly coordinating with, and raising money for, super PACs in complete violation of the law—and in total contradiction of the "independent expenditures" premises of *Citizens United*. Jeb Bush helped his Right to Rise PAC raise almost $100 million as he kissed babies in Iowa and shook hands in New Hampshire, two critical primary states. At one event, Bush said, "I'm running for president in 2016," before quickly adding ". . . if I run."[28]

None of this is meant to depress you, but neither should the magnitude of this enforcement problem be downplayed. The agencies tasked with ensuring that our elections are fair and lawful need to be reformed.

It's a law and order issue—one that anyone who believes in such laws—and order—should get behind.

Larry Noble says that at the end of the day, the effectiveness of enforcement agencies like the FEC comes down to the commissioners who are appointed.[29] Some good-government groups have recommended creating a bipartisan congressional task force to determine the best ways to fix institutional issues in the FEC, including how to replace the ineffectual six-member commission structure. Others have floated the idea adding a seventh commissioner to break deadlocked votes (that seventh, they stipulate, would have to have impeccable nonpartisan credentials).

Of the enforcement agencies at the state level, once again California is a model. We told you about the Fair Political Practices Commission earlier. Kathay Feng of California Common Cause calls it "an extremely effective agency."[30] The FPPC doesn't just review the paperwork—it actively goes after rule breakers. When political contributors hoping to avoid detection funneled over $12 million through out-of-state dark money groups to support two 2012 ballot initiatives in the state, the FPPC investigated and ended up imposing a jaw-dropping $16 million fine. Feng believes it's the largest campaign finance-related fine levied by any state, ever.

There's a lesson to be learned here. When an enforcement agency is given the resources it needs, it can both react quickly to potential infractions and follow through on holding violators accountable. Trevor Potter, in a speech praising the FPPC, helps explain just how important this one-two punch can be:

> The combined effect demonstrated to political players and the citizens of California that the law is enforced in this state. This in turn increases citizens' faith in the institution created to defend their interests.[31]

Our system of self-government relies, in part, on a citizen's belief that someone is enforcing the rules of politics, keeping the game clean. If the FEC were able to replicate California's model, how much of a difference would it make in our elections? Noble is positive that it would help to alleviate cynicism and bring Americans back into the process. "If they had a system that worked, an FEC that was really enforcing the laws," he says, "they might feel more connected to our democracy. They might feel like they have a shot at it."[32]

CHAPTER 10

The Makings of an
All-American Movement

I hold it that a little rebellion now and then is a good thing, and as necessary in the political world as storms in the physical ... It is a medicine necessary for the sound health of government.

—THOMAS JEFFERSON

Fellow citizens: it's time for a little rebellion, for a new patriotic force to reclaim our right to self-government.

Many, many times in our past we've had to rise up and transform our democracy. Powerful movements emerged that brought forth heroes like Frederick Douglass, Susan B. Anthony, and Martin Luther King, Jr. Their demands became part of the DNA of our government—the Thirteenth, Fourteenth, and Fifteenth Amendments to the Constitution, ending slavery and extending rights to African Americans; the Nineteenth Amendment, providing women the right to vote; and the Civil Rights Act, putting a legal end to many ingrained practices of discrimination

We should take a moment to appreciate what remarkable achievements these were, not just for our country but for the course of world history. Just as our revolution had a deep impact on the psyche of Europeans and provided inspiration for the French Revolution and the rejection of monarchy, the American political movements of the nineteenth and twentieth centuries inspired similar action all over the world—and still do.

Our present fight—whether you see it as a fight against cronyism and corruption or a fight for self-government—has the potential to write the next historic chapter.

Sure, you say, but how? How do we build the power necessary to enact the solutions laid out in the previous chapter? How do we move forward?

The beginnings of a movement already exists, comprising liberals and conservatives, Southerners and New Englanders, environmentalists and economic libertarians, business leaders, people of faith, former members of Congress, and everyone in between. From coast to coast, people are agreeing that they might not agree on everything, but they can agree that without a functional democracy, none of us has the power even to be heard, let alone to enact our bright ideas into laws. But the size of the movement right now is more comparable to a battalion than to an army. And it will take an army to win.

We two authors are by no means veterans of social or political movements. We're pretty normal Midwestern and Southern guys who have spent most of our lives in the media, are deeply concerned about the future of the country we love, and are willing to fight to get it back on track. Despite our lack of experience as activists, we do have some suggestions about goals that need to be achieved: (1) change the debate, (2) build a bigger, broader reform movement, (3) win at the state and local levels, (4) win at the federal level, and we can tell you about some groups and leaders who are helping make these things happen.

(1) Change the Debate

As we have shown in previous chapters, the vast majority of Americans are outraged by the current system. However, they don't understand how it connects to their daily lives, and they are skeptical that it can ever be fixed. Too many people have decided that the country might forever work this way, with wealthy people and special interests using their financial power to rig the rules in their favor. The Republican pollster Frank Luntz summed it up nicely in an editorial he penned for the *New York Times* after the 2014 elections:

> The current narrative, that this election was a rejection of President Obama, misses the mark. So does the idea that it was a mandate for an extreme conservative agenda. According to a

survey my firm fielded on election night for the political-advocacy organization Each American Dream, it was more important that a candidate "shake up and change the way Washington operates." I didn't need a poll to tell me that. This year I traveled the country listening to voters, from Miami to Anchorage, 30 states and counting. And from the reddest rural towns to the bluest big cities, the sentiment is the same. People say Washington is broken and on the decline, that government no longer works for them—only for the rich and powerful . . . The results were less about the size of government than about making government efficient, effective and accountable.

We believe this insight is as relevant a mandate for the 2016 elections—perhaps even more relevant than it was in 2014—because 2016 promises to be completely dominated by millionaires and billionaires.

So, step one in changing the debate: Just like the famous journalist Bob Woodward did, let's call it the "governing crisis" that it is. Let's not mince words. Money in politics isn't just something bad that's getting worse—it's paralyzing this country. It's destroying the American experiment. Prominent Republicans and Democrats are increasingly using the term "oligarchy" to describe our current system of governing. Warren Buffett says we're headed toward plutocracy because the political system is so controlled by the wealthy that it's no longer capable of steering the economy back to the middle class. And as you've seen throughout this book, nearly everyone recognizes how hard it is to get anything meaningful done on behalf of the common good these days. We're screwed if we don't fix this problem.

Step two: Recognize the cynicism while simultaneously rejecting it. We understand that this is a tough fight, but it will be a lot less hard as more people join it.

Congressman John Sarbanes, who has long been an advocate of this cause and is the sponsor of the Government by the People Act that we discussed in the previous chapter, speaks candidly about acknowledging the pessimism:

> If I stand in front of an audience of randomly selected Americans, I know that 95 percent of them sitting out there think that Washington is bought and sold by big interests and that their voice is inconsequential. So I can go right to talking about the

minimum wage, job creation, and infrastructure, knowing that
they're saying, "You can't get any of it done, because the system is
rigged."

Or I can start by tapping on the microphone, and saying: "I
know that 95 percent of people in this room think government is
bought and sold by big money special interests. And you're right."
All of a sudden they wake up and say, "Maybe this guy actually
knows how we feel and has something to say to me."

One of the many reasons the two of us prefer to talk about the right
to self-government—as opposed to discussing "money in politics" or
"campaign finance reform"—is because we believe that that's how this
fight should be viewed. It's about patriotism first and foremost, not just
about tweaking a campaign finance law here or there. It's not just about
shining a light on "dark money." It's not simply about enhancing ethics
laws on Capitol Hill and reducing conflicts of interest in the state capitals.
This is about the uprightness of the American way. Self-governing is
about believing in our collective problem-solving abilities. De-rigging the
system allows us to solve more problems. Bare minimum, it allows us to
have fairer fights about fixing problems.

We could repeat here the barrage of voices that we have highlighted
throughout this book that are sounding the alarm. We could list the
striking quotes from commentators ranging from CEOs to dignitaries to
former Supreme Court justices to entertainment moguls to former senators to celebrities to current elected officials to Nobel Prize and Pulitzer
Prize winners to the heads of major nonprofit organizations to leading
philanthropists to presidents and vice presidents. We could print dozens
of pages of public opinion polls that show how Republicans, independents, and Democrats feel the deck is stacked against them. But we don't
need to. This might be one of a dozen or so causes about which Americans
of all stripes agree.

So let's stop saying this is another one of those big problems that seem
hard to fix and realize it's a crisis we *can* fix, *have* to fix, and are willing to
come together to fix. All of the solutions laid out in the previous chapter,
wonky as they are, will hopefully provide inspiration and guidance for
anyone interested in how it can be done.

Step three: Set the problem on the kitchen table. This book is in large
part an effort to do exactly that. We hope we've shown you that we all pay
a price for a political system dominated by those who can afford to play.

We need to make more people aware of the connections between political and policy manipulations and the negative effects in their daily lives— why their neighborhood is still suffering the effects of foreclosure or why their grandma is paying so much for her prescription drugs or why their children are struggling with chronic health issues. Why is this step necessary? Because, although people readily recognize the problem of Big Money, it seems abstract, something that happens far away from home behind closed doors in the halls of power. When they are worried about putting food on the table, getting people motivated around abstractions is almost impossible. However, when they see that the problem is directly linked to pain points in their lives, they become more inspired to fight for reform—especially when they also see that there are many viable solutions at hand. The data to connect the dots is easy enough to find. Just check out the Center for Responsive Politics (CRP), the Sunlight Foundation, MapLight.org, Issue One (run by Nick Penniman), the Center for Public Integrity, ProPublica, or the National Institute on Money in State Politics (NIMSP).

Fourth: Let's make this issue a feature of every major political contest. The money raised and spent in 2016 will shatter all records. It'll be a Wild West–style Big Money shootout, right in front of us. The spectacle will offer reformers from all over the country the opportunity to press politicians and to organize pro-reform rallies, affinity groups, house parties, and voting blocs. Call such groups and voting blocs the Patriots for Democracy or something that connects with others at a gut level.

We need to make it crystal clear to politicians that they must take a strong stance on cleaning up Washington (or the state capital, or City Hall) if they want our votes. In the past thirty years, gun rights advocates have successfully made the Second Amendment an issue that can either make or break a political campaign. During that same period of time, "pro-choice" and "pro-life" advocates have accomplished the same thing for their primary issue. Now we have to do likewise for the issue we all have in common: restoring our democracy.

Efforts are already under way in the primary states of New Hampshire (called the New Hampshire Rebellion) and Iowa (called Iowa Pays the Price) to force presidential candidates to take clear, strong stances against the harm that Big Money is doing to the health of our republic. By the time this book is published, we should know whether those efforts have had the desired effect. And the state chapters of liberal organizations such as Common Cause or U.S. PIRG, and conservative organizations such as

Take Back Our Republic, continue to organize around this issue and ensure that politicians are feeling the heat.

Another way to exert pressure on our politicians is to provide feedback to all of the proxies, volunteers, and operatives who work in and around their campaigns. So when some young people knock on your door to talk to you about candidates they're hoofing for, tell them that you want to know what the politician will do to clean up the money-in-politics mess. You know those little handheld electronic devices they carry around while doing their door knocking? The data they collect—including your views on specific issues—is all assessed by the candidates' campaigns as a barometer of what the voters care about. Then lots of that data is dumped into master databases at the national level, where it is commingled with other data from other campaigns all over the country to inform the political parties and presidential candidates about which issues are hot and which are not. Similarly, if you get a fundraising phone call from a campaign, bring the issue up. When a polling firm asks you—those of you who actually still answer your phones—what issues you care about, make sure you mention this as a top priority. If it's not on their standard list of issues—jobs, education, national security, crime, health care, environment—then tell them to add it.

(2) Build a Bigger, Broader Reform Movement

Most of the organizations that work on this cause accomplish a tremendous amount with meager financial support, and there is nothing they would like more than to work themselves out of a job. These groups are full of bright, competent people who could be doing more lucrative work in the for-profit world. Or they could even stay in the nonprofit realm and put their shoulders to the wheels of causes that offer more immediate satisfaction. But, whether for love of country or hatred of corruption, they are spending their weeks—long weeks much of the time—fighting this Goliath. (And don't forget that David won that fight.)

You have doubtless heard of some of them: Common Cause, Public Citizen, Every Voice, People for the American Way. Others, you probably haven't, although the work they do—focused on making campaign finance data easily available to the public—you have probably benefited from. We mentioned them already: the Sunlight Foundation, the Center for Responsive Politics, MapLight.org, the National Institute on Money in State Politics. Others engage in legal battles over campaign finance law:

the Brennan Center for Justice, the Campaign Legal Center, Justice at Stake, Demos.

In recent years, a few organizations have been formed for the primary purpose of amending the United States Constitution, with an emphasis on effectively overturning *Citizens United* by constitutionally granting Congress and the states the authority to regulate and limit campaign fundraising and spending as they see fit. Groups such as Free Speech for People and Move to Amend are leading the charge. They've been remarkably successful in winning symbolic victories. More than six hundred anti–*Citizens United* resolutions have been passed by state and local governments.

A host of organizations that don't normally focus on defending democracy are now pitching in some of their time. In 2013, led by the Sierra Club, Greenpeace, the NAACP, and the Communications Workers of America, an effort called the Democracy Initiative was formed for the purpose of engaging environmental, labor, voting rights, civil rights, and good-government groups into a single coalition. Additional efforts are under way to connect the fight for self-government to #BlackLivesMatter and other vibrant social justice movements, including campaigns for raising the minimum wage and prison reform.

All of this momentum is promising. But don't let it lull you into thinking that that you're not needed. Most of the groups named above have very limited budgets, and most appeal almost exclusively to already activated liberals. As we said, it's a battalion, not an army. And a lot of the troops in it have been fighting this fight for a long time. It's time for new faces and new energy to emerge, especially from unexpected places. As the TV journalist Bill Moyers, who has written and spoken extensively about money in politics over the years, likes to say, our mentality should be: "Is this a private fight or can anyone get in it?"

This is an all-American cause. A democratic republic is the hardware that all of our software runs on. We may not enjoy one another's software choices all of the time, but we can agree that we all need the hardware to work.

Some unexpected organizations have cropped up in recent years, animated by that spirit, with a focus on generating support for reform with new constituencies. These types of groups include Issue One, Take Back Our Republic, and Represent.Us.

Josh Silver, the head of Represent.Us, is the reformer who successfully brought Tea Party activists and progressives together in 2014 to win the "anti-corruption" ballot initiative in Tallahassee, Florida. The experience led him to the conclusion that "This idea that reform is exclusively a pet project of the American left is 100 percent false." Says Silver, "If you ask conservatives where they stand on the policies we need to actually fix this problem, they're overwhelmingly in favor. We need to call out corrupt behavior regardless of party affiliation, and make it clear that we believe it should be illegal for anyone to use money to purchase political influence. Period."

As polling demonstrates, the problem resonates across political boundaries—at least, outside Washington, D.C.

- A comprehensive poll conducted by the *New York Times* and CBS News in the spring of 2015 showed that 84 percent of adults—including 90 percent of Democrats and 80 percent of Republicans—think that money has too much influence in American political campaigns. Even the richest Americans agreed: 85 percent of adults making $100,000 or more believe money has too much influence in the election process.
- In the same poll, another 85 percent said they want to see our campaign finance system either fundamentally changed or completely overhauled. Just a single example of such fundamental change: 80 percent of Democrats, 71 percent of Republicans, and 76 percent of independents favor contribution limits. The *New York Times* reporters Nick Confessore and Megan Thee-Brenan summarized it in their article on the poll: "The findings reveal deep support among Republicans and Democrats alike for new measures to restrict the influence of wealthy givers, including limiting the amount of money that can be spent by 'super PACs' and forcing more public disclosure on organizations now permitted to intervene in elections without disclosing the names of their donors."
- A November 2013 poll by Global Strategy Group showed that Republicans are as likely as any other voters to say that eliminating corruption in politics is very important (86 percent for Republicans, 85 percent for all voters). It also showed that Republicans are about as likely as Democrats to agree that politicians respond primarily to donors (65 percent of Republicans, 70 percent of Democrats) and that they are more likely to represent the moneyed interests than to do what is in the public interest (53 percent of Republicans, 56 percent of Democrats).

- A 2014 poll conducted by Public Citizen found that on a scale of 1 to 10, with 10 being extremely important, Democrats rated reducing the influence of money in politics a 7.7 and Republicans a 7.0.

In our conversations with prominent Republicans, a number of arguments against Big Money came up again and again.

First, there is a rising concern within the party about crony capitalism. We have devoted a lot of space in this book to detailing examples of such cronyism and highlighting the many conservative voices—from Luigi Zingales at the University of Chicago's School of Business to Peter Schweizer at the Hoover Institute—who are sounding the alarm.

Second, the political parties generally spend the same aggregate amount of money in election cycles. Although major Republican donors, such as the Koch brothers are chipping in huge amounts of money to outside groups, it isn't clear that either party has the financial upper hand. Witness the fact (see chart below) that there is nearly always, in aggregate money spent, basic parity between Republicans and Democrats in each election cycle.

Finally, as we have said over and over again, everyone is concerned about the health of the republic. We're all Americans who love this country. And we all—Republican, Democrat, independent—feel as if we have been kicked to the curb. We are losing faith, shutting down, tuning out. Republican

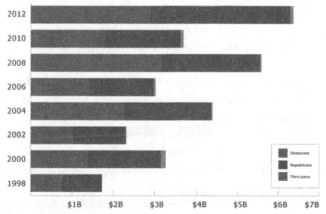

Total Cost of U.S. Elections (by Party) (1998–2012)

senator Lindsey Graham noted this emerging trend in the spring of 2015 when he said: "You're going to have money dumped in this [2016] election cycle that's going to turn off the American people." Graham has said we might need to amend the Constitution to reverse *Citizens United*. Other prominent Republicans who have joined the fight for reform include former senator Alan Simpson (R-WY), one of the leading voices of the need to reduce the national debt. Also in the phalanx is former senator Chuck Hagel (R-NE), who also served as President Obama's Secretary of Defense from 2013–2014. So is former representative Porter Goss (R-FL), who was President George W. Bush's director of the Central Intelligence Agency. Sean Hannity has devoted segments of his show to exposing lobbying and cronyism in D.C., at one point dedicating a whole show to the topic. The one-hour special featured a mini-documentary, produced by journalist Peter Schweizer and Stephen Bannon, then the executive chairman of the conservative site Breitbart News. The way Breitbart.com described the show: "'Boomtown: Washington, The Imperial City' reveals how Washington's power elite leverage their crony connections to vacuum taxpayer wallets, bankrolling their lifestyles of luxury and opulence—all under the guise of what's best for America."

There are more than one hundred such powerful Republican leaders who have gone on the record in support of reform, joining the tens of millions of Republican voters who feel the same.

John Pudner is an example of a reformer who understands the Beltway, but has chosen to work at the grassroots level for most of his career. A Republican political strategist with an uncanny record for winning underdog campaigns, he comes from Richmond, Virginia, and is the oldest of nine children. He cut his teeth in Southern conservative move- ment circles, where he married his love of grassroots organizing with his love of statistical data to launch surprising insurgent efforts that got him noticed, and got him good consulting contracts.

The biggest electoral feather in Pudner's cap is his work for Republican congressman Dave Brat, who ousted Eric Cantor (R-VA) in the 2014 Republican primary. At the time, Cantor was the Republican majority leader, the second most powerful member of the House, and was believed by all to be immune from serious primary challenges. But Brat and Pudner didn't accept that notion and launched an underfunded, outsider, Tea Party–style campaign that framed Cantor as being out of touch with his constituents and part of a system of cronyism. Brat relished landing lines against Cantor such as "All the investment banks in the New York and D.C.—those guys should have gone to jail. Instead of going to jail, they went on Eric's Rolodex, and they are sending him big checks." It was conservative populism, updated.

Months after Brat's victory, Pudner decided to launch the organization Take Back Our Republic to organize more conservatives to clean up the money-in-politics mess. His view:

> We are simply saying, "Look at the role of money in politics as a part of this—we know it influences the system, but how? Does it lead to increased spending in the interests of those who give money? Does it lead to regulations that benefit certain companies or special interests rather than the general interest? Does it force members of Congress to spend too much time raising money rather than spending time listening to ordinary citizens?" I think the answer is yes.

The organization's board consists of Bush-Cheney Republicans including Mark McKinnon, who was President George W. Bush's communications adviser; Juleanna Glover, who was a senior aide to Vice President Dick Cheney; and Richard Painter, who also served in the George W. Bush White House. Take Back Our Republic is young, but it has accomplished a lot in its short life—setting up chapters throughout the country, shining the light on foreign money affecting U.S. elections, and much more.

Pudner and Brat represent a strong vein of the conservative movement that is as deeply concerned about the dominance of Big Money as are the most progressive Democrats. To them, the Wall Street bailouts are Exhibit A. Hillary Clinton is Exhibit B.

A few weeks after Hillary officially announced her second run for the White House, Mark Meckler, formerly a major figure in the Tea Party Patriots, raked her over the coals in the pages of the *Washington Times*:

> The Clintons only sold nights in the Lincoln Bedroom to just a few hundred of their closest friends, right? And who can forget Clinton scandal figure Johnny Chung's defining quote: "I see the White House as like a subway: You have to put in coins to open the gates."

Other conservative leaders feel as if Big Money makes the party more wedded to the Beltway than to the base. Grassroots Republicans were particularly infuriated by the campaign finance rider we mentioned earlier that was attached to a $1.1 trillion appropriations bill signed by President Obama just before Congress left for Christmas recess in 2014. The provision significantly raised the cap on how much an individual could contribute to national political party committees from $97,200 to $777,600 per year. The conservative talk radio host Mark Levin perhaps best articulated outside-the-Beltway concerns when he called the rider "an outrage among many outrages" and an attempt by Mitch McConnell "to destroy any conservative—any group—that seeks to challenge an incumbent, to destroy the entire primary process."

Concerns of how money in politics leads to an increasingly rigged economic game are starting to mobilize business leaders as well. We've discussed in previous chapters some of the voices of business and finance speaking out against Big Money. Voices like theirs are backed up by pro-business groups like the Committee for Economic Development (CED). A 2011 report issued by the group, titled "Hidden Money," stated: "The influence of money [in Washington] can sustain inefficient or outmoded businesses, thereby subverting and frustrating the creative innovation that encourages new investment, spurs business development, and keeps jobs and investment at home."

In 2013, the CED conducted a survey of three hundred business executives—not just people who work in the corporate world, but folks who inhabit corner offices—about the influence of money in politics. The results were so stunning, and so thoroughly defied the conventional wisdom in Washington that "campaign finance reform" is somehow anti-business, that it's worth printing here one of the PowerPoint slides from the survey.

It's probably no surprise that a similar study conducted a year later by a group called Small Business Majority produced similarly resounding results: 72 percent of small business owners said major changes were needed to the campaign finance system; only 4 percent said the current system is fine.

As you can imagine, there are forces within the business community that want to keep the current system in place, perhaps because they benefit from it. The U.S. Chamber of Commerce, which spent $32 million in the 2014 midterm elections, has been customarily hostile to most campaign finance reform efforts, even the most modest efforts to increase transparency, claiming that such reforms would defang businesses. At an event hosted by the Chamber late in 2014, the group's head, Tom Donahue,

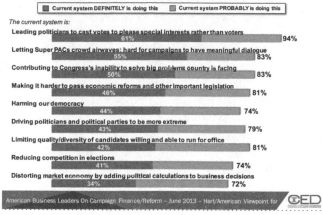

Current System Pleases Special Interest, Empowers Super PACs, Hurts Country In General

▪ Current system DEFINITELY is doing this   ▪ Current system PROBABLY is doing this

The current system is:

Leading politicians to cast votes to please special interests rather than voters
61% — 94%

Letting Super PACs crowd airwaves: hard for campaigns to have meaningful dialogue
55% — 83%

Contributing to Congress's inability to solve big problems country is facing
50% — 83%

Making it harder to pass economic reforms and other important legislation
46% — 81%

Harming our democracy
44% — 74%

Driving politicians and political parties to be more extreme
43% — 79%

Limiting quality/diversity of candidates willing and able to run for office
42% — 81%

Reducing competition in elections
41% — 74%

Distorting market economy by adding political calculations to business decisions
34% — 72%

American Business Leaders On Campaign Finance/Reform – June 2013 – Hart/American Viewpoint for CED

What Business Leaders Think of the Political System
Source: Committee for Economic Development's presentation, *American Business Leaders On Campaign Finance And Reform.*

hyperbolically stated: "They say it's about transparency, that's a laugh . . . the ultimate goal is to ban all corporate political speech and lobbying spending." As far as we know, not a single piece of legislation has ever been proposed that would do either of those things. No one in the reform community is talking about ending lobbying; they are talking about reforming it and delinking lobbying and money. Similarly, no one is talking about ending "corporate political speech." If corporate interests want to run campaigns to weigh in on legislation they either like or don't like, they should do so, just as nonprofit corporations like environmental and consumer watchdog groups should.

But, beyond the hyperbole, the Chamber wields an enormous megaphone in Washington and wants to convince business leaders that reducing the role of money in politics is somehow anti-corporate, as opposed to pro-America and anti-cronyism. Encouraging more business voices to emerge—like the vast majorities that are represented in the CED poll we just highlighted—is essential.

Just as we need more business leaders to stand up and speak out, we also need more representatives of mainstream groups to do so. We're thinking of groups, some of which are referred to throughout this book, that work to improve air quality, reduce obesity, get fewer kids to smoke, protect people from toxins in their food, improve product safety, engage young people in public service, alleviate poverty, improve education—all should see themselves as active players in improving the functioning of our government and the political system on which it rests.

Take Alan Khazei as an example of someone who has realized such connections. In 1988, after attending Harvard College, he and his roommate, Michael Brown, cofounded City Year—at the time, a first-of-its kind program to engage other college-aged kids from all backgrounds in a year of community service. The idea took off quickly, and in 1991 it caught the eye of then Arkansas governor Bill Clinton, who wanted to see up close how the program worked. As Clinton has said of his subsequent trip to Boston: "The lights came on in my mind and I said 'this is what I want to do.'"

Two years later, President Clinton, Eli Segal, Alan Khazei, Michael Brown, and others worked together to replicate City Year at the national level—the program was called AmeriCorps. To date, more than 900,000 people have served in AmeriCorps and have dedicated more than 1 billion hours of community service to our country.

Khazei now heads a group called Be the Change, which is committed to building coalitions on behalf of complicated issues such as national service, combating poverty, and empowering veterans. He feels that remaking the relationship between money and politics is necessary for anyone—or any organization—working to improve the public good. He told us,

> I've long believed we need two major reforms to make our democracy work and truly citizen-led: universal national service, in which there is an opportunity and expectation that all young people will spend a year in service to our communities and country; and reform of our currently corrosive money-in-politics system. If we don't enact sweeping campaign finance reform we will never see progress on the major challenges facing our country—in education, the environment, fighting poverty, income inequality, health care and more because the special interests and powerful lobbies will continue to get their way, crowding out the desires, hopes and dreams of the American people.

Good-government groups have been at this fight for a long, long time. Reinforcements from conservatives, business leaders, and mainstream nonprofit groups are needed to amplify the dire need for reform and make those calls reverberate across all sectors. When elected officials get phone calls from business leaders and public health leaders and

Republican leaders in their districts, that's when a new political reality will start to set in: Deal with this problem, or we'll all work together to find someone who will.

(3) Win at the State and Local Levels

Money's dominance of politics in the last forty years has been more defined by losses—many of them delivered by the Supreme Court—than by wins. That's why we're in the dismal shape we're in. We've let it go too long.

Obviously, we have to reverse the trend. Given how dysfunctional Washington currently is, cities and states provide the best near-term opportunities to pass transformational legislation or win major ballot initiatives. They are, as Justice Louis Brandeis once said, the laboratories of democracy. Such wins will demonstrate that there is a growing political will for reform.

This theory of change—from the states up to the federal level—has been embraced by many other movements throughout history. Regardless of where you stand on the issue of same-sex marriage, it has been one of the most successful social justice movements of our time. In 2003, not a single state allowed same-sex couples to marry, and less than 40 percent of Americans believed gays should have the right to do so. In the 2004 elections, the Republican strategist Karl Rove successfully deployed it as a key "wedge" issue to increase evangelical turnout for George W. Bush's reelection. A mere decade later, thirty-seven states allow same-sex couples to wed, the Supreme Court has validated the right to marriage for all, and public support for marriage equality is at an all-time high—more than 60 percent.

The recent wave of big victories for gay rights came after years of small ones. Bill Smith, who now runs a Washington strategy firm called Civitas Public Affairs, has spent nearly two decades immersed in political and grassroots organizing on behalf of the cause. Some of his time is now spent working on reducing the role of money in politics. About the need to start putting state and local points on the board, he told us:

> There's nothing that creates a winning culture better than winning. LGBT movement strategists knew that we couldn't go from an audacious idea to a national victory overnight. So while we created a steady drumbeat in the national conversation, we focused most of our energy on winning in the states, through legislatures, courts, and eventually at the ballot box. Recognition

of domestic partnerships, even at the municipal level, was a win.
Civil unions in state legislatures were wins, and of course full
marriage rights in a state were wins. Every win created
momentum, and even in our losses we learned lessons along the
way to get better at the game.

We need to amplify and broadcast wins when we get them, particularly to
combat the forces of resignation and cynicism. As we covered in the last
chapter, solutions are being implemented all over the country, but the
movement is doing a poor job of making sure citizens are informed
about them.

In the previous chapter we highlighted many effective laws that are
already in place in states and cities. Reform advocates have set their sights
on winning major reform measures in more than a dozen states by the
end of 2016. They are also aiming at counties and cities, including Denver,
San Diego, Buffalo, Chicago, and D.C. Such efforts are inherently fluid, so
by the time this book is published, some of the goals might have shifted.
But the agenda is ambitious, and it needs all the financial and grassroots
support that can be mustered. Strong victories in November of 2015 in
Seattle, Maine, and San Francisco—in which reformers passed new ethics,
lobbying, disclosure, and campaign finance laws—should encourage
more action and investment.

(4) Win at the Federal Level

Although we believe the best chance for major legislative progress in the
near term is at the state level, we are by no means writing Washington off.
Winning incremental victories in D.C. in the coming year is extremely
important for building the kind of momentum inside the Beltway that
will be needed to pass new and powerful laws down the road.

Remember, from the previous chapter, that President Obama has until
January of 2017 to use his authority over the executive branch to increase
transparency with federal contractors. "President Obama could bring the
dark money into the sunlight in time for the 2016 election," noted Michael
Waldman of the Brennan Center for Justice at the New York University
School of Law. "It's the single most tangible thing anyone could do to
expose the dark money that is now polluting politics."[1]

Also remember that the head of the Securities and Exchange Commission
has a similar opportunity to take meaningful action by making a rule that

would force corporations to disclose their political activity to their shareholders. Three former SEC chiefs, including Republican chairman William Donaldson, have pressed the SEC to approve the measure and more than a million comments have been submitted to the SEC in favor of it.

All of these are small steps that will help build momentum for an eventual major push for federal legislation that overhauls the way we finance politics in America. We firmly believe that the mightiest reform of all is some kind of citizen-funded system—one that positions regular people, who reside in the districts that our elected officials serve, at the center of political funding, and therefore political power.

We by no means mean to diminish the importance of transparency, stronger ethics and lobbying laws, and functional enforcement agencies. As we have said, there is no single silver bullet. But unless the funding of politics is placed in the hands of the many instead of being dominated by the few, we will never achieve, as Lincoln envisioned, a government of the people, by the people, for the people.

How will we know when we have developed the power to get such legislation passed? We'll know when politicians are winning elections in part because of their stance on the issue. We'll know when ending the reign of Big Money is regularly ranking in the top five concerns Americans are expressing in national polls. We'll know when legislative victories at the local and state level suddenly seem to be occurring everywhere. We'll know when the problem is seen as an all-American cause to preserve the right of self-government, with liberals, centrists, and conservatives putting their other differences aside to fight side by side on behalf of that right.

David Donnelly, who runs the group Every Voice, is a veteran of the reform movement. He's been working at it for twenty years and has helped establish some of the strongest citizen-funded systems in the country. In reflecting on the nature of the battle ahead, he told us:

> We need to build a broad-based, diverse movement of millions of Americans from all walks of life. And to do that, we must show that winning is possible and it starts in city councils, state legislatures, and through citizen-initiated petitions at the ballot box. When we pass real reform—including small donor policies—at the local and statewide level, we inspire hope that everyday people can get more involved in politics and have their voices heard. But winning isn't just about showing we can win; it's about building the apparatus and momentum to move Congress and the White

House. What we're doing now are the first flames of a prairie fire
that will sweep across the country and reach Washington, D.C.

Remember, this is what we Americans do.

*The gap between rich and poor has never been wider . . . legislative
stalemate paralyzes the country . . . corporations resist federal regulations . . . spectacular mergers produce giant companies . . . the
influence of money in politics deepens.*

The above snippets sound as if they were torn from recent news reports.
Actually, they're from Doris Kearns Goodwin's book *The Bully Pulpit*,
about Teddy Roosevelt, William Howard Taft, and the early-twentieth-
century era of investigative journalism. While reading the book, and
others about that time period, we were continually struck by the remarkable similarities between then and now. We described some of them in
part 1, but want to reiterate the point here.

America's last Gilded Age gave rise to rebellious fires, the flames of
which eventually spread to Teddy, a well-to-do Republican and progressive who was the single greatest champion of campaign finance reform
this country has ever seen. He didn't believe in reform as an end in itself.
He saw it as a means to reclaim the right to self-government, and the right
for every person to have an equal opportunity to get ahead in life—what
he termed a "square deal." In his words:

> Now, this means that our government, national and State, must
> be freed from the sinister influence or control of special interests.
> Exactly as the special interests of cotton and slavery threatened
> our political integrity before the Civil War, so now the great
> special business interests too often control and corrupt the men
> and methods of government for their own profit. We must drive
> the special interests out of politics . . . For every special interest is
> entitled to justice, but not one is entitled to a vote in Congress, to
> a voice on the bench, or to representation in any public office.

We're not sure where the next Teddy Roosevelt might come from, but we
do know that the fires have been lit. Throughout this book, we've cast a
spotlight on some of the colossal collateral damage that results from
coin-operated governing: money over merit; influence over evidence;

creeping cronyism; demoralized and distracted elected officials; and a pervasive sense throughout the country that things might never get better because we, the people, no longer have the power to make things better.

No one wants to stay stuck here. This is not the American mindset that has made us the envy of the world. We're the ones who overthrew a monarch and flew to the moon. We often let our differences divide us, we sometimes overreach, and we don't always fix things correctly. But then we try again, knowing that we might never arrive at a perfect union but that we always want to keep moving in that direction.

It's time to put aside our differences and move confidently together in that direction once again.

We started the book by quoting the Massachusetts constitution, which John Adams helped write. We want to remind you of that quote again:

> Government is instituted for the common good; for the protection, safety, prosperity, and happiness of the people; and not for the profit, honor, or private interest of any one man, family, or class of men; therefore, the people alone have an incontestable, unalienable, and indefeasible right to institute government; and to reform, alter, or totally change the same, when their protection, safety, prosperity, and happiness require it.

As we noted, these words were inspired by the Declaration of Independence and then provided inspiration for the crafting of the federal Constitution, seven years later. For us, these beautiful words best articulate our country's vision of a vibrant society. They also inspire all of us to constantly realize that we have an unalienable right to "reform, alter or totally change" our government when it has betrayed the common good. That's a weighty task, no doubt. But we should be comforted by the ease with which it is stated in so many of the founding documents and Founders' letters. The message to us citizens is: if it breaks, fix it, or get rid of it!

We hope you'll find it in your heart to join the very American struggle to fix our broken government.

Acknowledgments

This book was not just collaboration between the two of us. Many people chipped in, and to them we are immensely grateful. So, at the risk of sounding like two actors who just won Oscars and are trying to not get cut off by the music, here we go.

Thanks to: Anton Mueller, our editor at Bloomsbury, for his deep and thoughtful feedback and his patience; George Gibson, the publishing director of Bloomsbury USA, for his enthusiasm about this book and this topic; Gabrielle Sellei, our lawyer, who acted as so much more than that throughout this whole process; Nick Penniman IV, Nick's dad, for his contributions and thoughts about energy policy and corporate subsidies; Keenan Steiner for his copious research, reporting and insights and his lithe style; Laurie Roberts for helping us lay out the wonkery; Leigh Beasley for her "shock and awe" help early on; Erik Lampmann for his ruminations on cronyism; Jack Noland for his historical research and willingness to chip in whenever and wherever; Kyle Enochs for the same; Caitlyn Weber for the terrific info graphics and charts you see throughout the book; and Gleni Bartels for her expert eye and firm yet friendly nudging as the book trekked through production. Nick offers a special thanks to the staff and board of his organization, Issue One, for allowing him to write this book while also managing the expansion of a very busy startup nonprofit group.

We, of course, owe a huge debt of gratitude to our dear families, who cheered us on and gave us the time and space we needed to get this book into the end zone. Sarah, Nicky, Mac, Winnie, Linda, Da, Lou, Alex, and Morgan. Boundless love and thanks.

Notes

Introduction

1 https://www.opensecrets.org/overview/blio.php.

1. How We Got Here

1 "To George Logan," in *The Works of Thomas Jefferson: Volume* XII, Thomas Jefferson, edited by Paul Leicester Ford (G. P. Putnam's Sons, 1905), 44.

2 "George Washington Plied Voters with Booze," Paul Bedard, *US News & World Report*, November 8, 2011, http://www.usnews.com/news/blogs /washington-whispers/2011/11/08/george-washington-plied-voters-with-booze.

3 Robert E. Mutch, *Buying the Vote: A History of Campaign Finance Reform* (Oxford University Press, 2014), 46.

4 Zephyr Teachout, "The Anti-Corruption Principle," *Cornell Law Review* 94:341, accessed July 14, 2015, 374, http://www.lawschool.cornell.edu /research/cornell-law-review/upload/Teachout-Final.pdf?q=anti-corruption percent7Bporsyar_end percent7D.

5 Doris Kearns Goodwin, *The Bully Pulpit: Theodore Roosevelt, William Howard Taft, and the Golden Age of Journalism* (Simon and Schuster, 2013), 299.

6 Rebecca Edwards and Sarah DeFeo, "Trusts & Monopolies," *1896: The Presidential Campaign: Cartoons & Commentary*, 2000, http://projects.vassar. edu/1896/trusts.html.

7 Matthew O'Brien, "The Most Expensive Election Ever . . . 1896," *Atlantic*, November 6, 2012, http://www.theatlantic.com/business/archive/2012/11/the-most-expensive-election-ever-1896/264649/.

8 Mutch, *Buying the Vote*, 1.

9 Kenneth P. Vogel, *Big Money: 2.5 Billion Dollars, One Suspicious Vehicle, and a Pimp–On the Trail of the Ultra-Rich Hijacking American Politics* (PublicAffairs, 2014), 39.

10 John Milton Cooper Jr., "Theodore Roosevelt," *Encyclopaedia Britannica Online*, August 25, 2014, http://www.britannica.com/EBchecked/topic/509347/Theodore-Roosevelt/8429/The-Square-Deal#ref673089.

11 "The Northern Securities Case," Theodore Roosevelt Center, http://www.theodorerooseveltcenter.org/Learn-About-TR/TR-Encyclopedia/Capitalism-and-Labor/The-Northern-Securities-Case.aspx.

12 *A Compilation of the Messages and Speeches of Theodore Roosevelt*, vol. 1, edited by Alfred Henry Lewis, Bureau of National Literature and Art, 1906, 500.

13 "United States Presidential Election of 1904," *Encyclopaedia Britannica Online*, http://www.britannica.com/event/United-States-presidential-election-of-1904.

14 Mutch, *Buying the Vote*, 43.

15 "The Root of All Evil," *New York Times*, August 13, 1875.

16 "Fifth Annual Message," Theodore Roosevelt, UCSB American Presidency Project, December 5, 1905, http://www.presidency.ucsb.edu/ws/?pid=29546.

17 "Sixth Annual Message," Theodore Roosevelt, UCSB American Presidency Project, December 3, 1906, http://www.presidency.ucsb.edu/ws/?pid=29547.

18 Mutch, *Buying the Vote*, 74–76.

19 Ibid., 93.

20 "Message to Congress on the Hatch Act," Franklin D. Roosevelt, UCSB American Presidency Project, http://www.presidency.ucsb.edu/ws/?pid=15781.

21 Mutch, *Buying the Vote*, 106–107.

22 Ibid., 109.

23 Harry S. Truman, "On the Veto of the Taft-Hartley Bill," U.Va. Miller Center, June 20, 1947, http://millercenter.org/president/truman/speeches/speech-3344.

24 U.S. Government Brief in *United States v. Congress of Industrial Organizations*, quoted in Mutch, *Buying the Vote*, 109.

25 Mutch, *Buying the Vote*, 50.

26 "Appendix 4: Brief History," Federal Election Commission, http://www.fec.gov/info/appfour.htm.

27 "How Presidential Public Financing Works," *Public Citizen*, July 2012, https://www.citizen.org/documents/presidential-election-public-financing-how-it-works.pdf.

28 Comptroller General of the United States, "Report of the Office of Federal Elections of the General Accounting Office in Administering the Federal Election Campaign Act of 1971," U.S. Government Accountability Office, 1975, 23–24.

29 "Appendix 4," Federal Election Commission.

30 "About the FEC," Federal Election Commission, http://www.fec.gov/about .shtml.

31 Mutch, *Buying the Vote*, 9.

32 James Taranto, "Nine Decades at the Barricades," *Wall Street Journal*, August 1, 2014, http://www.wsj.com/articles/the-weekend-interview-nine-decades-at-the-barricades-1406931516.

33 *Nixon v. Shrink Missouri Government PAC*, 528 U.S. 377 (2000) (J. P. Stevens, concurring).

34 "Lincoln Bedroom Guests Gave $5.4 Million," *CNN AllPolitics*, February 26, 1997, http://www.cnn.com/ALLPOLITICS/1997/02/26/clinton.lincoln/.

35 Doug Weber, "Unlimited Presidential Spending: The Curse of Steve Forbes," Center for Responsive Politics, December 27, 2011, http://www .opensecrets.org/news/2011/12/unlimited-presidential-fundraising/.

36 Mutch, *Buying the Vote*, 10.

37 R. Sam Garrett, "The State of Campaign Finance Policy: Recent Developments and Issues for Congress," Congressional Research Service, April 30, 2015.

38 Robert Kelner and Raymond La Raja, "McCain-Feingold's Devastating Legacy," *Washington Post*, April 11, 2014, http://www.washingtonpost.com /opinions/mccain-feingolds-devastating-legacy/2014/04/11/14a528e2-c18f-11e3-bcec-b71ee10e9bc3_story.html.

39 "Happy Corporations," *New York Times*, June 17, 1906.

40 Mutch, *Buying the Vote*, 173–74.

41 James Bennet, "The New Price of American Politics," *Atlantic*, October 2012, http://www.theatlantic.com/magazine/archive/2012/10/the/309086/.

42 *Citizens United v. Federal Election Commission*, 558 U.S. 310 (2010).

43 Ibid.

44 Michael McConnell, "Reconsidering *Citizens United* as a Press Clause Case," *Yale Law Journal*, vol. 123, no. 2, November 2013.

45 Ibid.

46 *Citizens United v. Federal Election Commission*, 558 U.S. 310 (2010) (J. P. Stevens, concurring in part, dissenting in part).

47 Ibid.

48 "Democracy Corps Supreme Court Project: Frequency Questionnaire," Greenberg Quinlan Rosner Research, May 7, 2014, http://www.democracycorps .com/attachments/article/979/042214percent20DCORPSpercent20SCOTUS percent20FQ.pdf.

49 Norman Ornstein, "Citizens United: Corrupting Campaign Clarity," *Roll Call*, June 15, 2011, http://www.rollcall.com/issues/56_139/citizens_united_corrupting_campaign_clarity-206476-1.html.

50 Zephyr Teachout, *Corruption in America* (Cambridge, MA: Harvard University Press, 2014).

51 Jeffrey Rosen, "Ruth Bader Ginsburg Is an American Hero," interview with Ruth Bader Ginsburg, *New Republic*, http://www.newrepublic.com/article /119578/ruth-bader-ginsburg-interview-retirement-feminists-jazzercise.

52 Dave Helling, "Jack Danforth says the Citizens United campaign spending decision 'should not stand,'" *Kansas City Star*, June 17, 2015, http://www .kansascity.com/news/local/news-columns-blogs/the-buzz/article24793228 .html#storylink=cpy.

53 "More Voters Think They're on the Same Page with Congress," *Rasmussen Reports*, March 31, 2015, http://www.rasmussenreports.com/public_content /archive/mood_of_america_archive/congressional_performance/more_ voters_think_they_re_on_the_same_page_with_congress.

54 Stan Greenberg, James Carville, David Donnelly, and Ben Winston, "Voters Ready to Act against Big Money in Politics: Lessons from the 2014 Midterm Election," Democracy Corps, GQRR, Every Voice, November 10, 2014, http://everyvoice.org/wp-content/uploads/2014/11/EveryVoicePostElect Memo.pdf.

2. Rigged

1 Inflation Calculator, U.S. Bureau of Labor Statistics, accessed March 19, 2015.

2 "Pressure Groups Spent $3.85 Million on Lobbying in 1960," *CQ Almanac 1961*, 17th ed. (Washington, DC: *Congressional Quarterly*, 1961), 958, http:// library.cqpress.com/cqalmanac/cqal61-879-29202-1371585.

3 "Lobbying Database," Center for Responsive Politics, accessed March 19, 2015.

4 "Annual Lobbying by US Chamber of Commerce," Center for Responsive Politics, accessed March 19, 2015.

5 Peter Schweizer, *Extortion: How Politicians Extract Your Money, Buy Votes, and Line Their Own Pockets* (Houghton Mifflin Harcourt, 2013).

6 "461: Take the Money and Run for Office," *This American Life*, March 30, 2012, http://www.thisamericanlife.org/radio-archives/episode/461/take-the-money-and-run-for-office.

7 Ryan Grimm and Sabrina Siddiqui, "Call Time for Congress Shows How Fundraising Dominates Bleak Work Life," *Huffington Post*, January 9, 2013, http:// www.huffingtonpost.com/2013/01/08/call-time-congressional-fundraising_ n_2427291.html.

8 http://www.huffingtonpost.com/dan-glickman/congressional-campaign-funding_b_1830462.html.

9 Stephen Koff, "Senator George Voinovich talks about his decision to retire" (video), Cleveland.com, January 12, 2009, http://blog.cleveland.com/openers/2009/01/voinovich_talks_about_his_deci.html.

10 Lawrence Lessig, "Democracy After Citizens United," *Boston Review*, September/October 2012, http://new.bostonreview.net/BR35.5/lessig.php.

11 Rebecca Kaplan, "Watchdog groups: Jeb Bush, others violating campaign finance laws," *CBS News*, March 31, 2015, http://www.cbsnews.com/news/watchdog-groups-jeb-bush-others-violating-campaign-finance-laws/.

12 Thomas Beaumont, "Jeb Bush prepares to give traditional campaign a makeover," Associated Press, April 21, 2015, http://bigstory.ap.org/article/4098 37aa09ee405493ad64a94b8c2c3d/bush-preparing-delegate-many-campaign-tasks-super-pac.

13 Richard L. Hasen, "Jeb the Destroyer: Jeb Bush is tearing down what little campaign finance law we have left," *Slate*, April 22, 2015, http://www.slate.com/articles/news_and_politics/politics/2015/04/jeb_bush_destroying_campaign_finance_rules_his_tactics_will_be_the_future.single.html.

14 "Republicans Thwart New Campaign Finance Disclosure Rules As DISCLOSE Act Fails Procedural Vote in Senate," Michael Beckel, OpenSecrets.org, July 27, 2010, http://www.opensecrets.org/news/2010/07/republicans-thwart-new-campaign-fin/.

15 http://www.kentucky.com/2010/08/01/1372068/mcconnells-hypocrisy-on-campaign.html.

16 http://www.bloomberg.com/politics/articles/2014-10-14/the-darth-vader-moment-that-made-mitch-mcconnell.

17 https://www.youtube.com/watch?v=0_gPNGV79ko.

18 "Common Cause, Allies Urge Obama to Order Federal Contractors to Disclose Political Spending," *Common Cause*, March 2, 2015, http://www.commoncause.org/press/press-releases/common-cause-allies-urge-president-disclose-political-spending.html?.

19 Keenan Steiner, "New appointees are long overdue but is the FEC broken?" Sunlight Foundation, April 30, 2013, http://sunlightfoundation.com/blog/2013/04/30/new-appointees-are-long-overdue-but-is-the-fec-broken/.

20 Eric Lichtblau, "F.E.C. Can't Curb 2016 Election Abuse, Commission Chief Says," *New York Times*, May 2, 2015, http://www.nytimes.com/2015/05/03/us/politics/fec-cant-curb-2016-election-abuse-commission-chief-says.html?_r=0.

21 Ben Weider, Kytja Weir, Reity O'Brien, and Rachel Baye, "National donors pick winners in state elections," Center for Public Integrity, January 28, 2015, http://www.publicintegrity.org/2015/01/28/16661/national-donors-pick-winners-state-elections.

22 Zach Holden, "Overview of Campaign Finances, 2011-2012 Elections," National Institute on Money in State Politics, May 13, 2014, http://www.followthemoney.org/research/institute-reports/overview-of-campaign-finances-20112012-elections.

23 Edwin Bender, "Evidencing a Republican Form of Government: The Influence of Campaign Money on State-Level Elections," *Montana Law Review*, Winter 2013, http://scholarship.law.umt.edu/cgi/viewcontent.cgi?article=1007&context=mlr.

24 Zach Holden, "Overview of Campaign Finances, 2011-2012 Elections," National Institute on Money in State Politics, May 13, 2015, http://www.followthemoney.org/research/institute-reports/overview-of-campaign-finances-20112012-elections/.

25 Liz Essley Whyte, "Big business crushed ballot measures in 2014," Center for Public Integrity, February 5, 2015, http://www.publicintegrity.org/2015/02/05/16693/big-business-crushed-ballot-measures-2014.

26 Fredreka Schouten, "Federal super PACs spend big on local elections," *USA Today*, February 25, 2014, http://www.usatoday.com/story/news/politics/2014/02/25/super-pacs-spending-local-races/5617121/.

27 Ibid.

28 Theodore Schleifer, "Super PACs coming to a city near you," CNN, May 19, 2015, http://www.cnn.com/2015/05/19/politics/super-pac-local-elections-2015/.

29 Bert Brandenburg, "Justice for Sale: How elected judges became a threat to American democracy," *Politico*, September 1, 2014, http://www.politico.com/magazine/story/2014/09/elected-judges-110397.html#.VWjJPVxVhBd.

30 Adam Liptak, "U.S. Supreme Court Is Asked to Fix Troubled West Virginia System," *New York Times*, October 11, 2008, http://www.nytimes.com/2008/10/12/washington/12scotus.html.

31 "Money & Elections," *Justice at Stake*, http://www.justiceatstake.org/issues/state_court_issues/money-and-elections/.

3. Oligarchy, Gridlock, Cronyism

1 http://www.tulsaworld.com/test/okpreps/volleyball/lee-h-hamilton-money-and-politics-we-need-change-now/article_8db057f6-5c89-5131-adb4-b9520e94827f.html.

2 http://www.politico.com/story/2014/12/top-political-donors-113833.html#ixzz3fbgYpPBH.

3 Philip Rucker, "Governors Christie, Walker and Kasich woo billionaire Sheldon Adelson at Vegas event," *Washington Post*, March 29, 2014, http://

www.washingtonpost.com/politics/governors-christie-walker-and-kasich-woo-adelson-at-vegas-event/2014/03/29/aa385f34-b779-11e3-b84e-897d3d 12b816_story.html.

4 Matea Gold and Philip Rucker, "Billionaire mogul Sheldon Adelson looks for mainstream Republican who can win in 2016," *Washington Post*, March 25, 2014, http://www.washingtonpost.com/politics/billionaire-mogul-sheldon-adelson-looks-for-mainstream-republican-who-can-win-in-2016/2014/03/25 /e2f47bb0-b3c2-11e3-8cb6-284052554d74_story.html.

5 "The World's Billionaires," *Forbes*, http://www.forbes.com/billionaires/.

6 Nathan Vardi, "Sheldon Adelson Says He Is 'Willing to Spend Whatever It Takes' to Stop Online Gambling," *Forbes*, November 22, 2013, http://www .forbes.com/sites/nathanvardi/2013/11/22/sheldon-adelson-says-he-is-willing-to-spend-whatever-it-takes-to-stop-online-gambling/.

7 Tim Dickinson, "Inside the Koch Brothers' Toxic Empire," *Rolling Stone*, September 24, 2014, http://www.rollingstone.com/politics/news/inside-the-koch-brothers-toxic-empire-20140924?page=2.

8 Kenneth P. Vogel and Simmi Aujla, "Koch conference under scrutiny," *Politico*, January 27, 2011, http://dyn.politico.com/printstory.cfm?uuid=2EDE2 F1B-BE40-42F0-AF83-BAB96054F413.

9 Nicholas Confessore, "Koch Brothers' Budget of $889 Million for 2016 Is on Par with Both Parties' Spending," *New York Times*, January 26, 2015, http:// www.nytimes.com/2015/01/27/us/politics/kochs-plan-to-spend-900-million-on-2016-campaign.html?_r=0.

10 Andrew Restuccia and Elana Schor, "Tom Steyer backs Hillary Clinton despite Keystone caution," *Politico*, May 6, 2015, http://www.politico .com/story/2015/05/tom-steyer-hillary-clinton-keystone-117707. html#ixzz3bHD9ke1A.

11 Timothy Cama, "Billionaire environmentalist to host Clinton fundraiser," *The Hill*, April 29, 2015, http://thehill.com/policy/energy-environment /240460-billionaire-environmentalist-to-host-clinton-fundraiser.

12 Ed Rogers, "The Insiders: I'm embarrassed by our campaign finance system," *Washington Post*, April 21, 2015, http://www.washingtonpost.com /blogs/post-partisan/wp/2015/04/21/the-insiders-im-embarrassed-by-our-campaign-finance-system/.

13 Jesse H. Rhodes and Brian F. Schaffner, "Economic Inequality and Representation in the U.S. House: A New Approach Using Population Level Data," April 7, 2013, http://people.umass.edu/schaffne/Schaffner.Rhodes. MPSA.2013.pdf.

14 Paul Wiseman, "Unemployment rate for recent college grads rose in 2014," *Columbus Dispatch*, April 16, 2015, http://www.dispatch.com/content/stories /business/2015/04/16/0416-college-unemployment.html.

15 Lynn Sweet, "Inside the Fall of Aaron Schock," *Chicago Sun-Times*, Agust 23, 2015, http://chicago.suntimes.com/politics/7/71/900454/inside-fall-of-aaron-schock-investigation-ben-cole.

16 "Press Conference by the President," *The White House*, October 8, 2013, https://www.whitehouse.gov/the-press-office/2013/10/08/press-conference-president.

17 Ed O'Keefe, "Tom Harkin: It's somebody else's turn," *Washington Post*, January 26, 2013, http://www.washingtonpost.com/blogs/post-politics/wp/2013/01/26/tom-harkin-its-somebody-elses-turn.

18 Joseph Stiglitz, "Rewriting the Rules of the American Economy: An Agenda for Growth and Shared Prosperity," working paper, p. 15, accessed May 25, 2015, http://www.rewritetherules.org/report.

19 Bill Moyers, "David Stockman on Crony Capitalism," *Moyers & Company*, March 9, 2012, http://billmoyers.com/segment/david-stockman-on-crony-capitalism.

20 Luigi Zingales, *A Capitalism for the People: Recapturing the Lost Genius of American Prosperity* (New York: Basic Books, 2012), 2.

21 Desmond Lachman, "America's crony capitalism challenge," American Enterprise Institute, October 27, 2014.

22 Zingales, *Capitalism for the People*, 138.

23 Catherine Rampell, "Tax Breaks: A Primer," *New York Times*, February 22, 2012, http://economix.blogs.nytimes.com/2012/02/22/tax-breaks-a-primer/.

24 Timothy P. Carney, "The Case Against Cronies: Libertarians Must Stand Up to Corporate Greed," *Atlantic*, April 30, 2013, http://www.theatlantic.com/business/archive/2013/04/the-case-against-cronies-libertarians-must-stand-up-to-corporate-greed/275404/.

25 Timothy P. Carney, *The Big Ripoff: How Big Business and Big Government Steal Your Money* (Wiley, 2006).

4. Too Big to Beat

1 Jon Prior, "Fannie and Freddie to pay back taxpayers," *POLITICO*, February 21, 2014, http://www.politico.com/story/2014/02/fannie-mae-freddie-mac-bailouts-103768.html.

2 William D. Cohan, "The Final Days of Merrill Lynch," *Atlantic*, September 2009, http://www.theatlantic.com/magazine/archive/2009/09/the-final-days-of-merrill-lynch/307621/.

3 Matthew Karnitschnig et al., "U.S. to Take Over AIG in $85 Billion Bailout; Central Banks Inject Cash as Credit Dries Up," *Wall Street Journal*, September 16, 2008, http://www.wsj.com/articles/SB122156561931242905.

4 Chris Isidore, "Poll: 60% say depression 'likely,'" *CNN Money*, October 6, 2008, http://money.cnn.com/2008/10/06/news/economy/depression_poll/.

5 Tami Lubhy, "Foreclosures soar 76 percent to record 1.35 million," *CNN Money*, December 5, 2008, http://money.cnn.com/2008/12/05/news/economy /mortgage_delinquencies/.

6 Robin Sidel and Saabrina Chaudhuri, "U.S. Bank Profits Near Record Levels," *Wall Street Journal*, August 11, 2014, http://www.wsj.com/articles /u-s-banking-industry-profits-racing-to-near-record-levels-1407773976.

7 "Dow Jones Industrial Average," *Barron's* Market Data Center, http://online .barrons.com/mdc/public/npage/9_3050.html?symb=DJIA.

8 Floyd Norris, "Corporate Profits Grow and Wages Slide," *New York Times*, April 4, 2014, http://www.nytimes.com/2014/04/05/business/economy /corporate-profits-grow-ever-larger-as-slice-of-economy-as-wages-slide.html.

9 Elise Gould, "Average Real Wage Growth in 2014 Was No Better Than 2013," Economic Policy Institute, January 15, 2015, http://www.epi.org/blog/average- real-hourly-wage-growth-in-2014-was-no-better-than-2013/.

10 "Most Say Government Policies Since Recession Have Done Little to Help Middle Class, Poor," Pew Research Center, March 4, 2015, http://www.people- press.org/2015/03/04/most-say-government-policies-since-recession-have- done-little-to-help-middle-class-poor/.

11 Leslie Wayne, "Lobbyists for Financial Institutions Swarming All Over the Bailout Bill," *New York Times*, September 27, 2008, http://www.nytimes .com/2008/09/27/business/27lobbyists.html.

12 "American Bankers Assn," OpenSecrets.org, http://www.opensecrets.org /lobby/clientlbs.php?id=D000000087&year=2008.

13 "US Chamber of Commerce," OpenSecrets.org, https://www.opensecrets .org/lobby/clientsum.php?id=D000019798.

14 "Ranked Sectors: 2008," OpenSecrets.org, http://www.opensecrets.org /lobby/top.php?showYear=2008&indexType=c.

15 "Top Spenders: 2008," OpenSecrets.org, http://www.opensecrets.org /lobby/top.php?showYear=2008&indexType=s.

16 Harry Bradford, "10 Worst Single-Day Drops In Dow Jones History," *Huffington Post*, August 5, 2011, http://www.huffingtonpost.com/2011/08/05 /dow-jones-biggest-drops-falls_n_919216.html.

17 Paul Blumenthal, "Plunge in Wall Street Money Bolsters Populist Shift Among Democrats," *Huffington Post*, January 10, 2015, http://www.huffington post.com/2015/01/10/democrats-wall-street_n_6445276.html?ncid=tweetlnku shpmg00000016.

18 Ibid.; "Top Organization Contributors," OpenSecrets.org, http://www .opensecrets.org/orgs/list.php.

19 Russell J. Funk and Daniel Hirschman, "Derivatives and Deregulation: Financial Innovation and the Demise of Glass-Steagall," *Administrative Science Quarterly*.

20 Jerry Markham, "The Subprime Crisis—A Test Match for the Bankers: Glass-Steagall vs. Gramm-Leach-Bliley," 2009, http://scholarship.law.upenn .edu/cgi/viewcontent.cgi?article=1365&context=jbl.

21 Robert Dreyfuss, "How the DLC Does It," *American Prospect*, December 19, 2001, http://prospect.org/article/how-dlc-does-it.

22 James Shoch, *Trading Blows: Party Competition and U.S. Trade Policy in a Globalizing Era* (Chapel Hill: University of North Carolina Press, 2001).

23 "Finance/Insurance/Real Estate," OpenSecrets.org, http://www.opensecrets .org/industries/totals.php?cycle=2014&ind=F.

24 Jacob S. Hacker and Paul Pierson, *Winner-Take-All-Politics: How Washington Made the Rich Richer—and Turned Its Back on the Middle Class* (New York: Simon and Schuster, 2011).

25 John J. Pitney Jr., "Democrats Bring Back Their Hit Man: Tony Coelho, who rapped GOP ethics but took tainted S&L perks, returns to guide party," *Los Angeles Times*, August 16, 1994, http://articles.latimes.com/1994-08-16 /local/me-27581_1_tony-coelho.

26 Ibid.

27 Hacker and Pierson, *Winner-Take-All-Politics*, 177.

28 Bill Sing, "Coelho Joins Investment Firm," *Los Angeles Times*, October 3, 1989, http://articles.latimes.com/1989-10-03/business/fi-650_1_investment-banking-experience.

29 Ibid.

30 Ibid.; "National Republican Senatorial Cmte," Center for Responsive Politics, http://www.opensecrets.org/parties/indus.php?cmte–RSC&cycle=2008

31 Authors' analysis of House Financial Services Committee membership: Ryan Grim and Arthur Delaney, "The Cash Committee: How Wall Street Wins on the Hill," *Huffington Post*, March 18, 2010, http://www.huffingtonpost .com/2009/12/29/the-cash-committee-how-wa_n_402373.html.

32 Ibid.

33 Ibid.

34 Ibid.

35 Ibid.

36 Phil Angelides and Bill Thomas, "Financial Crisis Inquiry Report," Financial Crisis Inquiry Commission, Washington, D.C., January 2011, http:// www.gpo.gov/fdsys/pkg/GPO-FCIC/pdf/GPO-FCIC.pdf. Ibid.

37 "Byron Dorgan's Prophetic Words," Lauren Feeney, Moyers and Company, January 27, 2012, http://billmoyers.com/content/a-senators-prophetic-words-then-and-now/.

38 Stephen Labaton, "Congress Passes Wide-Ranging Bill Easing Bank Laws," *New York Times*, November 5, 1999, http://www.nytimes.com/1999/11/05/business/congress-passes-wide-ranging-bill-easing-bank-laws.html.

39 "The Long Demise of Glass-Steagall," PBS *Frontline*, http://www.pbs.org/wgbh/pages/frontline/shows/wallstreet/weill/demise.html.

40 Eric Lipton and Stephan Labaton, "Deregulator Looks Back, Unswayed," *New York Times*, November 16, 2008, http://www.nytimes.com/2008/11/17/business/economy/17gramm.html?pagewanted=all.

41 "Citigroup Inc," OpenSecrets.org, http://www.opensecrets.org/orgs/totals.php?id=D000000071&cycle=2014.

42 Ibid.

43 "Commerical Banks," OpenSecrets.org, http://www.opensecrets.org/lobby/indusclient.php?id=F03&year=2008.

44 Stephen Labaton, "Agreement Reached on Overhaul of U.S. Financial System," *New York Times*, October 23, 1999, http://partners.nytimes.com/library/financial/102399banks-congress.html.

45 Ellen Schloemer et al., "Losing Ground: Foreclosures in the Subprime Market and Their Cost to Homeowners," Center for Responsible Lending, December 2006, http://www.responsiblelending.org/mortgage-lending/research-analysis/foreclosure-paper-report-2-17.pdf.

46 Ibid.; Glenn R. Simpson, "Lender Lobbying Blitz Abetted Mortgage Mess," *Wall Street Journal*, December 31, 2007, http://www.wsj.com/articles/SB119906606162358773.

47 "Countrywide Financial," OpenSecrets.org, https://www.opensecrets.org/lobby/clientsum.php?id=D000021941&year=2006.

48 Simpson, "Lender Lobbying Blitz."

49 Ibid.

50 Joe Nocera and Bethany McLean, "All the Devils Are Here: The Hidden History of the Financial Crisis," *Portfolio*, 2011.

51 Board of Governors of the Federal Reserve System, Press Release, December 18, 2007, http://www.federalreserve.gov/newsevents/press/bcreg/20071218a.htm.

52 "Gretchen Morgenson on Corporate Clout in Washington," *Moyers and Company*, March 9, 2012, http://billmoyers.com/segment/gretchen-morgenson-on-industry-influence/.

53 Ibid.

54 Ibid.; "How Wall Street Defanged Dodd-Frank," Gary Rivlin, *The Nation*, April 30, 2013, http://www.thenation.com/article/174113/how-wall-street-defanged-dodd-frank.

55 Ibid.

56 "US Chamber of Commerce," Center for Responsive Politics, https://www.opensecrets.org/lobby/clientsum.php?id=D000019798&year=2015.

57 "American Fedn of State, County & Municipal Employees," Center for Responsive Politics, https://www.opensecrets.org/orgs/lobby.php?id=D000000061.

58 Kevin Conner, "Big Bank Takeover," Institute for America's Future, http://ourfuture.org/files/documents/big-bank-takeover-final.pdf.

59 "Citigroup Inc," Center for Responsive Politics, https://www.opensecrets.org/orgs/summary.php?id=D000000071.

60 Les Christie, "Foreclosures up a record 81 percent in 2008," CNN, January 15, 2009, http://money.cnn.com/2009/01/15/real_estate/millions_in_foreclosure/.

61 Paul Kiel and Olga Pierce, "Dems: Obama Broke Pledge to Force Banks to Help Homeowners," *ProPublica*, February 4, 2011, http://www.propublica.org/article/dems-obama-broke-pledge-to-force-banks-to-help-homeowners.

62 "Senator Obama Speaks in Golden, Col. on the Economy," CQ Transcriptwire, *Washington Post*, September 16, 2008, http://www.washingtonpost.com/wp-dyn/content/article/2008/09/16/AR2008091601767.html.

63 Adam J. Levitin, "Resolving the Foreclosure Crisis: Modification of Mortgages in Bankruptcy," *Wisconsin Law Review*, 2009:3, http://wisconsinlawreview.org/wp-content/files/1-Levitin.pdf.

64 Kiel and Pierce, "Dems: Obama Broke Pledge."

65 Brady Dennis and Renae Merle, "House Democrats push bill to use TARP funds for homeowner mortgage relief," *Washington Post*, December 8, 2009, http://www.washingtonpost.com/wp-dyn/content/article/2009/12/07/AR2009120703903.html.

66 Shaila Dewan, "Lew Unveils Small Steps to Augment Loan Modification Program," *New York Times*, June 26, 2014, http://www.nytimes.com/2014/06/27/business/treasury-secretary-unveils-small-steps-to-augment-loan-modification-program.html?_r=0.

67 Arthur Delaney, "HAMP: Obama Administration Lets Bank Out of Doghouse for Bad Mortgage Servicing," *Huffington Post*, March 2, 2012, http://www.huffingtonpost.com/2012/03/02/hamp-mortgage-barack-obama_n_1316873.html.

68 Olga Pierce and Paul Kiel, "By the Numbers: A Revealing Look at the Mortgage Mod Meltdown," *Pro Publica*, March 8, 2011, http://www.propublica

.org/article/by-the-numbers-a-revealing-look-at-the-mortgage-mod-
meltdown.

5. Drugged

1 FastStats, Centers for Disease Control and Prevention, last updated April 29, 2015.

2 http://www.oecd.org/unitedstates/Briefing-Note-UNITED-STATES-2014 .pdf.

3 The $3,484 figure is for 2012, the most recent year for which this OEDC information was available as this book was going to print.

4 Sheryl Gay Stolberg, "A Delicate Dance for 2 Health Lobbyists," *New York Times*, October 27, 2009.

5 https://www.opensecrets.org/politicians/summary.php?cid–00005372 &cycle=2004.

6 Paul Blumenthal, "The Legacy of Billy Tauzin: The White House-PhRMA Deal," Sunlight Foundation, February 12, 2010.

7 http://www.opensecrets.org/lobby/indusclient.php?id=H04&year=2009.

8 https://www.opensecrets.org/lobby/top.php?showYear=a&indexType=s.

9 Megan R. Wilson, "PhRMA comes out on top in trade group rankings," *The Hill*, July 24, 2013.

10 Bruce Bartlett, "Medicare Part D: Republican Budget-Busting," *New York Times*, November 19, 2013.

11 "Former Medicare administrator takes health care job at law firm," Baltimore *Sun*, December 19, 2003.

12 Richard S. Foster, "Actuary in the Hot Seat," *Contingencies*, November/ December 2004.

13 Noah Glyn, "Drug Deals," *National Review*, January 30, 2013.

14 Ibid.

15 Robert Pear, "Insurers and Drug Makers See Gain in Bush Victory," *New York Times*, November 5, 2004.

16 "Under the Influence," *60 Minutes*, season 30, episode 25, April 1, 2007.

17 *Congressional Record*, Senate, April 18, 2007.

18 Peter Baker, "Obama Was Pushed by Drug Industry, Emails Suggest," *New York Times*, June 8, 2012.

19 Ibid.

20 Paul Blumenthal, "The Legacy of Billy Tauzin: The White House–PhRMA Deal," Sunlight Foundation, February 12, 2010.

21 Dean Baker, "Reducing Waste with an Efficient Medicare Prescription Drug Benefit," Center for Economic and Policy Research, January 2013.

22 "Billy and the Beanstalk: Big Pharma's lobbyist has sold his CEOs on a political fantasy," *Wall Street Journal*, August 13, 2009.

23 Richard Anderson, "Pharmaceutical industry gets high on fat profits," BBC News, November 6, 2014.

24 Keith Speights, "10 Most Profitable Companies in Healthcare," *Motley Fool*, May 7, 2015.

25 Source: Yahoo! Finance, accessed July 15, 2015.

26 Marcia Angell, *The Truth About Drug Companies* (New York: Random House, 2004).

27 "Treating HCV—Is the Price Right?" Michael Smith, *MedPage Today*, February 18, 2014.

28 http://www.who.int/mediacentre/factsheets/fs164/en/.

29 Merrill Goozner, "Why Sovaldi shouldn't cost $84,000," *Modern Healthcare*, May 3, 2014.

30 Emory News Center, http://news.emory.edu/stories/2012/03/tech_transfer_highlights/campus.html.

31 Goozner, "Why Sovaldi shouldn't cost $84,000."

32 http://www.ncbi.nlm.nih.gov/pubmed/25646109.

33 Charles Ornstein, "New hepatitis C drugs are costing Medicare billions," *Washington Post*, March 29, 2015.

34 Andrew Ward, "Drug Pricing: Bitter Pill," *Financial Times*, July 31, 2014.

35 Dr. Val Jones, "When Chemo Saves Your Life: An Interview with Billy Tauzin," *Better Health*, January 29, 2009.

36 Bob Herman, "Genentech's distribution change for cancer drugs upsets hospitals," *Modern Healthcare*, September 30, 2014.

37 Jim Landers, "Your money or your life: Patients face painful choice," *Dallas Morning News*, April 3, 2015.

38 "High Price of Cancer Treatment Drugs Is 'Unsustainable,' Doctor Says," NPR, June 1, 2015.

39 Ed Silverman, "The Number of Drug Shortages—and Patient Frustration—Keeps Growing," *Wall Street Journal*, June 1, 2015.

40 "Medicines Use and Spending Shifts: A Review of the Use of Medicines in the U.S. in 2014," *IMS Health*, 2015.

41 "Trends in Retail Prices of Generic Prescription Drugs Widely Used by Older Americans, 2006 to 2013," AARP Public Policy Institute, May 2015.

42 Robert Pear, "Obama Proposes That Medicare Be Given the Right to Negotiate the Cost of Drugs," *New York Times*, April 27, 2015.

6. Fuel Follies

1 *New York Times*, September 20, 2011.

2 Daniel LeDuc, "Business Leaders Call for National Energy Policy," Pew Charitable Trusts, Clean Energy Initiative, October 5, 2012.

3 Ibid.

4 D. C. Rice, R. Schoney, and K. Mahaffey, "Methods and rationale for derivation of a reference dose for methylmercury by the US EPA," *Risk Analysis: An Official Publication of the Society for Risk Analysis*, 2003, www.ncbi.nlm.nih .gov/pubmed/11181111.

5 U.S. Environmental Protection Agency, "Mercury Study Report to Congress: An inventory of anthropogenic mercury emissions in the United States," 1997.

6 *American Lawyer*, August 1, 2005. Referenced at Institute for Agriculture and Trade Policy, http://www.iatp.org.

7 Ibid.

8 "Fact Sheet: EPA's Clean Air Mercury Rule," March 15, 2005. For more information, see www.epa.gov/air/mercuryrule/factsheetfin.html.

9 Connor Gibson, "Jeffrey Holmstead: The Coal Industry's Mercury Lobbyist," Polluterwatch Blog, December 21, 2011 (updated November 2012).

10 *New York Times*, October 11, 2011.

11 http://fusion.net/story/142473/the-american-coal-industry-is-collapsing/.

12 "Marcellus Shale: New Research Surprises Geologists," Geology.com. http://frack.mixplex.com/content/marcellus-shale-gas-new-research-results-surprise-geologists.

13 R. W. Hoise, "New Thinking Needed: Pa. Must Back Natural Gas Tax That Helps Local Governments," TheDailyReview.com, August 29, 2010.

14 Kevin McNellis, "Names in the News: Pennsylvania's Marcellus Shale Advisory Commission," National Institute on Money in State Politics, July 28, 2012, http://classic.followthemoney.org/press/PrintReportView.phmtl?r=455.

15 Pennsylvania Land Trust Association, "Marcellus Shale Drillers in Pennsylvania Amass 1614 Violations Since 2008," October 1, 2010, http:// conserveland.org/?s=marcellus.

16 Don Hopey, "Pennsylvania Environmental Secretary Mike Krancer to Step Down," *Pittsburgh Post-Gazette*, March 23, 2013, http://www.post-gazette .com/news/state/2013/03/23/Pennsylvania-environmental-secretary-Mike-Krancer-to-step-down/stories/201303230164.

17 Kristen Allen, *The Big Fracking Deal: Marcellus Shale—Pennsylvania's Untapped Resource,* 23 Villanova Envrionmental Law Journal 51 (2012).

18 McNellis, "Names in the News."

19 T. McDonnell, "Smelling a Leak: Is the natural gas industry buying academics?" *Grist,* July 30, 2012.

20 J. Efstathiou, "Penn State Faculty Snub of Fracking Study Ends Research," *Bloomberg,* October 3, 2012.

21 http://www.nytimes.com/2012/11/03us/pennsylvania-mitted-poison-data-in-water-report.html/.

22 http://stateimpact.npr.org/pennsylvania/2014/10/29/energy=companies-donate-more-than1-million-to-corbetts-campaign-coffers/.

23 http://www.marcellus-shale.us/political-contributions-htm/.

24 Ibid.

25 J. Elliott, "Another Layer to Rendell's Fracking Connections," *Pro Publica,* April 8, 2013.

26 http://www.elementpartners.com/team-edrendell.html.

27 http://www.Stateimpact.npr.org/pennsylvania/former-dep-chief-michael-krancer.

28 http://public-accountability.org/2013/02/fracking-and-the-revolving-door-in-pennsylvania/.

29 Personal interview with solar pioneer Neville Williams, July 14, 2015.

30 *International Business Times,* April 6, 2015.

31 Ibid.

32 See www.flsolarchoice.org.

33 *Wall Street Journal,* February 20, 2015.

34 www.heartland.org/newspaper-article/2015/03/02/solar-power-lobbyists-seek-subvert-florida-tea-party.

7. Fat Wallets, Expanding Waistlines

1 Cynthia Ogden, PhD, Margaret D. Carroll, MSPH, Brian K. Kit, MD, MPH, and Katherine M. Flegal, PhD, "Prevalence of Childhood and Adult Obesity in the United States, 2011–2012," *Journal of the American Medical Association,* February 26, 2014, http://jama.jamanetwork.com/article .aspx?articleid=1832542.

2 Ibid.

3 "Childhood Obesity in the United States: Facts and Figures," Institute of Medicine of the National Academies, September 2004, http://www.iom.edu

/~/media/Files/Reportpercent20Files/2004/Preventing-Childhood-Obesity-Health-in-the-Balance/FINALfactsandfigures2.pdf.

4 Arthur H. Rubenstein, "Obesity: A Modern Epidemic," *Transactions of the American Clinical and Climatological Association*, 2005, http://www.ncbi.nlm.nih.gov/pmc/articles/PMC1473136/?report=classic.

5 "Obesity Threatens to Cut U.S. Life Expectancy, New Analysis Suggests," National Institutes of Health, March 16, 2005, http://www.nih.gov/news/pr/mar2005/nia-16.htm.

6 Eliana Dockterman, "Study: Obesity May Shorten Life Expectancy by Up to 8 Years," *Time*, December 4, 2014, http://time.com/3619251/obesity-life-expectancy/.

7 "Early Childhood Obesity Prevention Policies: Goals, Recommendations, and Potential Actions," Institute of Medicine of the National Academies, June 23, 2011, http://www.iom.edu/Reports/2011/Early-Childhood-Obesity-Prevention-Policies/Recommendations.aspx.

8 "Vital signs: obesity among low-income, preschool-aged children—United States, 2008–2011," Centers for Disease Control and Prevention, August 9, 2013, http://www.ncbi.nlm.nih.gov/pubmed/23925173.

9 "Evaluating Obesity Prevention Efforts: A Plan for Measuring Progress," Institute of Medicine of the National Academies, August 2013, http://www.iom.edu/~/media/Files/Reportpercent20Files/2013/Evaluating-Obesity-Prevention-Efforts/EPOP_rb.pdf.

10 Elizabeth Mendes, "Americans' Concerns About Obesity Soar, Surpass Smoking," *Gallup*, July 18, 2012, http://www.gallup.com/poll/155762/americans-concerns-obesity-soar-surpass-smoking.aspx.

11 "Scientific Report of the 2015 Dietary Guidelines Advisory Committee: Advisory Report to the Secretary of Health and Human Services and the Secretary of Agriculture," Dietary Guidelines Advisory Committee, February 2015, http://www.health.gov/dietaryguidelines/2015-scientific-report/PDFs/Scientific-Report-of-the-2015-Dietary-Guidelines-Advisory-Committee.pdf.

12 Anahad O'Connor, "Nutrition Panel Calls for Less Sugar and Eases Cholesterol and Fat Restrictions," *New York Times*, February 19, 2015, http://well.blogs.nytimes.com/2015/02/19/nutrition-panel-calls-for-less-sugar-and-eases-cholesterol-and-fat-restrictions/.

13 Authors' analysis of Center for Responsive Politics records.

14 "Who needs lobbyists? See what big business spends to win American minds," Center for Public Integrity, January 15, 2015, http://www.publicintegrity.org/2015/01/15/16596/who-needs-lobbyists-see-what-big-business-spends-win-american-minds#!6.

15 Robert Pear, "Congress Approves Child Nutrition Bill," *New York Times*, December 2, 2010, http://www.nytimes.com/2010/12/03/us/politics/03child. html.

16 Authors' analysis of Center for Responsive Politics data.

17 Authors' analysis of Center for Responsive Politics data.

18 Nick Confessore, "How School Lunch Became the Latest Political Battleground," *New York Times*, October 7, 2014, http://www.nytimes. com/2014/10/12/magazine/how-school-lunch-became-the-latest-political-battleground.html.

19 Ibid.

20 Jim Spencer and Mike Hughlett, "Pizza still counts as a veggie in schools," *Minneapolis Star Tribune*, November 21, 2011, http://www.startribune.com/lifestyle/health/134208058.html.

21 Brett Neely, "Washington pizza sauce fight has deep Minnesota ties," Minnesota Public Radio, November 18, 2011, http://www.mprnews.org/story/2011/11/18/schwan-foods-pizza-as-vegetable-minnesota-delegation.

22 Duff Wilson and Janet Roberts, "Special Report: How Washington went soft on childhood obesity," Reuters, April 27, 2012, http://www.reuters.com/article/2012/04/27/us-usa-foodlobby-idUSBRE83Q0ED20120427.

23 "School Meal Program Regulations," National Potato Council, http://nationalpotatocouncil.org/issues/health-and-nutrition/.

24 Sam Rosen-Amy, "Congress Passes Year's First Spending Bill With Plenty of Riders, Declares Pizza a Vegetable," Center for Effective Government, November 21, 2011, http://www.foreffectivegov.org/node/11915.

25 Confessore, "How School Lunch Became the Latest Political Battleground."

26 Ron Nixon, "Nutrition Group Lobbies Against Healthier School Meals It Sought, Citing Cost," *New York Times*, July 1, 2014, http://www.nytimes .com/2014/07/02/us/nutrition-group-lobbies-against-healthier-school-meals-it-sought-citing-cost.html.

27 Authors' interview with spokesperson for the School Nutrition Association.

28 www.stateofobesity.org/states/al/.

29 www.americashealthrankings.org/AL/.

30 Peter Overby, "Lobbyists Loom Behind the Scenes of School Nutrition Fight," NPR, June 11, 2014, http://www.npr.org/blogs/thesalt/2014/06/11 /320753007/behind-the-scenes-of-school-nutrition-fight-big-food-money-flows.

31 Jay Sjerven, "Congress eases whole grain and sodium requirements in school meals," *Food Business News*, December 16, 2014, http://www

.foodbusinessnews.net/articles/news_home/Regulatory_News/2014/12
/Congress_eases_whole_grain_and.aspx?ID=percent7B29827895-2A79-
4F20-9ED5-CFD960523BE7 percent7D.

32 Letter to the Senate and House Members of Committees on Agriculture
Appropriations, School Nutrition Association Past Presidents Initiative, May
27, 2014, http://www.democraticleader.gov/sites/democraticleader.house.gov
/files/SNA percent20Past percent20Presidents.pdf.

33 "SNA President Testifies on School Meal Successes and Challenges," School
Nutrition Association, April 15, 2015, https://schoolnutrition.org/PressReleases
/SNAPresidentTestifiesonSchoolMealSuccessesandChallenges/.

34 http://www.fns.U.S.D.A.gov/pressrelease/2014/009814.

35 D. Ludwig, K. Peyterson, and S. Gortmaker, "Relation between consumption of sugar-sweetened drinks and childhood obesity: A perspective, obser-
vational analysis," The Lancet, 2001.

36 K. Brownell and K. Warner, "The Perils of Ignoring History: Big Tobacco
Played Dirty and Millions Died. How Similar Is Big Food?" Milbank Quarterly
87(1): 259–94.

37 Kelly D. Brownell, PhD, and Thomas R. Frieden, MD, MPH, "Ounces of
Prevention—The Public Policy Case for Taxes on Sugared Beverages," New
England Journal of Medicine, April 30, 2009, http://www.nejm.org/doi
/full/10.1056/NEJMp0902392.

38 Roberta R. Friedman, ScM and Kelly D. Brownell, PhD, "Sugar-Sweetened
Beverage Taxes: An Updated Policy Brief," Yale Rudd Center for Food Policy
and Obesity, October 2012, http://www.yaleruddcenter.org/resources/upload
/docs/what/reports/Rudd_Policy_Brief_Sugar_Sweetened_Beverage_Taxes
.pdf.

39 Erin Quinn, "Who needs lobbyists? See what big business spends to win
American minds," Center for Public Integrity, January 15, 2015, http://www
.publicintegrity.org/2015/01/15/16596/who-needs-lobbyists-see-what-big-
business-spends-win-american-minds#!1.

40 Washington Post, June 25, 2014.

41 Americans Against Food Taxes Form 990s, https://www.citizenaudit.
org/270514291/.

42 "Pennies," Americans Against Food Taxes TV ad, September 11, 2009,
https://www.youtube.com/watch?v=sxIwwrO2JYg.

43 Christine Spolar and Joe Eaton, "The food lobby's war on a soda tax,"
Center for Public Integrity, November 4, 2009, http://www.publicintegrity
.org/2009/11/04/2758/food-lobbys-war-soda-tax.

44 Swati Yanamadala et al., "Food industry front groups and conflicts of interests: The case of Americans Against Food Taxes," Public Health Nutrition 15,

no. 8, 2012, http://journals.cambridge.org/download.php?file=percent2FPHN percent2FPHN15_08 percent2FS1368980012003187a.pdf&code=ebb31e0749a886 bc3a840b894cced959.

45 "The Masterminds Behind the Phony Anti-Soda Tax Coalitions," Nancy Huehnergarth, *Huffington Post*, September 2, 2012, http://www.huffington post.com/nancy-huehnergarth/soda-ban-new-york_b_1644883.html.

46 New York State lobbying records.

47 "2010 A $weet year for Albany lobbyists," NYPIRG, March 4, 2010, http:// www.nypirg.org/media/releases/goodgov/NYPIRG-percent202010percent20 Lobbying.pdf.

48 Duff Wilson and Janet Roberts, "Special Report: How Washington went soft on childhood obesity," Reuters, April 27, 2012, http://www.reuters.com/ article/2012/04/27/us-usa-foodlobby-idUSBRE83Q0ED20120427.

49 Anemona Hartocollis, "Failure of State Soda Tax Plan Reflects Power of an Antitax Message," *New York Times*, July 2, 2010, http://www.nytimes .com/2010/07/03/nyregion/03sodatax.html.

50 William Harless, "Beverage lobbyist funds 'community' campaign against soda tax," *California Watch*, June 13, 2012, http://californiawatch.org/dailyreport /beverage-lobbyist-funds-community-campaign-against-soda-tax-16585.

51 "Group Fighting Proposed Richmond Soda Tax Files Lawsuit," CBS San Francisco, September 5, 2012, http://sanfrancisco.cbslocal.com/2012/09/05 /group-fighting-proposed-richmond-soda-tax-files-lawsuit/.

52 Fernando Quintero, "Advocates bulking up for the next battle with Big Soda," Berkeley Media Studies Group, January 8, 2013, http://www.bmsg.org /blog/advocates-bulking-up-for-the-next-battle-with-big-soda.

53 http://articles.latimes.com/2012/dec/09/opinion/la-oe-zingale-soda-tax-campaign-funding-20121209.

54 Representative Marvin Jones of Texas, one of the sponsors of the bill, was later recognized with the industry's Dyer Memorial Award as "Sugar Man of the Year."

55 Alexandra Wexler, "Bulk of U.S. Sugar Loans Went to Three Companies," *Wall Street Journal*, June 26, 2013.

56 Brian Riley, "U.S. Trade Policy Gouges American Sugar Consumers," Heritage Foundation, June 5, 2014.

57 www.aei.org/AmericanBoondoggle.

58 Ibid.

59 *Wall Street Journal*, October 13, 2013.

60 Fran Smith, "Sugar—Congress' Favorite Sweetener," Competitive Enterprise Institute, December 9, 2013.

61 Jennifer Comiteau, "When Does Brand Loyalty Start?" *Adweek*, March 24, 2003, http://www.adweek.com/news/advertising/when-does-brand-loyalty-start-62841.

62 Kristen Harrison, PhD, and Amy L. Marske, MA, "Nutritional Content of Foods Advertised During the Television Programs Children Watch Most," *American Journal of Public Health*, September 2005, http://www.ncbi.nlm.nih.gov/pmc/articles/PMC1449399/#r6.

63 Mark Bittman, "The Right to Sell Kids Junk," *New York Times*, March 27, 2012, opinionator.blogs.nytimes.com/2012/03/27/the-right-to-sell-kids-junk/.

64 "Preliminary Proposed Nutrition Principles to Guide Industry Self-Regulatory Efforts," Interagency Working Group on Food Marketed to Children, https://www.ftc.gov/sites/default/files/documents/public_events/food-marketed-children-forum-interagency-working-group-proposal/110428foodmarketproposedguide.pdf.

65 Lyndsey Layton and Dan Eggen, "Industries lobby against voluntary nutrition guidelines for food marketed to kids," *Washington Post*, July 9, 2011, http://www.washingtonpost.com/politics/industries-lobby-against-voluntary-nutrition-guidelines-for-food-marketed-to-kids/2011/07/08/gIQAZSZu5H_story.html.

66 Katy Bachman, "Industry Group: Feds Would Muzzle Advertising of Popular Foods," *Adweek*, August 4, 2011, http://www.adweek.com/news/advertising-branding/industry-group-feds-would-muzzle-advertising-popular-foods-133878.

67 Kraft Foods lobbying report, http://soprweb.senate.gov/index.cfm?event=getFilingDetails&filingID=0697C58D-9493-4C44-AFFD-30384F45A76F&filingTypeID=69.

68 "Limiting Food Marketing to Children," Center for Science in the Public Interest, https://www.cspinet.org/new/pdf/limitingfood_marketing.pdf.

69 "Restore FTC Authority to Regulate Food and Beverage Marketing Aimed at Children," Partnership for Prevention, https://www.prevent.org/Prevention-Policy-Agenda-for-the-110th-Congress/Restore-FTC-Authority-to-Regulate-Food-and-Beverage-Marketing-Aimed-at-Children.aspx.

70 "Foods and Beverages That Meet the CFBAI Category-Specific Uniform Nutrition Criteria That May Be in Child-Directed Advertising," Better Business Bureau Children's Food and Beverage Advertising Initiative, http://www.bbb.org/globalassets/local-bbbs/council-113/media/cfbai/cfbai-product-list-january-2014.pdf.

71 http://www.fightchronicdisease.org/media-center/releases/new-data-shows-obesity-costs-will-grow-344-billion-2018.

72 "F as in Fat: How Obesity Threatens America's Future," Trust for America's Health, 2012, http://www.rwjf.org/content/dam/farm/reports/reports/2012/rwjf401318.

73 "The medical care costs of obesity: An instrumental variables approach," John Cawleya and Chad Meyerhoeferd, *Journal of Health Economics*, 2012.

74 "Economic Costs of Obesity," National League of Cities, http://www.healthycommunitieshealthyfuture.org/learn-the-facts/economic-costs-of-obesity/.

75 Eric Pianin and Brianna Ehley, "Budget Busting U.S. Obesity Costs Climb Past $300 Billion a Year," *Fiscal Times*, June 19, 2014, http://www.thefiscaltimes.com/Articles/2014/06/19/Budget-Busting-US-Obesity-Costs-Climb-Past-300-Billion-Year.

76 "10 Flabbergasting Costs of America's Obesity Epidemic," *PHIT America*, April 11, 2013, http://www.phitamerica.org/News_Archive/10_Flaggergasting_Costs.htm$hash.kHzrdOHp.dpuf.

77 "Adult Obesity Facts," Centers for Disease Control and Prevention, http://www.cdc.gov/obesity/data/adult.html.

78 Ross A. Hammond and Ruth Levine, "The economic impact of obesity in the United States," *Diabetes, Metabolic Syndrome and Obesity: Targets and Therapy*, August 17, 2010, http://www.brookings.edu/~/media/research/files/articles/2010/9/14 percent20obesity percent20cost percent20hammond percent20levine/0914_obesity_cost_hammond_levine.

79 Sharon Begley, "As America's waistline expands, costs soar," *Reuters*, April 30, 2012, http://www.reuters.com/article/2012/04/30/us-obesity-idUS-BRE83T0C820120430.

80 Ibid.

81 Whit Johnson, "Too fat to serve: Military wages war on obesity," *CBS News*, March 8, 2012, http://www.cbsnews.com/news/too-fat-to-serve-military-wages-war-on-obesity/.

82 Authors' analysis of comments submitted to Federal Trade Commission and lobbying records, https://www.ftc.gov/policy/public-comments/initiative-378.

83 "Accelerating Progress in Obesity Prevention: Solving the Weight of the Nation," Institute of Medicine, May 8, 2012, http://www.iom.edu/Reports/2012/Accelerating-Progress-in-Obesity-Prevention.aspx.

8. Enough to Make You Sick

1 "Lumber Liquidators Linked to Health and Safety Violations," *60 Minutes*, CBS News, March 1, 2015, http://www.cbsnews.com/news/lumber-liquidators-linked-to-health-and-safety-violations/.

2 *Lila Washington et al. v. Lumber Liquidators, Inc.* (N.D. Cali. 2015), http://www.hbsslaw.com/Templates/media/files/case_pdfs/Lumber_Liquidators/3_31_Filing.pdf.

3 David Heath, "How politics derailed EPA science on arsenic, endangering public health," Center for Public Integrity, June 28, 2014, http://www.publicintegrity.org/2014/06/28/15000/how-politics-derailed-epa-science-arsenic-endangering-public-health.

4 "Questions and Answers Regarding Laminate Flooring," United States Environmental Protection Agency, http://www2.epa.gov/formaldehyde/questions-and-answers-regarding-laminate-flooring-0.

5 "What Is Formaldehyde? Why Is Formaldehyde Chemistry So Special?" American Chemistry Council website.

6 "Answers to Frequently Asked Questions about the Health Effects of Formaldehyde," American Chemistry Council, April 6, 2011, http://www.americanchemistry.com/ProductsTechnology/Formaldehyde/Answers-to-FAQs-about-the-Health-Effects-of-Formaldehyde.PDF.

7 Liz Szabo, "Study links formaldehyde to more common cancers," *USA Today*, May 12, 2009, http://usatoday30.usatoday.com/news/health/2009-05-12-formaldehyde-cancer_N.htm; "Mortality From Lymphohematopoietic Malignancies and Brain Cancer Among Embalmers Exposed to Formaldehyde," Michael Hauptmann et al., *Journal of the National Cancer Institute*, November 20, 2009, http://jnci.oxfordjournals.org/content/101/24/1696.full#ref-1.

8 Authors' interview with Becky Gillette.

9 "Formaldehyde and Cancer Risk," National Cancer Institute, June 10, 2011, http://www.cancer.gov/about-cancer/causes-prevention/risk/substances/formaldehyde/formaldehyde-fact-sheet.

10 "Katrina, Rita victims get $42.6M in toxic FEMA trailer suit," Associated Press, *CBS News*, September 28, 2012, http://www.cbsnews.com/news/katrina-rita-victims-get-426m-in-toxic-fema-trailer-suit/.

11 "Prepared Testimony of Lindsay Huckabee: Government Reform and Oversight Committee, U.S. House of Representatives," NPR, July 19, 2007, http://www.npr.org/documents/2008/may/huckabeetestimony.pdf.

12 *Toxicological Profile for Formaldehyde*, Research Triangle Institute, Agency for Toxic Substances and Disease Registry of U.S. Department of Health and Human Services, July 1999.

13 Liz Szabo, "Study Links Formaldehyde to More Common Cancers," *USA Today*, May 12, 2009, http://usatoday30.usatoday.com/news/health/2009-05-12-formaldehyde-cancer_N.htm.

14 "Formaldehyde in Your Products," Occupational Health and Safety Administration, https://www.osha.gov/SLTC/hairsalons/formaldehyde_in_products.html.

15 "National Poll Shows Bipartisan Support for Stronger Protections from Toxic Chemicals," National Resources Defense Council, July 19, 2012, http://www.nrdc.org/media/2012/120719.asp.

16 "Poll of Small Business Owners on Toxic Chemicals," American Sustainable Business Council, September 2012, http://asbcouncil.org/toxic-chemicals-poll#.VUvGhNNVhBc.

17 "High-Risk Series: An Update," GAO-09-271, January 2009, Washington, DC: Government Accountability Office, http://www.gao.gov/new.items /d09271.pdf.

18 Daniel Stevens, "Chemical Industry Increases Contributions and Lobbying as Congress Takes Up Chemical Bill," MapLight, March 16, 2015, http://maplight.org/content/chemical-industry-increases-contributions-and-lobbying-as-congress-takes-up-chemical-bill.

19 Erin Quinn, "Who Needs Lobbyists? See what big business spends to win American minds," Center for Public Integrity, January 15, 2015, http://www.publicintegrity.org/2015/01/15/16596/who-needs-lobbyists-see-what-big-business-spends-win-american-minds.

20 Joaquin Sapien, "How Senator Vitter Battled the EPA Over Formaldehyde's Link to Cancer," *ProPublica*, April 15, 2010, http://www.propublica.org/article /how-senator-david-vitter-battled-formaldehyde-link-to-cancer.

21 Alex Knott, "Lobbyists bankrolling politics," Center for Public Integrity, May 6, 2004, http://www.publicintegrity.org/2004/05/06/7511/lobbyists-bankrolling-politics.

22 Sapien, "How Senator Vitter Battled the EPA."

23 Laura E. Beane Freeman et al., "Mortality from Lymphohematopoietic Malignancies Among Workers in Formaldehyde Industries: The National Cancer Institute Cohort," *Journal of the National Cancer Institute*, May 20, 2009, http://www.ncbi.nlm.nih.gov/pmc/articles/PMC2684555/.

24 "The Grizzle Company," The Grizzle Company, http://www.grizzleco.com/.

25 Jennifer Sass and Daniel Rosenberg, "The Delay Game: How the Chemical Industry Ducks Regulations of the Most Toxic Substances," Natural Resources Defense Council, October 2011, http://www.nrdc.org/health/files /irisdelayreport.pdf.

26 "EPA nomination held up amid debate over formaldehyde risks," Jonathan Tilive, *Times-Picayune*, September 24, 2009, http://www.nola.com/politics /index.ssf/2009/09/epa_nomination_held_up_amid_de.html.

27 "Fundraising Dinner for David Vitter," *Political Party Time*, March 24, 2010, http://politicalpartytime.org/party/19825/.

28 Richard Denison, PhD, "The chemical industry says formaldehyde and styrene don't cause cancer. Only one of 52 scientists agree," Environmental

NOTES 257

Defense Fund, March 26, 2013, http://blogs.edf.org/health/2013/03/26/the-chemical-industry-says-formaldehyde-and-styrene-dont-cause-cancer-only-one-of-52-scientists-agree/.

29 David Heath, "Obama's EPA breaks pledge to divorce politics from science on toxic chemicals," Center for Public Integrity, January 23, 2015, http://www.publicintegrity.org/2015/01/23/16641/obamas-epa-breaks-pledge-divorce-politics-science-toxic-chemicals.

30 "Department of the Interior, Environment, and Related Agencies Appropriation Bill, 2012: Report, together with Dissenting Views," U.S. House of Representatives, July 19, 2011, http://www.gpo.gov/fdsys/pkg/CRPT-112hrpt151/pdf/CRPT-112hrpt151.pdf.

31 David Heath, "How politics derailed EPA science on arsenic, endangering public health," Center for Public Integrity, June 28, 2014, http://www.publicintegrity.org/2014/06/28/15000/how-politics-derailed-epa-science-arsenic-endangering-public-health.

32 Heath, "Obama's EPA breaks pledge."

33 Bruce Alpert, "American Chemistry Council 1st $100,000+ donor to David Vitter Super PAC," *Times-Picayune*, July 16, 2014, http://www.nola.com/politics/index.ssf/2014/07/american_chemistry_council_1st.html.

34 Eric Lipton and Rachel Abrams, "The Uphill Battle to Better Regulate Formaldehyde," *New York Times*, May 3, 2015, http://www.nytimes.com/2015/05/04/business/energy-environment/the-uphill-battle-to-better-regulate-formaldehyde.html.

35 Wendell Potter, *Deadly Spin: An Insurance Insider Speaks Out on How Corporate PR Is Killing Health Care and Deceiving Americans* (New York: Bloomsbury, 2010).

36 Bill Perdue, "Formaldehyde Emissions Standards for Composite Wood Products: Comments of the American Home Furnishings Alliance," American Home Furnishings Alliance, http://www.compositepanel.org/userfiles/filemanager/5266ea97165ad/.

37 Eric Lipton and Rachel Abrams, "The Uphill Battle to Better Regulate Formaldehyde," *New York Times*, May 3, 2015, http://www.nytimes.com/2015/05/04/business/energy-environment/the-uphill-battle-to-better-regulate-formaldehyde.html.

38 Richard Denison, "EDF comments at EPA's public stakeholder meeting on its IRIS program," Environmental Defense Fund, November 14, 2012, http://blogs.edf.org/health/2012/11/14/edf-comments-at-epas-public-stakeholder-meeting-on-its-iris-program/.

39 Lee Drutman, *The Business of America Is Lobbying: How Corporations Became Politicized and Politics Became More Corporate* (Oxford University Press, 2015), 45.

40 Ibid., 44–45.

41 Ibid.

42 Heath, "How politics derailed EPA science."

43 Ibid.

44 James Hamblin, "The Toxins That Threaten Our Brains," *Atlantic*, March 18, 2014, http://www.theatlantic.com/features/archive/2014/03/the-toxins-that-threaten-our-brains/284466/.

45 "Chemical Regulation: Observations on the Toxic Substances Control Act and EPA Implementation," U.S. Government Accountability Office, June 13, 2013, http://www.gao.gov/products/GAO-13-696T.

46 Kate Sheppard, "Senators Introduce Bill to Overhaul U.S. Chemical Regulations," *Huffington Post*, March 10, 2015, http://www.huffingtonpost.com/2015/03/10/toxic-chemicals-senate-bill_n_6842524.html.

47 Timothy Cama, "Chemical safety bill picks up support in Senate," *The Hill*, May 7, 2015, http://thehill.com/policy/energy-environment/241339-chemical-safety-bill-picks-up-support-in-senate.

48 David McCumber, "Questions raised on authorship of chemicals bill," *San Francisco Chronicle*, March 16, 2015, http://www.sfgate.com/nation/article/Questions-raised-on-authorship-of-chemicals-bill-6137823.php.

49 Return of Organization Exempt from Income Tax: American Chemistry Council, Internal Revenue Service, 2013, https://s3.amazonaws.com/s3.documentcloud.org/documents/1371629/american-chemistry-council-2013.pdf.

50 Eric Lipton, "Tom Udall's Unlikely Alliance with the Chemical Industry," *New York Times*, http://www.nytimes.com/2015/03/07/us/tom-udalls-unlikely-alliance-with-the-chemical-industry.html.

51 "Written Commentary of Lindsay Huckabee: Prepared for the Committee on Science and Technology," NPR, April 1, 2008, http://www.npr.org/documents/2008/may/huckabeetestimony08.pdf.

52 "Prepared Testimony of Lindsay Huckabee: Government Reform and Oversight Committee, U.S. House of Representatives," NPR, July 19, 2007, http://www.npr.org/documents/2008/may/huckabeetestimony.pdf.

53 Sarah Maslin Nir, "Perfect Nails, Poisoned Workers," *New York Times*, May 11, 2015, http://www.nytimes.com/2015/05/11/nyregion/nail-salon-workers-in-nyc-face-hazardous-chemicals.html.

54 "FDA Authority over Cosmetics," U.S. Food and Drug Administration, August 3, 2013, http://www.fda.gov/Cosmetics/GuidanceRegulation/LawsRegulations/ucm074162.htm.

55 "Personal Care Products Council: Report Images," OpenSecrets.com, 2015, http://www.opensecrets.org/lobby/client_reports.php?id=D000028328&year=2015.

56 Hamblin, "The Toxins That Threaten Our Brains."

57 Stefanie Knoll, "Harmful chemicals and neurotoxins: Slightly eroding intelligence, damaging societies," *Journalist's Resource*, March 21, 2015, http://journalistsresource.org/studies/environment/pollution-environment /neurobehavioral-effects-developmental-toxicity#.

Philippe Grandjean, MD, and Philip J. Landrigan, MD, "Neurobehavioral effects of developmental toxicity," *The Lancet*, February 14, 2014, http://www.thelancet.com/journals/laneur/article/PIIS1474-4422percent2813percent2970278-3 /abstract.

58 Leonardo Trasande, "Further Limiting Bisphenol A in Food Uses Could Provide Health and Economic Benefits," *Health Affairs*, January 2014, http://content.healthaffairs.org/content/early/2014/01/16/hlthaff.2013.0686.

59 Lynne Peeples, "BPA Among Toxic Chemicals Driving Up Health Care Costs, Experts Say," *Huffington Post*, January 24, 2014, http://www.huffingtonpost.com/2014/01/22/bpa-health-care-costs_n_4644372.html.

60 Knoll, "Harmful chemicals and neurotoxins."

9. It's Fixable

1 http://reason.com/poll/2014/04/03/americans-say-75-percent-of-politicians.

2 http://www.demos.org/sites/default/files/publications/FreshStart_PublicFinancingCT_0.pdf.

3 http://apr.sagepub.com/content/31/5/520.full.pdf.

4 Ibid.

5 http://www.demos.org/sites/default/files/publications/FreshStart_PublicFinancingCT_0.pdf.

6 Ibid.

7 Ibid.

8 Ibid.

9 http://www.brennancenter.org/publication/donor-diversity-through-public-matching-funds.

10 http://www.brennancenter.org/press-release/study-public-financing-contributes-greater-diversity-participation-nyc-elections.

11 http://www.nydailynews.com/opinion/mouth-money-article-1.2011596.

12 http://missoulian.com/news/state-and-regional/montana-house-backs-bill-to-require-dark-money-groups-disclose/article_72bd75d5-6371-5b6b-b1d7-026d09be7d9f.html.

13 "Political Contribution Disclosure Survey Results," CFA Institute, August 2014, http://cfainstitute.org/Survey/political_contribution_survey_final.pdf.

14 http://www.usnews.com/opinion/articles/2015/04/23/obama-should-sign-order-to-force-contractors-to-disclose-political-spending.

15 http://www.washingtonpost.com/blogs/monkey-cage/wp/2015/04/16/what-we-get-wrong-about-lobbying-and-corruption/.

16 http://billmoyers.com/2015/04/07/living-high-life-congress/.

17 http://www.reddit.com/r/IAmA/comments/1qk2aa/we_are_dc_super_lobbyists_jack_quinn_and_john/cddkjnt.

18 Jack Abramoff, *Capitol Punishment: The Hard Truth About Washington Corruption From America's Most Notorious Lobbyist* (Washington, D.C., WND Books, 2011) 273.

19 http://www.politico.com/news/stories/0710/40207.html.

20 http://thehill.com/blogs/floor-action/house/238743-gop-lawmaker-proposes-permanent-lobbying-ban.

21 http://www.nytimes.com/2015/05/03/us/politics/fec-cant-curb-2016-election-abuse-commission-chief-says.html.

22 http://www.publicintegrity.org/2013/12/17/13996/how-washington-starves-its-election-watchdog.

23 Ibid.

24 Larry Noble, personal communication, May 28, 2015.

25 http://www.publicintegrity.org/2013/12/17/13996/how-washington-starves-its-election-watchdog.

26 Larry Noble, personal communication, May 28, 2015.

27 http://www.nytimes.com/2015/05/03/us/politics/fec-cant-curb-2016-election-abuse-commission-chief-says.html.

28 http://abcnews.go.com/Politics/jeb-bush-presidential-candidate-seconds-today/story?id=31027090.

29 Larry Noble, personal communication, May 28, 2015.

30 Kathay Feng, personal communication, May 28, 2015.

31 http://www.campaignlegalcenter.org/news/publications-speeches/californias-fppc-provides-example-dysfunctional-federal-agencies-follow.

32 Larry Noble, personal communication, May 28, 2015.

10. The Makings of an All-American Movement

1 Nick Kristof, "Polluted Political Games," *New York Times*, May 28, 2015, http://www.nytimes.com/2015/05/28/opinion/nicholas-kristof-polluted-political-games.html.

Index

A Note on the Authors

Wendell Potter is an author and journalist whose work has appeared in *Newsweek*, the *Guardian*, the *Nation*, the Center for Public Integrity, and at WendellPotter.com.

Nick Penniman is executive director of the organization Issue One. He was previously publisher of the *Washington Monthly* and director of the Huffington Post Investigative Fund.

Nick lives in D.C., a few miles from the U.S. Capitol Building; Wendell lives in Philadelphia, a few miles from Independence Hall.